PRINCE ALBERT AND VICTORIAN TASTE

WINSLOW AMES

✳

Prince Albert and Victorian Taste

✳

*'Je ne désire que de n'avoir pas
de goût, parce que les grands hommes n'en ont pas,
et en inventent un nouveau'.*

GUY DE MAUPASSANT

✳

NEW YORK : THE VIKING PRESS

for my Wife
in Memory of
our Parents

CONTENTS

[vii]

ILLUSTRATIONS

ILLUSTRATIONS

appearing between pages 142 *and* 143

appearing between pages 174 *and* 175

FOREWORD

One day in 1951 William Sebastian Heckscher, now Professor at the University of Utrecht, noticed in our house the Victorian and Edwardian memoirs which my wife and I had been reading. In talking about them, we agreed that an account of the Prince Consort's activity in the arts was needed. Later the same year I read John Steegman's *Consort of Taste* (1950), an admirable book in which the same need is expressed but which is based throughout on previously printed sources. When Dr Heckscher returned to Europe, he kindly ceded to me any presumptive right he had in what otherwise might have been a joint work.

There has been ample documentation building up, at least since the younger Eastlake, on the development of taste or tastes in Victorian Britain; references to much of it will be found in my notes. If one did no more than read *Punch* from the beginning, he could learn much about the slow but noticeable changes from Melbourne's 'done thing' to Ruskin's moral judgements and the conscious aestheticism of the eighties.

For that aspect of the subject with which this book is concerned, special importance attaches to the comments made by Queen Victoria in her journal. Large portions of her diary have appeared in print in the five volumes of Sir Theodore Martin's *The Life of His Royal Highness the Prince Consort* (1875-80), Lord Esher's *The Girlhood of Queen Victoria* (1912), the Queen's own *Leaves from the Journal of Our Life in the Highlands* (1868), and (though this covers the years after the Prince's death) *More Leaves from the Journal of a Life in the Highlands* (1884). In addition to these, I have been most generously allowed the use of numerous further extracts, both from the diary and from other papers in the Royal Archives at Windsor Castle. For this courtesy as well as for the gracious permission of Her Majesty Queen Elizabeth II

[xi]

to print such quotations as I might need, I cannot sufficiently express my thanks. To Her Royal Highness Princess Alice Countess of Athlone and to the Lady Patricia Ramsay I am indebted for a good deal of background, particularly for a sense of the character of Osborne House as it was when Queen Victoria lived there.

Sir Owen Morshead and his successor as Librarian at Windsor Castle, Mr R. C. Mackworth-Young, have put me under the most pleasant and bearable obligation; Miss Scott-Elliot, Miss Price-Hill, Miss Hedley, and other of their associates have worked many hours finding answers to my questions. I am grateful to Sir Anthony Blunt, Keeper of the Queen's Pictures, his deputy Mr Oliver Millar, Mr Francis J. B. Watson, Keeper of the Queen's Works of Art, and his deputy Mr Geoffrey de Bellaigue, and Mr John Charlton of the Ministry of Works. Dr Gertrude Bing and Dr Leopold Ettlinger of the Warburg Institute allowed me to shelter under the wing of their organization, and otherwise helped to make the rough places plain. For many kindnesses I am indebted to Mr Hugh Murray Baillie, Professors Quentin Bell and Arnold Noach of the University of Leeds, Dr T. S. R. Boase, President of Magdalen College, Oxford, Mr Hector Bolitho (one of the best biographers of Prince Albert), Mr Humphrey Brook, Secretary, and Mr Sidney C. Hutchinson, Librarian of the Royal Academy, Mr and Mrs J. Byam Shaw, Lt.-Gen. Sir Neil Cantlie, former Governor of Osborne House, Col. the Hon. Sir Martin Charteris, Sir Trenchard Cox and Mr C. H. Gibbs-Smith, Mrs Shirley Bury, Miss Helen Lowenthal, Mrs Betty O'Looney, Mr H. D. Molesworth, and the late Peter Floud of the Victoria and Albert Museum, Mr H. S. Ede, Dr Joan Evans, Mr Lindsay Fleming, Mr Peter Fleetwood-Hesketh, Mr E. T. Floyd Ewin, Mr and Mrs Helmut Gernsheim (who have made vast photographic contributions to Victorian iconology), Professor Lawrence Gowing, Dr Carmen Gronau, Mr and Mrs John Gurney, Mr John Hayes of the London Museum, Mr John Harris of the Royal Institute of British Architects, Mr George Howard, Mr and Mrs K. E. Maison, Mr Christopher Norris, Sir Richard Nosworthy, Professor Nikolaus Pevsner, Mr and Mrs Robert Ponsonby, Mr C. N. P. Powell, Miss Margit Rostock of the German Institute in London, the late Earl of Sandwich, Mr John Steegman, Mrs Stirling and her son the Hon. Bernard Bruce and Mrs Bruce, Mr W. D. Sturch, Secretary to the Royal Commission for the

Exhibition of 1851, Sir John Summerson, the Duke of Wellington and Mr Francis Needham his librarian, Lt.-Col. L. H. Yates of the Prince Consort's Library in Aldershot, and others to whom I apologize if I have omitted them by forgetfulness or error.

In my own country I have received valuable help from my wife and from our daughter Eliza Ames Nimmo (who helped with some work at Windsor), from Dr Edgar Breitenbach, the Revd. T. Huntington Chappell, the Revd. Robert L. Jacoby, Dr Hans Huth, Professor Henry-Russell Hitchcock, Mr A. Hyatt Mayor (who pointed out to me the set of Minutoli's *Vorbilder* in the Metropolitan Museum of Art), Miss A. Margaret Potter, the late George Haines IV, the late Francis Henry Taylor, Mr E. J. Rousuck, Mrs H. Thomas Clark, Dr Adolf K. Placzek, Mr George N. Kates, Miss Anna Wells Rutledge, and Mr and Mrs Whitney Stoddard.

In Germany, Prince and Princess Friedrich Josias of Coburg, Marie-Louise Freifrau von Erffa, Dr Heins of the Bavarian State Archive, and Dr Kohlhaussen, curator of Veste Coburg, were all exceedingly kind. Frau Maria-Carla Gräfin von Pfeil-Minutoli (now Frau Hübschle von Lingen) helped in the search for material on Alexander von Minutoli of Liegnitz. I was also aided in that inquiry by two Polish correspondents, Dr Stanislawa Sawicka of the University of Warsaw and Dr Jan Reiter of the University of Breslau. From Belgium I have had useful information on Laeken through the Vicomte G. du Parc, Chamberlain to H.M. the King of the Belgians.

I am obliged to several foundations for their prompt answers to requests.

Never shall I forget the visit my wife and I paid to Osborne on a grey day in November 1954. We had the good fortune to go accompanied only by the House Governor. The sense of being able to penetrate, on the spot, those cobwebs of memory which the Queen had spun, and to see the Osborne of her husband's labours and pleasures, came unbidden and strong; it was echoed in the physical pleasure of turning back the brown linoleum to see the starch-blue and white, the red and green and yellow, of the tiles. So is it necessary, often, to penetrate layers of neglect, as Prince Albert could do with the darkened paintings at Hampton Court, and really to *look* at what the Prince and Queen created. Some of it does not stand inspection; some is outrageous, some

[xiii]

is as qualified as 'works of royal and noble authors' must usually be; some is poignant, some is solid. The objects and the places themselves are the best witnesses; but just after them come the written sources.

The Prince's diary in German, which by the Queen's own account was brief, was in part made available by her to Martin through abstracts and an occasional short quotation. But the journal itself has vanished; one can hardly imagine the Queen's having destroyed it, though her executor Princess Beatrice may have done so; or perhaps it went with the Queen to her tomb. Her attachment to people and places and tokens, which I shall be mentioning a good deal, was a sort of misuse of the well-trained royal memory. Against this attachment her husband had to work steadily. She could not tear herself away from a much loved place without complaint, yet when she arrived at the next she would often say, 'It is as if we had never left dear Osborne.' Her extraordinary mixture of toughness and dependence was much of her husband's making, and perhaps he made her too dependent upon him. That she eventually modified her extravagant mourning for him is to her own credit as well as to the Prince of Wales's and Disraeli's.

Prince Albert was a person of such self-control, and often so deliberate in forming decisions, that his breadth rather than his depth, his knowledge rather than his intenseness, is what comes forward in his writing. Even in those letters to his wife written during moments borrowed from elaborately-scheduled journeys, there is more of light jocosity than of intimacy or revelation (the heavier jocosities appear in letters to Stockmar, and seem still heavier in translation). The quick sights of the Prince given by many good observers who, however, did not know him, are more often chilly than not (e.g., those of the Americans Nathaniel Hawthorne, G. P. A. Healey, and Herman Melville). For more rewarding insights, real knowledge on the part of the reporter was needed. The passionate devotion of those who did know him tells almost as much about him as if he had given himself more openly to the written word – but not quite. There remain mysteries, for which one is always a little grateful.

Prince Albert was so upright and had been so thoroughly briefed by Stockmar that he almost expected to disapprove of the 'well-born and idle' British who were supposed by Stockmar not to be pulling their weight in this earnest world. The Prince himself had all the necessary accomplishments and even some small talk; but he did not warm to anyone who had nothing more than small talk, and it was abundantly clear to those whom he did not care to know that he was not disposed to make undue efforts. To those who drew close to him through shared work, whether or not they came from the class he expected to disapprove of, he was the greatest of men. They, like the professional consultants whom he chose, the government men who confronted his enormous knowledge, and the Court people who saw him not quite *en pantoufles* but certainly very closely and steadily, all adored him. He was able to get much work and true devotion out of a capable but lazy man like Lord Granville, who might never have gone into public service without the Prince's demands upon him; those demands gave Granville backbone. Prince Albert was also able to keep an ambitious but over-enthusiastic and sometimes overbearing man like Henry Cole on the right track.

Cole's papers in the library of the Victoria and Albert Museum and the great file of material relating to the Royal Commission for the Exhibition of 1851, which was compiled by the Prince and which covers the whole South Kensington work up to 1861, are invaluable.

The evidences of Ernest I's tastes and plans, chiefly architects' projects in the Bavarian State Archive at Coburg, were apparently not seen by Mr Bolitho although he was able to see some Coburg interiors, particularly at the Rosenau, which have been stripped since his visits.

Queen Victoria stood at the elbow of her husband's official biographers Grey and Martin. Perhaps for that reason, Martin was so circuitous in avoiding harsh words that, unless one knows facts from other reports, it is difficult not to draw wrong conclusions from some of his pages; for his desire not to give offence makes his work read as if it had been roses, roses all the way. Opposition to the Prince as a foreigner is mentioned, but his own doings appear to have no flaw. For instance, in writing of the public meeting on 21 February 1850 which prepared a climate of opinion favourable to the coming Exhibition, Martin says that 'Lord Brougham and the Bishop of Oxford helped with others to sustain the discussion at a level far beyond that of most public meetings.' In fact, Brougham was strongly opposed, and said so; Wilberforce, who was in eclipse at the time because of his

[xv]

stuffiness about Hampden's appointment as Bishop of Hereford, was also a speaker in opposition.

To Martin, however, and to all other biographers of the Prince, for their labours and insights, we must all be grateful – as also to the even larger number, and most recently and notably Lady Longford, who have wrought upon the image of Queen Victoria. In the long run, even the sneers of Douglas Jerrold and his associates in *Punch*, the rather caustic but willing-to-be-fair remarks of Claire Jerrold in *The Married Life of Queen Victoria*, the absurd adulation of the many popular volumes issued at the two Jubilees and immediately after the Queen's death, will all have been useful – even perhaps the grovellings of such an early work as *The University of Bonn its rise, progress, and present state, with a concise account of the college life of His Royal Highness Prince Albert of Saxe Coburg and Gotha*, by a Member of the Middle Temple (1845), which was an elaborate demonstration of the Prince's simon-pure Protestant status. Such harm as has been done recently by colloquial or fictionalized biographies is more readily corrected than the ancient and quite erroneous and unfounded whispers about the Prince's mother; some latter-day interpretations have been more comic than anything else, but they have sometimes carried with them lessons in the dangers of false inference to which playful interpretations may lead their readers. To be imaginative, it is not necessary to invent.

While I was gathering material, my wife and I were taken by an historian (who believed that life has not been worth living since the Hohenstaufens) to see a film called *Mädchenjahre einer Königin*, which described itself as based on documents and expert advice of many sorts. As if the facts of Victoria and Albert's long-forecast engagement and marriage were not in themselves sufficiently fascinating, the script transferred to the young Queen Victoria an escapade of her cousin the Princess Charlotte, and combined with it a wholly fanciful clandestine meeting with Prince Albert at an inn, and other absurd fancies. The film was visually charming, for it had been photographed in a number of Baroque and neo-Classic palaces near Vienna; but it was whipped cream in all other respects, and included so hilarious a 'boner' as the appearance of the Archbishop of Canterbury at an evening party in cope and mitre. I trust I may have blundered into no such howlers, nor been guilty of 'selective Victorianism' (W. L. Burn's phrase), but I succumb once for all to the temptation of an imaginary conversation (for which I have good evidence) in the style of *Punch:*

The scene is a highway near Lichfield, and the Queen and Prince, who have been married some years, are in their carriage in sight of the Cathedral.

The Queen (remembering that as a young girl she had passed this way and had been told that Lichfield Cathedral was unique): 'See, Albert, Lichfield Cathedral – it has three spires, is it not splendid?[1] There is no other like it.'

Prince Albert: 'It is beautiful, *Liebchen*; but what about Bamberg and Gelnhausen and Worms? If it comes to that, what about Durham and Peterborough?'

WINSLOW AMES

Saunderstown, Rhode Island
3 July 1966

---

[1] Daniel Defoe: *A Tour through the Whole Island of Great Britain by a Gentleman,* 1724–7, vol. II, Letter III: ' . . . the three beautiful spires; the like of which are not to be seen in one Church, no not in Europe.'

1

Background in Germany

When the small Prince Albert was baptized at the Rosenau near Coburg on 19 September 1819, his godparents (present or absent, chosen by his parents or by fate) were clues to the curious position of his family and to his own future tastes and activity.

Ernest I of Sachsen-Coburg-Saalfeld chose as godfathers for his second son, Francis Albert Augustus Charles Emanuel, the following persons:

> The Emperor Francis I of Austria-Hungary, who as Francis II had been the last Holy Roman Emperor, and whose daughter had become Napoleon's second wife;

> The Emperor's uncle by marriage, Albert Casimir, Duke of Sachsen-Teschen;

> The baby's maternal grandfather Augustus, Duke of Sachsen-Gotha-Altenburg;

> The baby's uncle by marriage, Emanuel Count Mensdorf-Pouilly.

The one godmother was the baby's paternal grandmother, the Duchess Dowager of Coburg, who was of course also grandmother of the Princess Victoria. It might be said that certain fairy godparents also gave their aid: Uncle Leopold (who had had the Emperor Leopold II as one of *his* godparents), Baron Stockmar, and that midwife of distinction, Frau Siebold, who had brought both Victoria and Albert into the world.

Coburg (now administratively part of Bavaria) lay on the borders of Saxony and Bavaria; to the north and east the Thuringian mountains were full of a Gothic darkness partly lightened by Lutheran individualism; to the south and west the easy, fat Franconian land was rich enough to support the late-Baroque ecstasies of Vierzehnheiligen. Coburg and Gotha produced hereditary rulers who never forgot their ancestors' partisanship with Luther, but who also remembered that the chief power in their involved family lay with the younger branch who had been successful in Dresden and Poland. Of the five godparents, three were Roman Catholic, two Lutheran; but among them they seem to suggest the mixture of monarchical principle, dynastic ambition, interest in the arts, system combined with perception and drive, and a strong sense of service, which could be considered typical of Prince Albert in his maturity.

Family, and family alliance, were as important as religious connexion or geographical attachment. In Ernest I's generation, in which Prince Ferdinand made a valuable Roman Catholic marriage in Hungary and Prince Leopold a more valuable Protestant one in England, the elder branch of the dynasty began to fulfill the promise of the younger. Ernest I's grandmother, wife of Duke Ernst Friedrich, was, in Prince Leopold's phrase, 'too great a person for a small dukedom'; her son Friedrich Anton, though the mother's extravagance left him small means, yet managed to rival Albert Casimir and the contemporary Fürst Liechtenstein as a print-collector. But Franz Friedrich Anton's own extravagance left his son Ernest I really poor.

The passion of many of the Saxon electoral family and their cadets for works of art and collecting is well known. Augustus the Strong and his porcelain, Friedrich August II in the following century with his prints and drawings, and between them at a lucky time, Albert Casimir, are perhaps the most notable. Albert Casimir, born a prince of Saxony and Poland, and created Duke of Teschen at his marriage to Maria Theresa's daughter, Maria Christina, was the founder of the Albertina in Vienna, one of the greatest collections of graphic art in the world. A failure as a military man and not very good as a joint governor in the Netherlands, he was a connoisseur of both old and new who, after the death of his wife in 1798,[1] devoted himself for more than twenty years to acquisition and the exercise of discrimination. His godson never knew him, for he died in 1822, but Prince Albert certainly knew and

---

[1] Employing, as usual, an artist abreast or ahead of the style, he engaged Canova to create her tomb, the extraordinary and aesthetically debated semi-pyramid with a tableau of mourning figures in the Capuzinerkirche, completed about 1805.

felt something of the old Sachsen-Teschen's passion and method. King Leopold lived for many years in the château of Laeken near Brussels, which Albert Casimir and the Archduchess had built during their governorship, and there Prince Albert and his elder brother Ernest made their uncle a long visit in 1836-7. Laeken left an impression, as we shall see. So did Florence, where Prince Albert stayed as long (three months) as anywhere else but Brussels and Bonn during his youthful travels. Brussels, which has two Anglican churches (one high, one low) within a few minutes of each other, and Florence (which has had a British colony of as many as twenty thousand) were both great places for expatriates, and much English was spoken there. It was in pursuit of King Leopold's, the Coburg dowager's and Baron Stockmar's plans that a nice young Seymour was sent out to Florence while Prince Albert was there to improve his English. We may imagine the young Prince and Lieutenant Seymour, some years ahead of Browning and Pater, walking about Florence and speaking English. We have few direct testimonies from the Prince for his love of Florence, but he later bought many Florentine pictures, and Queen Victoria repeatedly mentioned his fondness for the city in later years when she visited it herself.

The Gotha grandfather was in many ways a silly man, but he too had some of the interests of the collector: he had a library of 150,000 volumes, six thousand manuscripts, a more interesting picture gallery than that of Coburg, and an Oriental collection. Most of this he had inherited, to be sure, from his father, who had been a friend of Diderot and an early patron of Houdon. Uncle Mensdorf-Pouilly, a French refugee, made a career for himself in Austrian government service, in which he was followed by his sons and a grandson (who was Austrian ambassador in Edward VII's time.) The Coburg grandmother was described by Queen Victoria as 'a most remarkable woman, with a most powerful, energetic, almost masculine mind, accompanied with great tenderness of heart and extreme love for nature'.

Ernest I made a great point of being a Saxon prince, and the assiduity with which he and his family pursued the right to the title of Royal Highness was almost absurd (indeed Queen Victoria may have asked Sir Theodore Martin, the Prince Consort's biographer, to soft-pedal it, for her mention of the *Hoheitssache* in her abstracts from her husband's diary, prepared for Martin's use, is not taken up in the *Life*).[1] It is hardly an accident that the *Almanach de Gotha* began and continued in the domain of a family with so strong and conscious a feeling for the dynastic, nor that the *Almanach,* which had been printed in German up to Napoleon's time, was produced thereafter in both German and French, the language of courts and diplomacy. Coburg and Gotha, though provincial now, were closer in the early nineteenth century to the main stream of European diplomatic traffic than, say, Berlin. The new 'culture capital', Goethe's Weimar, was a Saxon city.

Those German princes whose land and authority came originally through fiefdom from the Holy Roman Emperor were responsible immediately to the Emperor and to no one else except nominally the Pope; after the Reformation the Protestant princes were effectively sovereign in their often tiny territories. Always proud, sometimes accumulating great treasure, they nevertheless often kept a rather cosy relationship with their people, which is reflected in the fairy stories with carpet-slippered kings which the brothers Grimm began to publish in 1812 just as their time was ending. The mediatization which followed the downfall of the Holy Roman Empire in 1806 put many of these princelings under the *mediate* authority of kings, as for instance the king of Bavaria. They felt demoted, and in fact were often also deprived of property or uprooted during the Napoleonic wars, as the Leiningens were uprooted. Hence the *Hoheitssache.*

Prince Albert's early surroundings are important to his later life. Besides his love of the arts, he had in him something of the mind of an appeals judge; he was a methodical man of retentive memory and, being by his own admission sentimental, he was quite willing to train and use his eyes and his mind for the pleasures of memory as well as for the work of creating an admirable monarchy. Little escaped him. Though he had not that passionate attachment to persons, and to tokens of persons, which was one of his wife's prime characteristics, he was interested in meanings and purposes, and in meaning itself: so that the connexion between people and things was important to him.

---

[1] Draft note by the Queen in Royal Archives, Windsor, Additional MSS. Z. 491. Hereafter such documents will be cited as *Archives* with the volume and document numbers.

If we made a scale of degrees of attachment, with a Gandhian non-attachment at one end, Queen Victoria would be found at the other end. It is probably fair to say that to her an object (however intrinsically valuable) had extrinsic value in direct proportion to its associations as a souvenir or reminder. To Prince Albert an object (regardless of intrinsic value but not of design) was a token of creation, of work in progress; and if it had some personal connexion, that was simply an added value. His collecting of autographs kept interest in persons rather separate from interest in their real works, and after his marriage he did not keep autographs by him very long; but he continued to collect them, and sent them to Coburg.

Having a trained memory like his wife's he often mentioned the resemblances of newly-seen British landscapes to German or Italian terrain that he had known before; this is not evidence either of 'German' sentimentality or of an immature stage of emotional development, but rather of a classifying mind. He was using his eyes and memory not in order to bathe in remembrance of things past, but as an art-historian does. When he was nineteen he wrote to his father from Florence that the house of the Marchese Cerini, where he was staying, had 'very airy and pretty rooms, still furnished in the style of Louis XIV';[1] but he wrote more appraisingly to his tutor Florschütz that 'it is all shabby and has lost all its freshness and glamour'.

There is no denying that Coburg is a lovely part of the world. The Rosenau, where Prince Albert was born and where he spent much of his youth, stands on the shoulder of a hill a few miles from the city, with broad, not quite dramatic, views of farm and forest. It was, and still is, in its present use as an old people's home, a simple geometric mass with one exciting accent.[2] The size of a very large barn, it is a stone oblong, one storey high on the uphill side and two on the downhill, with three layers of garrets showing at the gable-ends; at the centre of the long uphill side a circular stair tower stands just free of the walls, being connected with the house by a narrow passage at each level (Cézanne would have enjoyed these two steep-roofed forms). The gable-ends

---

[1] Grey, *Early Years of the Prince Consort*, 1867, p. 192.

[2] Mr Bolitho's description in *The Reign of Queen Victoria*, 1948, is based on his own visits to the interior before the building was dismantled for its present use.

consist largely of windows; with their balconies, late-Gothic tracery, and bull's eye glass, they are oddly reminiscent of Venetian late Gothic; but a trace of the *Bierstube* style has crept in.

When Ernest I succeeded his father the Rosenau and, indeed, all the buildings which came into his ownership, were in bad repair. Between that time and his marriage (i.e., 1806-17) he put much of his revenue into rebuilding, and when Gotha became part of his duchy in 1825-6 he undertook interior revisions at Schloss Friedenstein and a drastic re-modelling of the ruinous Reinhardtsbrunn; he even managed to afford Jägersruh, a hunting lodge hidden in the forest, scene of the appalling drive of beasts during Victoria and Albert's visit to Ernest II in 1845. With the definite fall of Napoleon, Ernest I did the proper thing by first building a mausoleum (1815-16) at Coburg for his father Franz Friedrich Anton: a charming neo-Greek aedicule in the Hofgarten near the foot of the long ascent to the Festung; sphinxes guard the door, and the ceiling has white relief ornament on a blue ground. Either the cost of this building or the approach of his marriage sent him to the Roths-childs of Frankfurt for a loan, and with this help he continued to work: from 1822 to 1831, for instance, he was planning and decorating the throne room in Schloss Ehrenburg. It is in full-dress Empire style, with red velvet (embroidered in gold laurel-leaves) covering the walls, ormolu candelabra in the manner of Thomire, chairs by Jacob-Desmalter, a handsome moulded ceiling in rather seventeenth-century style, and an up-to-date inlaid floor.

The description of the enchanting rooms which Ernest I arranged for his bride has come down to us in her letters.[1] The Coburg *Staats-archiv* contains also a number of watercolour elevations for rooms at the Rosenau, perhaps by Renié who remodelled the Ehrenburg; and the souvenir albums at Windsor include watercolours of Coburg and Gotha interiors, many of which (signed Rothbarth) were commissioned by Queen Victoria after her husband's death; but a few are earlier. When-ever these can be checked with the Queen's account of her first visit in 1845, or with the elevations in the Coburg archive, they prove to re-present accurately the décor by his father in which the Prince grew up. If there were not already ample evidence to disprove the old charges of

---

[1] Ebart, *Louise Herzogin von Sachsen-Coburg-Saalfeld*, 1903.

illegitimacy, we might find in Ernest I's persistent architectural oc-
cupations some useful proof that his second son came by his tastes
honestly.

No doubt Ernest was, as Bolitho called him, 'not a pleasant man in
manner or culture',[1] or as Fulford said, 'selfish and extravagant',[2] but
he had (or was skilful enough to command) a pretty taste in housekeeping. It was based on acceptance of the bare rooms, with their few
windows in high thick walls, as they came into his hands; he kept most
of the surfaces simple and hard. Parquet floors seldom had more than a
hearth-rug or a small bedside mat; walls were distempered in plain
colours, sometimes subdivided by wallpaper 'pilasters' or topped with
friezes of neo-Gothic tracery in wallpaper or stencilling; or elswhere
charmingly painted with trellises and morning-glories or with landscapes seen as through a trellis (Ernest's sister Victoire painted one
such room). What the Duke had to buy of a portable nature was chiefly
sound standard Empire cabinet furniture in blond wood with marble
tops, or black with ormolu mounts; beds in matched veneers, sofas with
striped covers, and diaphanous curtains (not for him the expensive and
light-excluding drapery of Carlton House). Later he added chairs in the
styles of Charles X and Louis Philippe. It is all a little too simple and
even sometimes chic to be called quite Biedermeier.

The one room of architectural pretension at the Rosenau was the
Marble Hall; on the lowest level of the house, it opened through many
windows, perhaps enlarged by Ernest I, to a garden; its half-elliptical
vaults were carried on clustered columns, and the whole, which might
have been rather gloomily grotto-like, was made luminous by a white
marble sheathing with an over-all pattern of gilt curlicues, and by
ormolu chandeliers of a 'Gothick sort'; it was really in what the French
call the Troubadour taste, and a little silly, precisely because pretentious; Ernest seems to have worked best on a low budget.

Though somewhat limited indoors by existing brick and mortar, he
could be fancy-free outdoors; so he created a Fishing Temple with
tree-trunks as columns, topped by a proper cornice and a ventilating
clerestory, all suggesting Soane or Schinkel rusticized; and then a

---

[1] Bolitho, *Albert the Good,* 1933, p. 22.
[2] Roger Fulford, *The Prince Consort,* 1949, p. 21.

Bathing House built like a permanent tent, with lead 'canvas' striped in green and white, gilt-topped poles, and red-piped scallops to the awnings; all very gay. Is it possible that these constructions date from after his sight of Virginia Water? I can find no date for them.[1] My descriptions come from water-colours.

At Schloss Ehrenburg in what might be called 'downtown' Coburg, there was not so much to do; by the same token, there was a more mixed background for Prince Albert's youth. The Ehrenburg that one now sees has a sixteenth-century base-court fronted by a larger U-shaped seventeenth-century building to which Renié, over the years 1816-40, gave a rather papery Tudorish or 'Jacobethan' facing. Within, it is a typical German provincial mixture of styles, and a pleasant mixture of periods. The standard tall entrance-way, by which carriages could drive under the main block to the court, leads to the equally standard vast stairway and the two honorific upper floors. The newish throne room in the east wing has been mentioned; the most interesting other apartments are the *Riesensaal* of mirrors and caryatids with its flanking chambers, dating from the last decade of the seventeenth century; the small rooms contrived by Renié for comfort rather than *Prunk*; and the chapel on the ground floor of the west wing.

The caryatids or rather atlantides are twenty-eight noble giants in stucco, who carry a ballroom ceiling of superb oval wreaths in high relief; part of the ceiling is frescoed in a warm earthy palette, and there is much armorial display. At each end of the ballroom, separated only by a screen of caryatids, is a smaller mirrored room with a fireplace (not the usual German stove). The brothers Luchese (from Melide in the Ticino) began the work in 1697; in an adjacent room the ceiling by Carlo Tagliata bears wreaths animated with oak leaves, lilies, and other pendent details in wood, wire, and lead, some gilded some whitened. The Bamberg *Neues Residenz* is almost exactly contemporary; its frescoed ballroom by other hands has much the same hot palette as the Coburg *Riesensaal* and church.

This *Schlosskirche* is a remarkable example of Lutheran Baroque

---

[1] Martin quotes (I, 94) a letter from Prince Albert to his father dated from Windsor 14 August 1840, which mentions a cottage of George IV's and the Fishing Temple 'which were to have been taken away. These are now safe.'

which nevertheless has, like many later German provincial palaces, a certain flavour of Versailles (it is earlier – 1690–1700 – than the Versailles chapel, though its decoration was not completed until 1735). The ducal family, sitting at balcony level as usual in such chapels, had a sort of closet for partial privacy. At the opposite end, a Berniniesque canopy rises over the altar, but this whole end of the room is complicated by the presence of a high pulpit *behind* the altar; and above the pulpit in turn, at balcony level, rises the organ. The entire church is stuccoed and frescoed, again in a warm palette, with standard Christian symbols, some emblems of Lutheran reference, and subjects from the Apocalypse; the ceiling by the Luchese, the rest by Germans. The total effect, with the yellow ochres and oranges of the walls, some gilding, the complex construction in the chancel and not very much light, is splendid, but crowded and a bit oppressive. In view of the ducal family's tendency to agree that 'Paris vaut bien une messe', it is interesting that the chapel is used even now for both Lutheran and Roman Catholic services. The low-church Queen Victoria remarked, *à propos* of the crucifix on the *Schlosskirche* altar, that this usage in Lutheran churches seemed right to her.[1]

When Ernest I wanted some up-to-date but less grandiose rooms in the Ehrenburg, he commissioned a pupil of Percier, André Marie Renié (1789-1853) who, while clothing the building in its timid 'English neo-Gothic' dress, also did the far more sympathetic work indoors. Here, as in England at the same time, Gothic was all very well for churches and garden-houses, but not quite comfortable in dwellings.[2] Except for the throne room and the duke's startling bedroom, the new interiors are as modest and charming as the duke's work mentioned above. The bedroom, within its striped wallpaper enclosure and upon its tiled floor,

---

[1] The Queen's *Journal*, 31 August 1845. Hereafter all dated quotations from Queen Victoria, unless otherwise identified, are to be understood as from her diary, and they will not be footnoted.

[2] One of the marks of eighteenth-century or Regency Gothic of the offhand sort, as opposed to Gothic Revival, is the breadth of the windows and the relatively large window area, the result of three generations of sash-windows and steadily enlarging sizes of window-panes. Such a fine archaeological piece of Gothic Revival domestic work as Peckforton Castle, Cheshire – by Salvin for John Tollemache, 1846–50 – used plausibly small windows, and the interiors must have been correspondingly dark.

bore a sort of Jeffersonian bed-alcove which took the form of a triumphal arch in marbleized plaster, with trophies painted in the spandrels; the sitting-room next to it had a monumental *Kachelofen*, poison-blue walls, and (for once) intricately draped curtains with rose fringe.

Several of Renié's drawings are preserved in the *Staatsarchiv*, including one in which, carefully rendered, we see one of the still-existing French eighteenth-century 'Nouveaux Indes' tapestries; this drawing is dated 1822. Two others are for the oddly-shaped library and the octagonal dressing-room which Renié made by rearranging the Ehrenburg stairs. There had been near the end of each wing a circular staircase, the eastern one of which the architect now gutted; he made new, light, straight-run stairs in part of the old corridors, provided breakneck service stairs in a corner, and floored over the circular stairwell at two levels for the dressing-room and for a library (shaped in plan as a long D, a semicircle attached to a half-square whose long side is the diameter). The bookcases on the curved wall are mahogany with stretched curtains, rather French-looking.[1] An adjacent square reception room with light-and-dark lemonwood inlays in the panelling is more German-looking: one of the few approaches to Biedermeier in Ernest I's interiors.

Elsewhere in the Ehrenburg is a long sixteenth-century gallery, remodelled in Empire style and having a black marble chimneypiece said to have been designed by Schinkel in 1817; the *Staatsarchiv* has a plan, perhaps from Schinkel's drafting-room, for a remodelling (never carried out) of the *Marstall,* the old stable range next to the Schloss. One might suppose there was little reason to send to Schinkel for small matters when Renié was in charge, but a token from Potsdam would be of a piece with the *Hoheitssache*. Among other designs preserved is one for a restyling of the *Platz* in front of the Ehrenburg, dated 1835 and apparently signed Lenni – this is probably by Peter Joseph Lenné (1798–1866), who became chief garden-designer and manager for Schinkel at Potsdam in 1815. The *Platz* was finally cleared, towards the

---

[1] There has been confusion in some accounts of Coburg between this library and another, which had ceiling-panels bearing the names of Goethe, Schiller, and other literary giants, and which was installed at the Rosenau for Ernest II's wife, Alexandrine of Baden.

end of Ernest's building campaigns, of an accumulation of old houses and palace dependencies.

One of the Duke's most diverting ideas was to propose a sort of guest house for royal visitors only, literally an *Hôtel des Princes;* for this there is a scheme by Renié dated 1823, and another by Gutensohn, dated 1830, which includes the hotel, a new opera house, and an orangery to be built under the slope leading up to Veste Coburg. Johann Gottfried Gutensohn (1792–post 1844) also designed many of the remodellings of ceilings in the Ehrenburg, which either replaced damaged older work or simply reduced the scale of certain interiors to make them more suitable to Empire furniture. Gutensohn is connected with other personages of our inquiry: as a young man in Rome he was noticed by Ludwig I of Bavaria, then crown prince, who later sent him to Greece as building superintendent to the bungling Otho I; the second edition of Gutensohn's *Denkmäler der Christlichen Religion* (Munich, 1843) had a new text by Baron Bunsen, later Prussian ambassador in London; an English edition of Gutensohn's *Sammlung von Denkmälern und Verzierungen der Baukunst in Rom aus dem 15. und 16. Jahrhundert* was published by Ludwig Gruner in 1844; and with one Thürmer he produced a set of engravings of the Villa Madama with attempts (different from Geymüller's) to restore missing sections; this was used by Prince Albert and Ruland for their Raphael corpus.

When Gotha came also into Ernest I's domain in 1825–6, he extended his campaigns. At Friedenstein his rooms were much like those in the Rosenau and the Ehrenburg, though a shade richer in detail; but again there was a decent absence of clutter; the floors were bare, perhaps only to show their beautiful cube-pattern parquetry. Reinhardtsbrunn had once been a cloister, and had a long history of fire, damage in the Peasants' War of 1525, two seventeenth-century revisions, and additions; thereafter gradual decay. Ernest rebuilt its church completely, beginning in 1828; in 1827 he put Gustav Eberhard in charge of restoring the *hohe Haus* of 1607–11. Without altering the disposition of the main rooms or floor levels, Eberhard was to make the house liveable, with larger windows and other amenities. The result is a symmetrical late-Gothic dress of freshly-quarried red sandstone, with Tudorish labels over the windows, tracery here and there, and heraldic flourishes carved at some of the doorways; again there is a faintly British flavour, as of quick-dried Wyatville. The *Staatsarchiv* has some of the drawings, dated 1831. Eberhard (1805–80), though a pupil in Paris of Leclerc, was a native of Gotha. He completed Reinhardtsbrunn in 1833, thereafter designing a theatre, ducal stable, and Roman Catholic church for Gotha (1837–40); Prince Albert and Ernest II chose Eberhard to execute the ducal mausoleum (1854–8) in Coburg, to which we shall return.

Queen Victoria, visiting after her father-in-law's death, described Reinhardtsbrunn as 'furnished in dear Papa's best taste' and was pleased more by it than by anything but the Rosenau. When it was damaged by fire in March 1852 she bewailed 'those lovely rooms so beautifully furnished . . . dear Albert's father's last, and favourite work'. The Rothbarth watercolours at Windsor almost certainly show Ernest I's work rather than Ernest II's restorations. Once more there are handsome floors normally bare, Gothic decoration on ceilings or carved tracery on doors and in windows embrasures; walls in strong plain colours (bright green, staring blue, gold) with wallpaper borders; white tile stoves or black marble chimneypieces; simple white curtains, sometimes with ball fringe, seldom with pelmets or draped valances. Once, the routine early nineteenth-century pedestal table covered with potted plants appears; and in the Duke's own sitting-room chairs with loop or ribbon backs like flattened pierced hearts.

In all Ernest I's decoration, besides things which the reader will already have noticed, there is one repeating rich note: his fondness for ormolu candlesticks and for partly gilt clocks, often under glass domes and sometimes of a fearful fantasy. One timepiece at the Ehrenburg is a standing Athena in bronze, with the clock-hands and numerals in gold on her shield. Queen Victoria and Prince Albert's remarkably numerous purchases of clocks and candelabra *en suite* did not go in for freaks, but they liked bronze and gold, or blue enamel with bright-and-matte gold; and, particularly in the early years of their marriage, they repeatedly chose ornament of Bacchanalian subjects, or such as Daphnis and Chloe.

All this circumstantial matter is pertinent not only on the Prince's account but because the Queen was brought up with Empire furniture of her mother's.

It remains to mention the Callenberg and the *Festung* or Veste Coburg itself. The former has been so extensively romanticized and Anglicized by successive English-born or Anglophile dukes that it is impossible to say what it was like in 1830. The Festung, a truly romantic feudal stronghold having a sort of resemblance to the Hohensalzburg, was in disrepair during the childhood of the Prince and his brother, though the memorabilia of Luther, the old carriages, and the armoury (with its heaps of pikes and breastplates from the Thirty Years War) were evidently safely kept. Under Ernest II and his successors the Festung became again a dwelling as well as a museum of the family and of local history. The works of art gathered there from various Wettin houses survived the war of 1939–45, but unhappily the accession records were destroyed by fire after a bombing; this has made it impossible to guess what came there when. But Prince Albert certainly knew the documents of Luther and Wallenstein and the long series of New Year's greetings from generations of Thuringian neighbours; and he sent additions to the autograph collection almost every time he wrote to his brother from England. As a boy he collected the tin-glazed earthenware of the short-lived (1738–86) Coburg pottery; around this and the early glass collected in the late nineteenth century by Prince Alfred Duke of Edinburgh, an admirable systematic collection has been formed. Franz Friedrich Anton's 300,000 prints are also at the Festung (230,000 of them German), and four thousand drawings, many of them important (e.g., Dürer and Kulmbach).

The didactic features of Prince Albert's early travel, which was part of King Leopold's and Baron Stockmar's plan of study, have been amply reported upon; I need only give a list of place-names: 1835, Strelitz, Berlin, Dresden, Prague, Budapest; 1836, London, Ostend, Brussels; 1837–8, the University of Bonn; 1838–9, Switzerland, Italy, England. When his uncle or Stockmar was not present, their letters followed him Polonius-like; in the last year a young English officer was sent out as companion and language teacher. We know that the nineteen-year-old at Florence (where Jérôme Bonaparte was 'very civil' to him) admired the Pitti Palace, perhaps because it was still a palace and not purely a picture-gallery; but we can only guess that he may have liked especially the 'warm room' of the Pitti, with the polychrome tile floor and the frescoes by Pietro da Cortona. We know that he was disappointed by most of the ceremonies of Rome, where he talked art to the Pope and received the honorary diploma of the Academy of St Luke; he was even a little disappointed with himself because he was not more enthusiastic about the Sistine Chapel.[1] But we do not know for sure whether he met the remnant of the Nazarenes, many of whom by 1839 were back in Germany as influential directors of academies, leaving in Rome perhaps only Overbeck (by no means a fixture), Ramboux, Johannes Veit, the marginal von Rohden, and old Reinhart who, though German, was not really sympathetic with the Nazarenes (the heroic landscape-painter Joseph Anton Koch died in January while Prince Albert was in Florence).[2]

If he got anything from direct contact with the Nazarenes it was probably their double emphasis on vocation: in the religious sense and in the practical sense of insisting on professional standards of craftsmanship which had latterly been neglected. The earnestness, the sense of mission, the tendency to substitute moral or ethical criteria for aesthetic ones, and to test beauty by supposed virtue – all Nazarene characteristics – find an echo in Prince Albert. Whether or not he saw the group's work in the Casa Bartholdy and the Villa Massimo, his interest in fresco has roots in the Nazarene programme. He had met Julius Schnorr von Carolsfeld in December 1838 at Munich and visited his studio at the Academy,[3] and must have seen Cornelius's great schemes of fresco decoration in Ludwig I's new buildings. It is therefore more than likely that he met the Roman remnant of the Nazarenes, as well as J. M. von Wagner, who was installed in Ludwig I's Villa Malta in Rome as buyer of antique sculpture for the Glyptothek. He almost certainly met Ludwig Gruner for the first time in Rome; Gruner became one of his steadiest advisers on works of art, buying sculpture for the Osborne terraces and fifteenth-century paintings for both Queen and Prince, publishing the Buckingham Palace fresco experiment, and designing a jewel-casket shown at the Exhibition of 1851, candelabra, inlaid table-tops, and the like.

We wonder whether the young Prince, with Goethe's *Italienische*

---

[1] This is a not uncommon reaction for sensitive persons upon first experiencing a much-touted *Sehenswürdigkeit;* witness Oscar Wilde's famous remark on Niagara Falls. Ruskin at 21 wrote, 'St Peter's I expected to be *disappointed* in. I was *disgusted.*'

[2] For an admirable account of the group see Keith Andrews, *The Nazarenes,* 1964.

[3] Letter to Florschütz; *Archives,* vol. A/6.

1. Ferdinand Rothbarth: *Ernest I's Bedroom at the Ehrenburg in Coburg*; water-colour, commissioned by the Queen, 1845

2. *The Riesensaal in the Ehrenburg*, Coburg; about 1693

3. Caleb Robert Stanley: *Aviary, Frogmore*; watercolour, April 1845

4. Douglas Morison: *The Picture Gallery, Buckingham Palace*; watercolour, 1843

5. Joseph Nash: *The Queen's Birthday Table*; watercolour, 24 May 1849

6. Julius Troschel: *La Filatrice Addormentata*; marble; gift of the Prince to the Queen, 24 May 1849

7. Sir Edwin Landseer: *The Queen and Prince with the Princess Royal*; canvas, $44\frac{1}{2} \times 56\frac{1}{2}$ in.; commissioned by the Queen, 12 June 1841

8. Franz Xaver Winterhalter: *Queen Victoria*; canvas, $25\frac{7}{8} \times 20\frac{7}{8}$ in.; gift of the Queen to the Prince, 26 August 1843

9. Sir Edwin Landseer: *Prince Albert with the Princess Royal*; coloured crayons, $15\frac{1}{2} \times 11\frac{1}{2}$ in.; gift of the Prince to the Queen, 26 August 1842

10. *Wreath, Earrings, and Pair of Brooches*; engraved gold, porcelain, and green enamel; gifts of Prince Albert and the Duchess of Kent to the Queen, Christmas 1845 and 10 February 1846

11. *Cradle*, carved and gilded wood; German late seventeenth century; acquired by the Queen and Prince in March 1843

12. W. L. Leitch: *Osborne House under Construction*; watercolour, 11 March 1847

13. *Osborne House*: 1845 and following years

14. *Hall Chair*, mahogany; designed by Henry Whitaker, 1847

15. *Candelabrum*, one of a pair made by Oslers of Birmingham for Osborne; glass, 8 ft tall; gift of the Prince to the Queen, 24 May 1848; shown at the Great Exhibition, 1851

Reise (1816–17) in hand, followed the great man's footsteps all the way to Naples, as many a pious German has done since. And we wonder how much influence certain well-known professors may have had upon Ernest and Albert during their sixteen months at Bonn. Immanuel Fichte, son of the eminent J. G. Fichte, was professor of philosophy, and emphatic upon the need for what he called 'moral experience' (this again sounds Nazarene).[1] August Wilhelm von Schlegel, brother to the great Friedrich and a weighty person in his own right, became professor of history in 1818 and, although he was seventy when the Coburgers matriculated, and may no longer have been teaching, he was active in philological study and publication. Perhaps he or someone of his general mind was the source of Prince Albert's belief that History was the best instructor of princes.[2]

In Antwerp, it is safe to guess, the Prince probably saw the van Ertborn collection of 'primitives', which was the foundation of the Antwerp picture gallery; formed substantially before 1828, it was as much a pioneer collection as that of the brothers Boisserée, which Ludwig I bought for the Alte Pinakothek and which the Prince knew. He will also surely have made the rounds of many of the Franconian seats and collections, as well as those courts and works of art to be seen by well-born travellers on the Rhine and Danube. The Fürstenberg collection at Donaueschingen, which was started about 1829, was one of the possible outreaching ones, not merely an inherited accumulation. For the treasure of English houses, Prince Albert will have been prepared by Passavant's *Kunstreise durch England und Belgien* (Frankfurt, 1833), to which King Leopold probably introduced him.

---

[1] A rather typical English view of the contemporary German earnestness is James Dennistoun's in 'Pictures and Picture-Dealing' (*Foreign Quarterly Review*, 1845): '. . . the Germans are plodding students, bound to each other, and to their common pursuit, by every tie of country and sympathy; whilst the English are loiterers, left to waste or misapply their opportunities. Under it [their Nazarene discipline], Overbeck and Cornelius, Veit and Schnorr, Schwanthaler and Gruner, have effected an entire renovation of art, and have enshrined their names in a niche far higher than their British contemporaries, as yet, approached.'

[2] Letter to his daughter the Princess Royal, later the Empress Frederick, 16 March 1858, quoted by Corti, *Wenn . . . Sendung und Schicksal einer Kaiserin*, 1954, p. 73. The Nazarene brothers Veit were stepsons of Friedrich von Schlegel; their mother was a Mendelssohn, an aunt of the composer.

The King's own house of Laeken outside Brussels had been stripped by Albert Casimir of Sachsen-Teschen when he fled in 1789, but the Gobelins tapestries of Achilles which were installed for Napoleon were still there. The château, built from 1782 by Louis Montoyer of Hainault and Antoine Payen of Tournai, is in a good international Louis XVI style; before the modern partition of the Low Countries it had been an occasional residence for the King of Holland. There is a domed central salon, expressed as a semi-circular projection, and at each end a three-storey pavilion crowned by statues; it rather suggests Buckingham House before Nash began to enlarge it.[1] There were also in King Leopold's time a Chinese orangery and a *Temple d'Amitié* in the garden; the temple was circular, with ten Tuscan columns and a statue (it may have influenced the design of the Duchess of Kent's mausoleum).

Prince Albert's visual memory was stocked, by the time of his marriage, with images from the Italian grand tour, Flemish Baroque and Mannerist art, Gothic of various places and periods, German Rococo, the neo-Classic architecture of Schinkel, Gärtner, and von Klenze, in short everything from Rhenish Romanesque to the Nazarenes. He had also perhaps had enough experience of trial and error in the visual arts to know that his hand would never be as skilled in that field as his eye. In music, however, he had not only historical knowledge but a skilled hand and voice.

Without apologizing for the amount of conjecture to which the incomplete records of the Prince's early travel lead us, we may say that his other and better-documented studies made him at twenty a very well-informed young man. He and John Ruskin were, in their generation, outstanding among young men who had been most carefully prepared by their elders for the careers which they undertook. As we shall see later, one of the puzzles of the period is the apparent almost complete absence of contact between them.

---

[1] Louis Joseph Montoyer followed Albert Casimir back to Vienna and there designed for him the Albertina (1800–4). The big room with its statues of Apollo and the Muses is a nice bit of romantic classicism and a good place to work in. The statues, to be sure, are by Josef Klieber and date from the second quarter of the century.

2

The Queen's Taste

When Russell Lynes coined his now famous word, *tastemaker*, he was thinking, I believe, of the way in which really original choices become acceptable to less original people through the activities of popularizers (*vulgarisateurs* the French would call them) who mediate between the real finders or inventors and the consumers. Mr Lynes has been amusing us ever since with lists of the preferred music, furniture, works of art, drink, drama, and clothing of highbrows, upper and lower middlebrows, and lowbrows at given moments in the history of taste.

It would be fair to say that Queen Victoria was a consumer, better able than most to command what she wanted, but a consumer nevertheless in matters of taste, admiring so impeccable a person as the Duchess of Sutherland, who could do no wrong in the Queen's eyes, and whose taste the Queen could not imagine herself as equalling. The Duchess herself was not of course an artist, but a superb arranger and chooser, just such as a recent observer describes in general terms:

'Creative people very often do not have what is commonly known as "taste" in their manner of living. . . . Perhaps they are so greatly absorbed in their art that they have no need to look outside of it. On the other hand, I have observed that there are people who are not remotely creative and yet are extremely artistic. These people have irreproachable taste and are only happy when surrounded by beauty. They can decorate a house beautifully, arrange flowers charmingly, design exquisite clothes, and blend colours faultlessly. It would seem that creativeness in the artist is something quite different from the mere production of beauty.'[1]

The Prince was neither a mere consumer nor (in the arts) a great originator, but a brilliant popularizer, mediator, and organizer, and

[1] Mercedes de Acosta, *Here Lies the Heart*, 1960, p. 120.

one of the creators of the modern general art museum. Before we go on to his confrontation with British taste and British activities in the arts at the time of his marriage, I must say a little about his bride's orientation.

The Princess Victoria was brought up (her father having died before she was a year old) by her mother and a team of instructors chosen by Sir John Conroy, the Duchess of Kent's major-domo, and approved in principle by King Leopold, Dr Stockmar, the Coburg grandmother, and Lehzen the 'Lady Attendant on the Princess'. Uncle Leopold interfered often, not only because of his strong dynastic interest but also because he paid most of the bills up to the time when Parliament, after the accession of William IV, began to grant an allowance for the heir. Upon Leopold's election to the throne of Belgium in the following year (1831), he put into trusteeship the £50,000 a year which he himself had from Parliament, and some help to his sister and her daughter continued from that source.

The Princess was, I think primarily an auditory receptor. To the extent to which her visual taste was formed by things rather than people, we can name an interesting mixture of first causes: Kensington Palace and her mother's furniture, and after them the worldly mode. The rooms given over to the Duchess of Kent and her household were fine seventeenth-century ones, with tall windows (narrow for their height) looking out eastward upon the Park. The Duchess had fetched from Amorbach a good deal of the new furniture with which she had lived as Princess of Leiningen, or which she had acquired in her first widowhood (1814-18). This furniture was German, from Frankfurt and Aschaffenburg and Mainz, in Empire style, some of it white and gilt. The Leiningens had been uprooted by the French from their old land on the west bank of the Rhine, and the superb Baroque abbey and Benedictine cloister of Amorbach, which they received in exchange shortly before Princess Victoire married Emich von Leiningen, meant little to them; they sold most of the portable contents and started over again. Amorbach is only about a hundred miles west-south-west of Coburg, and the Princess must, therefore, have seen her brother Ernest I's remodelling of the Ehrenburg in process; during her first widowhood she herself decorated rooms there and at Saalfeld.

Queen Victoria always noticed good Empire furniture on her travels and, in her invariable reminder-association habit, tied it to 'Mama's furniture from Amorbach'. What stayed with her chiefly from Kensington Palace's handsome inconvenient parade rooms was a dislike of inconvenience and a desire for privacy. She often noticed in later years the awkwardness of an enfilade of rooms without *dégagements*. Her acquaintance with the beauties of Wren's work and the only lesser beauties of William Kent's work in Kensington Palace does not seem to have caused any association with the late seventeenth century to rise in her mind when she became mistress of the splendours of Charles II's rooms at Windsor; but she often remarked resemblances to Hampton Court in Continental palaces. As a girl she may well have admired the Merry Monarch, and she thought William III a 'cruel bad man'.[1] Claire Jerrold says that only two years before the Prince Consort's death the couple planned to write a new life of Charles II.[2] As the Prince felt that William III was 'the greatest sovereign this country has to boast of,'[3] he may well have changed his wife's mind in this as in some other opinions; in her old age she would buy only under pressure the portrait of Charles II by Michael Wright, annotating her approval of the purchase with the comment that she did not care for that king.[4]

When she came to the throne, Queen Victoria inherited (along with her father's clocks and debts) a monarchy at the low point of its repute. George IV, William IV, and their cruel, rowdy, or eccentric brothers had brought the Crown almost down and out. The very taste of George IV, costly to the public purse as it had been, was under suspicion by many. The first king since Charles I to be a fountain of taste, he was also at the end of the old progression of styles developing one from another. The almost complete break with that long tradition was

---

[1] *Journal*, 25 August 1839; Melbourne said no, the 'only cruel thing he ever did was at Glencoe' in 1692.

[2] Claire Jerrold, *The Married Life of Queen Victoria*, 1913, p. 384; no authority is given for the statement.

[3] From his speech to the S.P.G., 16 June 1851; the opinion may have been influenced by Hallam's *Constitutional History*, which he and the Queen read together in 1842; the Queen notes on 17 November that – whatever William III may have felt – she did not believe a sovereign's right came from the people alone.

[4] Information from Oliver Millar, M.V.O., in letters of 16 and 30 December 1964.

marked, during his regency and reign, by the triumph of the politically-motivated Empire style concoted (though not without precedents) by Napoleon's designers. In its various versions, from Hope's British to Biedermeier, it helped to let loose the flood of new styles which provided the eclectic delights of the next four generations.

Queen Victoria never knew the real and short-lived beauties of Carlton House, and what she liked at the Brighton Pavilion, at her first exposure to it in 1838, was the riding-school; when she and her husband went there in 1842, they were 'struck by the strangeness of the place', and 'strangeness' became her key word in noting further visits in her journal. Prince Albert can hardly have liked the aggressively exotic flavour of the Pavilion, and the Queen, after trying it in the interest of sea air for their older children, came to dislike its total lack of privacy. When she gave it up, some of its 'Chinesey' furniture and fittings came to the new east wing of Buckingham Palace.

The Queen's own early taste was rather uncritical: what she really liked was what was new and modish in clothes, music, and the theatre. In the first two and a half years of her reign she was guided by the ancient upper-class taste of Lord Melbourne, who was flat, old-fashioned and supercilious in his judgements. He disliked landscapes, said of the Dutch paintings at Buckingham Palace, mostly chosen by Lord Farnborough for George IV, that they were of a 'low style', and thought Murillo 'even lower than Raphael'. He approved the Queen's idea of buying Italian paintings (meaning presumably the Bolognese school) after her father's debts should be cleared away. In May 1838 she wrote of her 'wishing, but fearing to buy pictures'.

Lord Esher in *The Girlhood of Queen Victoria* (1912) quoted such full particulars of her early enthusiasms that I need repeat only enough for flavour. Though the Princess was steadily drilled by her clerical and lay tutors in constitutional history and other suitable subjects, she was certainly provided with all the entertainment that the small Kent purse afforded. A mixture of quiet amusement with instruction was offered by the albums and annuals, the habit of looking at which seems to have been inculcated for evenings when there was not an opera or ballet. The 'picture-book' device was already an old one in popular chap-books; for the Princess it was developed as a way of learning history, even recent history, including royal genealogies. Thomas

Roscoe's *Landscape Annual,* beginning in 1830, with engravings after Prout and Harding and Roberts, is typical of the ones that came ready-made; others were specially put together. After the Queen's accession the habit grew upon her, and became exercise taken with real pleasure, notably if Melbourne was at her elbow to expatiate upon a volume of mezzotints after Reynolds portraits. Prince Albert later built upon this habit and upon his own methodical foundations the great stock of illustrated records which he intended as resources for the training of the Prince of Wales and sovereigns after him.

Perhaps the Duchess of Kent's chief outlay of an exceptional sort was for those late-summer travels in England and Wales which William IV referred to slightingly as 'royal progresses', at the beginning of which (1 August 1832) the Princess undertook to keep a journal. She was a remarkable observer; these journeys and her notes on them were the best possible illustration to her studies, and an admirable intro-duction to the sovereign-subject relationship, as well as to British topo-graphy. The splendid establishments visited were treasure houses of works of art and of history; reservoirs of styles, manners, even folkways. A variety of mayors, dukes, rich commoners, rural deans, servants, and interesting ladies left impressions upon the small Princess. With her charming voice, her enchanting way of moving, and her acceptable parlour accomplishments, she was received as precisely what she was, an heir presumptive, refreshing and welcome.

The four or five years for which we have her journals as heir were years when the Regent Street quadrant still had Nash's arcades, when Norfolk House (with its rococo interiors) stood in St James's Square, the Royal Mews dominated what is now Trafalgar Square, Burlington House was still a dwelling, and Apsley House had just been remodelled for its new owner. The Coburg Theatre, named for Uncle Leopold, had many years to go before it should become the Old Vic. The young Victoria's Church was in effect Queen Anne's, her State a subdued form of George IV's. The London that she knew (unless one went to the Abbey or the Temple Church or the Southwark Inns or St Barth-olomew the Great) was the London shaped by Wren and Adam and Nash; Windsor, because her mother quarrelled even more with William IV than with George IV, she hardly saw. The novelties that excited her eye and ear were those of the stage and those observed *en voyage.* In country visits the random character of greater age, the proximity of Stuart houses to Gothic parish churches, the clashes of old and new within a house (which she never liked) were noted down along with the awkward bows of beadles, the new coiffures, and the pleasures of driving fast. Her journal was overseen by her mother and Lehzen, perhaps occasionally looked through by a bishop or the Duchess of Northumberland. Esher remarks on the complete change of tone from the day when the Princess became Queen and had some privacy, at least when she was diarizing.

Let us see what changes she made (other than having a room of her own and enjoying a minor unconstitutional triumph) between accession and marriage. First, she entered with pleasure upon the tenancy of great possessions. 'My' this and 'my' that appear promptly in her journal. Repeatedly, after dinner at Windsor, she looks at Domenichino drawings; she counts the Canalettos; with Melbourne, she turns the pages of other albums of drawings (the 'uneligible' pages have been tacked together);[1] in the spring of 1838 she notes that she was out of the Palace only one hour when she went to the Old Water Colour Society's show, and that at the Academy she liked Landseer (including a picture of one of her own dogs), Grant, Lucas, Callcott, Maclise, and Hayter (a portrait of Melbourne).

In 1838 she is already enthusiastic about Highland costume; she hangs the Wilkies inherited from George IV; in the season she admires Lansdowne House and the new Stafford House ('beautifully fitted up'). In the autumn she hangs the Gainsboroughs of George III's family for Lord Melbourne to admire (he said this was wise, for it pleased 'old people' – meaning the Princess Augusta – who thought themselves forgotten). In November, her saying that Haydon's colouring is 'not English' sounds like unadulterated Melbournism.

In March 1839 she has a new piano, painted with monkeys, which may sound rather *dix-huitième* (Melbourne approved); she dislikes almost all the official paintings of her coronation; she hangs her dressing room with Partridge's portrait of Stockmar, Hayter's Melbourne

---

[1] These, it seems to me, can only have been some of the Leonardo da Vinci anatomical drawings (Clark, *A Catalogue of the Drawings of Leonardo da Vinci in the Collection of His Majesty the King at Windsor Castle*, 1935, I, 178-9).

(which she now finds 'coarse . . . but like'), and a first Winterhalter (Louise Queen of the Belgians with her infant, the future Leopold II). At Windsor, between dinner and dessert, she causes perfume to be burned at table (Lady Holland did this, too, and perhaps Lady Blessington; the young Queen and the older *salonnières* whom she could not receive were inquisitive about one another, and Lord M. was glad to act as gossip). When the dinner table has bisque porcelain ornaments, she asks Lord M. his opinion as usual (he in his grudging-oracular fashion said they were nice 'for a small party'). With her watch, the Queen wears a little coral hand against the evil eye; she gives her mentor a gold one with the same gesture, for his watch-chain. It is a wonder that he did not more fatally mould her; really he was outrageous but he did build up her self-confidence.[1]

A week after her marriage in February 1840 she still deferred to Melbourne by removing, from a room in Buckingham Palace where the Court sat after dinner, certain landscapes and inserting in their place portraits of William and Mary and some others. On 11 March at the Ancient Concert there was 'too much Handel for my taste;' but the next day there was talk of Prince Albert's becoming a Director of the Concerts; and so he did; not to mention his persuading her that Handel was really rather fine.

The Queen's attachment to things and people made her sensitive to *likeness* (lack of which was her main reason for objecting to the Coronation pictures); once a likeness was found satisfactory it was multiplied so that it might be found in some form in any house of the Queen's, and

---

[1] Lady Longford (*Queen Victoria/Born to Succeed*, 1964, p. 577) calls Melbourne a 'dedicated pessimist', but he was more than that, being outrageously and almost comically reactionary. He believed (though he admitted he 'mustn't say it') that there ought to be one law for the rich and another for the poor; 'blotting paper no use – sand the only thing'; the penny post would do no good at all; it was 'not social' if you did not spend four thousand pounds on your first visit to Paris; 'when people talk of bridges and railroads, they generally are liberal'; 'a very singular thing, but all these Temperance people are Radicals'; 'these Quakers are all knaves'. In fairness to him it should also be said that he thought Bishops should be chosen young, that 'those who fight custom against grammar are fools', and that 'monuments don't add to the man's reputation; his works are his best monument'. All these quotations are from the Queen's *Journal*. It is curious that the late President Kennedy should have been fascinated by Lord Melbourne.

smaller copies (miniatures or enamels) were made as gifts, still smaller ones becoming bracelets for ladies-in-waiting. In her girlhood, every new visitor had left a powerful after-image which had to be fixed by the exchange of hair and handkerchiefs, sometimes portraits; in later years, while the multiplication of images had certain real uses, the attachment to places and persons was in danger of becoming pathological, and Prince Albert had to hold it in check. But the Queen's taste was circumstantial. She thought nothing more beautiful than a beautiful horse; if you gave her a silver statuette of her horse or of a favourite dog, she would be pleased if the likeness was good and pleased that you gave her silver.

The Prince's view was much broader than Lord Melbourne's, and he began to open the Queen's eyes and ears immediately. Though he was probably a visual receptor, and visual order was his work, it seems clear that music was his emotional outlet, and that playing the organ was a real release for him whom Lytton Strachey called 'so full of energy and stress and torment, so mysterious and so unhappy, and so fallible and so very human'.[1] During the early years of the marriage the couple played, in piano-duet form, through most of the Mozart and Beethoven symphonies and much other standard literature; when Lablache, the Queen's singing teacher, came to the Palace, the Prince often joined them (he sang bass); and when private concerts were given, the three took part with various sound Court amateurs and occasional professionals in sextets and small choruses. Much more of this joint music-making is reported in the Queen's *Journal* than of the joint drawing and etching in the first few (and least busy) years. To judge by the remaining evidence, their work was romantic but timid,[2] like the Prince's paintings. In 1846 they tried lithography briefly, but by this time there were greater enterprises; and they may have turned against these activities when an unauthorized individual somehow got hold of some of their plates and uttered a publication as well as trying to exhibit the prints.[3] Neverthe-

---

[1] Lytton Strachey, *Queen Victoria*, 1921, p. 318.

[2] A. H. Scott-Elliot, 'The Etchings by Queen Victoria and Prince Albert' in *Bulletin of the New York Public Library*, 65, No. 3, March 1961, pp. 139–53.

[3] According to Claire Jerrold, *op. cit.*, pp. 274–84, Jasper Tomsett Judge, a gadfly journalist who lived at Windsor, came to grief over trying to exhibit a hundred of the Royal couple's etchings; but the author, who seems to have

less, both Queen and Prince continued to sketch on holiday, and the Queen's illustrations to her journal, some of which were preserved when Princess Beatrice did her great editorial work, are sometimes skilful as well as pungent.

A few samples of change in the Queen's taste may suffice. She had never attended a performance of *The Magic Flute* until after her marriage; on 12 June 1840 an amateur Palace concert included excerpts, and on 11 June 1841 the Queen heard the whole opera for the first time, finding it beautiful but long. By 10 July 1851 her note on a performance showed that she loved the piece but thought the story 'too simple, trivial, and rather absurd for our times' (the costumes were all carefully copied 'from a German book lent by Albert' – Schinkel's designs?). On 11 May 1852, when the two eldest sons were taken to *The Magic Flute,* she found the singers good but the production 'slovenly'. When she first heard Verdi she noted with evident approval Lablache's severe judgement on his music, but she came to like both *Rigoletto* and *Trovatore.* The Royal couple's delight in the art and personality of Mendelssohn is well known.

The Prince's interest in the Ancient Concerts, of which he became a Director in March 1840, helped to keep alive, sometimes to resurrect, certain otherwise 'dated' or neglected composers. The Queen's reason for not going very often to these Concerts was not so much a dislike of Handel as a newspaper statement that the Ancient Concerts were the best place to see the Queen plainly; on 8 May 1844 she noted that, as a result of that paragraph, the 'ignorant public (I must call them so, as their taste is so bad)' came in vast numbers. She therefore preferred the greater privacy of the Royal box at theatre or opera, where at least it was dark during the performance; and the Prince would sometimes

---

inherited most of the Jerrold prejudices against Victoria and Albert, was chiefly concerned to show the heavy hand of the Court and of the Prince's secretary Anson. Another version of this story appears in *The Times* for 9 February 1949, which recapitulates an article of one hundred years before, about the theft of an early Welsh travel sketchbook of the Queen's, a catalogue of the contents of which was published along with the promise of a facsimile autograph of the Queen; Prince Albert had secured an injunction against the publication, and the Lord Chancellor, in confirming the injunction granted by his subordinate, gave a ruling which, said *The Times,* had proved important in the later history of copyright in works of art.

join her there after one of his own early-evening engagements. By the end of his life, his wife found herself able to absorb the music of Wagner and indeed of almost everyone except Berlioz (a noise as of 'cats and dogs', she said). I believe her judgements on music are her own, however much she may have been led to them; while her judgements on visual art reflect her husband; more often she simply says that he pointed out to her this or that painted splendour at Antwerp or Burghley.

On 23 April 1859 the Queen heard, apparently for the first time, Bach's *St Matthew Passion* at Windsor (Bach was almost forgotten by the large public); 'so fine', she wrote, '. . . a little fatiguing'.

On 30 June 1860 Glück's *Orfeo* 'beautifully given . . . music in parts old-fashioned'. For their last wedding anniversary they had at Buckingham Palace sixteen singers with an orchestra and organ to do Haydn, Beethoven, Bach's *St Ann* organ fugue, Mendelssohn, a forgotten Marcello quartet, and the Hallelujah Chorus. By this time they had, besides several organs and an harmonium, a French mechanical piano to which the children danced.

Queen Victoria was, at her marriage, an unusually well-informed woman rising twenty-one; Prince Albert, three months younger, was equally well-informed, his education overlapping his wife's in history but otherwise stronger in what we should now call general culture. He was far more interested than she in synthesis, though by no means to the extent of seeking all-embracing Utopian systems. She was more interested in the right way of doing things then and there than in finding universal order. His understanding of his wife's character and needs was, however, as instinctive as his remarkable depth-perception (which gave him insight into mechanical devices) and his physical tact (which made him a good fencer, skater, and dancer).[1] Further, he had like Disraeli an almost feminine intuition (but, being no snob, he did not flatter like Disraeli). A memorandum by his first private secretary, G. E. Anson (Claremont, 8 June 1843), says, 'The Prince is systematically going over the Queen's education and reforming her mind – &

---

[1] By *depth-perception* I mean the ability to read, using one's binocular vision, relationships among three-dimensional objects in space, and thus to recognize from a new viewpoint an object already seen and understood. By *physical tact* I mean the kinaesthetic equivalent of verbal tact or tactfulness (an example might be a blind man's 'sensing' of the nearness of a wall).

drawing out her Powers, and the progress he has made, especially in fairness & candor, has been quite wonderful. . . .' He continues on the good new relationship which the Prince had brought about between the Queen and her mother. The drawing-out went on necessarily throughout the twenty years of the marriage, for the Queen's hotness of temper called for her husband's revision, and he could annoy her by occasional vacillations. Yet he was a broadener, and she a ritualist. By this I do not mean that she was a ritualist in the ecclesiastical sense: far from it. But she had been trained for a particular life and work, she expected those who helped her to have had proper preparation for their share in the work, and she was offended if standard operating procedure was transgressed. At her coronation, the Archbishop of Canterbury tried to force her ring onto the wrong finger; even worse than the physical hurt was her annoyance with his blunder. How could she be patient if an archbishop, who should have known, got things wrong? So, throughout her life, she insisted anxiously upon method. At her marriage she had already worn a rut for herself which was in danger of narrowing her further, so well had she learned her routine. Her toughness saved her; this toughness and her husband's skill in management must, taken together, have electrified anyone who was so foolish as to suppose that a queen was going to let government have its own way.[1]

Both Queen and Prince were lop-sided on the work-play-love-worship quadrilateral:[2] both were long on work and rather short on worship; she mistook idolatrous worship of her husband for love; he could not abandon himself to play except with his children, for his games tended to be elaborate or highbrow, and his sport to become as serious as that of blue-kneed winter bicyclists; the Duke of Wellington once complained of having to play tactical games at Windsor. And if the Prince drew spiritual strength of a re-creating sort from his solitary

---

[1] The aged James Northcote once told the young painter Leslie that George IV was 'the best king of his family we ever had. It has been remarked that this country is best governed by a woman, for then the government is carried on by able men; and George IV is like a woman, for he minds only his own amusements, and leaves the affairs of the country to his ministers, instead of meddling himself, as his father did.' C. R. Leslie, *Autobiographical Recollections*, 1860, I, p. 69.

[2] R. C. Cabot, M.D., *What men Live By/Work, Play, Love, Worship*, 1914.

music, the Queen – though in many ways a much 'stronger' character – drew spiritual re-creation from him.

In the course of the drawing-out, the Prince began to introduce artists and scientists to his wife; she may have been at first either a little troubled or a little boastful in telling her uncle about the new people, for there is a letter to her from King Leopold which says that dealing with artists and scientists requires 'great prudence . . . they are acquainted with all classes of society, and for that very reason are dangerous' (10 October 1845). Not only these but technicians and craftsmen, such as men of the building trades, were agreeable to the Prince: 'Ich habe diese Art Leute so gern; sie sind so intelligent', he said.[1] In time, the Queen heard that the King of Prussia also entertained the learned and the creative; this she took for a testimony to the Prince's forward step.

Just as we should not let ourselves be blinded to certain of Prince Albert's faults by his wife's worshipful attitude, so we should not permit ourselves to be misled about his taste by her accumulations. If we compare the Nash watercolour-and-gouache drawings of the Queen's bedroom and dressing-room at Windsor, dated 1847,[2] with recent colour photographs of her rooms at Osborne,[3] we see that the famous Victorian clutter was a late growth; if we look also at the tinted photographs of her rooms at Windsor taken in 1862,[2] we can guess that this affective clutter began as soon as the Prince was dead. In other words, in the 1847 arrangement even the Queen's rooms show some of her husband's taste: a few portraits hung high in the eighteenth-century fashion, but a new flowered carpet and a modern bed; a French eighteenth-century commode; deep strong colours, red damask on the walls, green on bed and sofa. In 1862 the basic objects are the same, but there are far more things on the chimneypiece, and indeed the only emptiness is in the wastepaper-basket. A lower row of pictures has crept in.

An interesting contrast may be useful. Shortly before her marriage the Queen commissioned of the excellent but aged and 'safe' Sir Francis

---

[1] Remembrance by the Queen, *Archives*, vol. Z/491.

[2] Windsor, Souvenir Album No. 1.

[3] Dust-jacket to *Connoisseur Period Guide No. 6: The Early Victorian Period 1830–1860*, 1958.

Chantrey three marble busts for the Corridor at Windsor: herself, William IV, and Wyatville. In 1876 she took rather a bold step into unfamiliar territory by commissioning of Jules Dalou (who had been in England since 1871) an angel with five children; this work (in the private chapel at Windsor) is of a remarkably Renaissance spirit and even has a Stevens-like *morbidezza*. The Queen may have been moved by some of Dalou's small mother-and-child terracottas, but she would hardly have made this choice without the experience of the twenty years during which she and Prince Albert were decorating Osborne terraces with replicas of standard classical sculpture, buying occasional classic originals, and commissioning work of almost all the accepted sculptors of their day (Calder Marshall was the only one never employed directly, and even he was represented by 'Parian' porcelain reductions among the figurines in glass cases).

Her other late acquisitions were seldom distinguished (they included some work of women artists), and of course she no longer had her husband to find successors to those artists who were superannuated. After 1873, the year in which both Landseer and Winterhalter died, no artist was admitted to the private Royal circle; on the suggestion of the Empress Frederick, the old Queen had herself painted by von Angeli, and on that of the Prince of Wales she allowed herself to be looked at for twenty minutes by J. J. Benjamin-Constant, who then painted from memory.

In subsequent chapters we shall see what share the Queen took in the choices made by her husband. Though it is sometimes hard to tell which of them led the way in some acquisitions for the Royal collection, such a fascinating object as the Darnley Jewel[1] will have appealed to them for different reasons: to the Prince for its design and craftsmanship, its quaint but poetic inscriptions, and its meaning as a rare survival of its time; to the Queen for its probable connexion with some of the most romantic of her ancestors, and perhaps for its obvious preciousness. Her taste was always for intrinsic value and for personal associations.

---

[1] A heart-shaped gold locket with precious stones and enamel; the internal evidence makes it fairly sure that it was made for Margaret Douglas, the mother of Lord Darnley, husband to Mary Queen of Scots. It is reproduced by Dr Joan Evans in *English Jewellery,* 1921.

3

British Tastes in 1840

At the time of the Queen's marriage there existed a fission of tastes which showed that the Rule of Taste was over[1], and which expressed more or less a shift from stratification of taste by class to compartmenting by occupation and interest. Stratification was far from being dead, and obviously there was stratification of quality within each category which I am about to suggest; but there were by 1840 large clusters of people whose work and play and dwellings were those neither of the old ruling class (whatever its political label) nor of the wage-earning classes. The tastes which I shall try to classify transcended the variety of styles which the new eclecticism permitted, although certain styles tended to appeal chiefly to certain tastes. Eclecticism itself must be seen as a natural consequence of the collapse of the Rule of Taste, and as a normal nineteenth-century condition.

One of Max Beerbohm's satirical drawings shows the eighteenth century viewing the future as a minuscule copy of itself while the nineteenth sees the future as an inflated imitation of itself.[2] Eclecticism may be considered in one way as a function of optimism: whereas the old rule had found certain categories right and others wrong, the new rules said all categories were good – take your pick but behave yourself.[3]

If taste, in the long view, is the making of choices which produce rewarding experience, then the marking-out of categories (within each of which one may find the best) is helpful to all who must choose. Such marking-out became, in the fifties, the great work of Prince

---

[1] John Steegman, *The Rule of Taste from George I to George IV*, 1936.
[2] The twentieth century is drawn by Beerbohm as a hunched-over weedy youth who sees the future as a question-mark somewhat like his own silhouette.
[3] Even Soane would, like Repton, show alternative elevations in some cases for one set of plans.

Albert's team in South Kensington; and over against it Ruskin's casting out of certain categories and his idolatry of some others can only seem like a return to eighteenth-century attitudes. When Ruskin said, 'Taste is not only a part and an index of morality; it is the *only* morality',[1] he sounded even more like Oscar Wilde than like the eighteenth century; and Prince Albert would not have agreed with him.

The split – it would be better to call it a trifurcation – had become clear ten or a dozen years after Waterloo, but the sources or reasons for it lay, naturally, a generation farther back.

The old upper class had its houses, as Boston women are said to have their hats. During the long years of comparative peace and prosperity (without war on British soil since 1746), the great building and furnishing campaigns of the eighteenth century had provided the nobility and gentry with all that they could need for several generations if they did not feel pressed by changes in their own Rule or by a rising birthrate among their own numbers. Chambers and Dance and the Adams, Capability Brown and Humphrey Repton, Gainsborough and Reynolds, the Worcester porcelain factory and the Bristol potters and Wedgwood, the Chippendales and Gillows, Roubiliac and Nollekens, had served them well; and Lawrence painted the last of them. The French Revolution gave them a terrible fright.[2] In their alarm, they tended naturally to see their safety and comfort so much in terms of the *status quo* that they froze the liveries of their servants at the breeches-and-hair-powder stage. They had had their flirtations with Gothic and Chinoiserie; Hepplewhite had made a French note pleasant and acceptable; the purchase of *ébénisterie* from French refugees (with the Prince Regent's cook as one of the principal brokers) was perhaps their latest adventure within the old rule.

Of the Regent's two personal buildings, Carlton House was the last splendour of eighteenth-century development, going out in a flourish of Sheratonian draperies and strong post-Adam colours; while the Brighton Pavilion was the lushest outbreak of the romantic taste for novelty, nourished by the eclectic information which a growing British

---

[1] Quoted in Buckley, *The Victorian Temper*, 1951, p. vii, but without source. Mr Buckley tells me it is from Ruskin's *Traffic*, 1864.

[2] The American revolution they rather ignored as a civil commotion taking place on remoter soil; it was an 'unpopular' war.

empire provided. The interior and exterior remodellings of Windsor Castle had differing effects, to which we shall come. The new official face which John Nash gave to the Regent's London was something else: its bones were traditional, its lineaments so modern as to provide a sort of form for the buildings of a new class, who populated by day the offices and lecture-rooms of the coming Establishment and the new clubs in and near Nash's Waterloo Place, by night the new Terraces or the newer Bloomsbury, and Torrington and Fitzroy Squares.[1] The Greek Revival style which this class liked was in a sense a revolt against the Chippendale–Hepplewhite–Sheraton continuum, although Sheraton's *Designs for Household Furniture* (1812) made concessions to it.

This class came forward during the Regency and reign of George IV in response to such stimuli as the development of University College (later the University of London), the growing business of the Law Courts, the increase of the civil service, the improved science of medicine, the pressure on Parliament which led to the Reform of 1832, and the presence of capable youngish or middleaged officers, retired after Waterloo, who would not play the old gentleman and who could not live on half-pay. For the men of this well-instructed and sometimes even learned professional group, the new clubs of the twenties were created. Some of these, such as the 'highbrow' Athenaeum in Decimus Burton's building, were in Greek Revival houses; some were not; but to a very great extent the furniture and interior decoration of these buildings, even of the Travellers', were and are of the Greek Revival family in its more intellectual and restrained forms. Indeed, it is difficult to think of a British corporate dining-room of a certain dignity and masculinity without seeing in the mind's eye *klismos* chairs, pedestal

---

[1] Fitzroy Square, two sides of which have Adam façades, was favoured by professional men and successful artists. Ludwig Gruner lived 1848–55 at No. 12 (not one of the Adam elevations, but a good tall house now the rectory of St Pancras). The Eastlakes lived for years at No. 7; Alfred Stevens lived in the forties around the corner in Robert Street. Maclise lived close by in the thirties. But Trollope said in 1862 in *The Small House at Allington*, 'We know how vile is the sound of Baker Street, and how absolutely foul to the polite ear is the name of Fitzroy Square. The houses, however, in those purlieus are substantial, warm, and of good size.' But they would not do for an earl's daughter whose old house was in Portman Square (Trollope lived in Montagu Square). Here quoted is the Tauchnitz edition of 1864, p. 281.

tables, walls with stencilled anthemia, and sideboards with faint suggestions of altars; and it is worth noting that in Maclise's 'Gallery of Illustrious Literary Characters' (in *Fraser's Magazine,* 1830-8) by far the commonest chair shown as a seat of the mighty was the modified *klismos* with turned front leg, followed by the pure *klismos* and by an editorial easy-chair; the series included one Chippendale chair, occupied by a Scot, and one Sheraton, used by an Irishman – both doubtless conservative. America and France were more faithful than Britain to the pure *klismos*: the chairmakers of Wycombe and thereabouts owned many lathes, and therefore had a vested interest in turning which was threatened by the sabre leg; they took effective countermeasures.

Although the taste of this new engineer-lawyer-don-officer class, which I like to call Grec, favoured the Greek Revival and its later developments, it also liked the more archaeological sort of Gothic (as for instance Savage's St Luke's church Chelsea, 1824, which has true vaulting – a performance both scholarly and practical). The strong engineering element among the upholders of this taste (despite occasional vagaries of pasted-on 'architecture') *generally* moved towards emphatic structure, smooth or even taut surfaces, and correctness rather than fancy. The roots of the taste are in Soane: the long slow curves of his segmental arches, the sharp edges, the arbitrary use or even disuse of mouldings, the rather flat ornament, all turn up in the Britannic version of Empire and in the engineer's architecture (despite those vagaries of dress) seen in bridges.

By 1840 the Grec taste was mature and ready for mutation. Its prime architect was C. R. Cockerell, whose classical training combined with his own genius to make possible excellent work in both Roman and Greek accents (not to mention at least one Gothic performance), and who in his ripe age nevertheless seems as unmistakably Victorian as Barry. Cockerell could be quite as splendid as Barry (especially when he was enriching Elmes's St George's Hall or Basevi's Fitzwilliam Museum), but he always kept a degree of restraint reminiscent of the more purely Greek Burton (who incidentally was a dozen years the younger but had done his own best work when *very* young).

The Empire style itself, propagated at a high level by Thomas Hope's *Household Furniture and Interior Decoration* (1807) and at a lower one by George Smith's *Collection of Designs for Household Furniture and Interior Decoration* (1808), was merged with the Sheraton and older native streams by the efforts of the cabinet-makers, the rising manufacturers of serial furniture, and such influential periodicals as Ackermann's *Repository*.[1] By 1826 Smith's *Cabinet Maker's and Upholsterer's Guide* and rival publications showed the appearance of new Chinese, Egyptian, French, and presumably Indian forms, and was both vulgarizing in the English sense and a *travail de vulgarisation*. By 1840 there were great modifications in the Greek style, but the spirit of the Grec taste continued as a light, blond and smooth sort of counterblast (with classical and academic sanctions) to the inorganic crockets, ebonized lumps, and ballooned upholstery of other eclectic styles and tastes. Its elegance was of rosewood and brass, maple, birch, inlaid mahogany (but not the red-dyed mahogany of the seventies); of muslin, watercolour, clear glass, and single (not double) flowers. It would be fair to add that certain legacies of the Adam brothers lingered long with this taste, especially the fondness for pale tints; the strong deep tones favoured by the Continental Empire style appealed more to the taste which I call Lusso, as did the Continental Empire fondess for veneers of very rich burlwood, for satin, and for great immobile set-pieces of furniture.

As the old upper class held largely to its own old clubs in St James's Street, so it tended not to look for anything new except when it had new sources of money. During the Napoleonic wars it had done almost no building; if thereafter it wanted something, it wanted a setting for its Dubois and Weisweiler commodes. The palace style of Wyatville's Windsor interiors, with elements of Louis XIV and Louis XV, was exactly right; and Wyatville's cousin Benjamin Dean Wyatt became its promoter. For those who liked to gamble in luxurious surroundings he built Crockford's Club (1826-7) with tall panels, *rocaille* detail, and coved ceiling-to-wall transitions; in 1825 he began York House and in 1828 the remodelling of Apsley House in the same French style. Sir John Summerson (in *Georgian London*, 1946) has doubted that Wyatt or his assistant, Harper, was capable of 'this brilliant mimicry of Op-

---

[1] *The London Chair Makers Book of Prices*, 1808, was quick on the uptake, for it, too, included 'Grecian' chairs and sofas.

penordt, Boffrand, and Verberckt', and he suggests that there must 'have been foreign master-hands employed both in design and execution'.[1] He adds that 'In the fifties and sixties it [the style] became a riot, fed by the professional decorators', and I should say much forwarded by the Duchess of Sutherland, who took over York House[2] and completed it as Stafford House[2] with the help of Wyatt himself, Smirke, and Barry (who did two other splendid but Italianate rebuildings for her). It may be significant that the Leveson-Gowers were precisely old upper-class people with new sources of money in the Potteries and canals, on top of the old revenues of Sutherland.

It is also interesting that although Wellington (with new money from public grants) had the new parts of his London house done in this almost royal fashion, the portable objects given him by merchants and bankers, 'noblemen and gentlemen' in syndicates, and Continental royalty, were almost all in the international Empire style: porcelain from German, Austrian, and French State works, and silver that was sumptuous in the assembled-looking Empire way but un-silverish; yet

---

[1] Why not? Henry Holland had employed French decorators at Carlton House, and both his master the Prince of Wales and the second Earl Spencer bought furniture from Dominique Daguerre and other *marchands-merciers* in Paris before the days of the refugees. See F. J. B. Watson, *Louis XVI Furniture*, 1960. 'Scrutiny of the sale catalogues of London auction rooms during the years between 1820 and 1850 reveals that the demand for French furniture in London continued to be sufficiently great to make it more profitable to export Parisian collections for sale here.' *Ibid.*, p. 92.

[2] The history of York-Stafford-Lancaster House is confused. The Duke of York borrowed money from the Marquess of Stafford, but died insolvent in January 1827. Stafford took over the house, meant to give it to his eldest son Gower, but moved in himself, and was entertaining there in October 1830. He was created Duke of Sutherland shortly before he died in 1833. Upon her husband's succeeding, the Duchess Harriet began such a campaign that he gave out in 1838 that he was somewhat 'reduced by building' expense. The noise of constructing an additional storey in 1834 woke up William IV and Queen Adelaide early on summer mornings at the Palace, and Sir Robert Smirke had to apologize. Barry's grand stair was opened with a ball early in July 1835. Hitchcock's date for the Sutherlands' acquisition (1841) is a pardonable mistake; in that year the proceeds of the sale of the crown lease were spent on Victoria Park. The Queen herself, godmother at a christening party, found the house 'beautifully fitted up' on 4 July 1838, when it must have been reasonably complete; a new dining room was opened in her presence on 1 July 1841.

Wellington's *own* choices were careful and suitable (witness the contrast between his grand ambassadorial service of 1810-12 by Paul Storr and Rundell & Bridge, which was 'representation', Empire style, and his travelling service of 1814-15, used on the Waterloo campaign and perfectly plain except for gadrooned edges.[1]

By 1840, of course, B. D. Wyatt had been superseded as architect to the fashionable by Charles Barry. Like most of the sound men of his generation and the preceding one, Barry could find ways to produce satisfactory designs in two or more styles; he had not only designed the Italianate Travellers' and Reform Clubs and the Greek-Revival Manchester Art Gallery but also three Gothic churches in London and the 'Jacobethan' Highclere; and his new Palace of Westminster, to be detailed by Pugin, was under construction. From Barry's time forward, the sort of luxurious *rocaille* interior of which I have been speaking was likely to be enclosed in an Italianate exterior.

The taste which on this account I like to call Lusso was not absolutely restricted to these styles. Sometimes very splendidly detailed Elizabethan, as at Salvin's Harlaxton, appealed to it; and in Roman Catholic quarters it might find a rich Gothic palatable, as at Pugin's Scarisbrick.[2] Lusso was a taste for brilliance and abundance and breadth rather than subtlety: its elegance was of tuberoses and peonies, ormolu and velvet and Boulle marquetry (which, oddly, it often called *Buhl*). It was expensive but the expenditure was conspicuous only to those who were invited. Though by intention part of a large landscape, the houses of the Lusso taste tended not to have the lawns and shrubberies of the Picturesque style to their very doors, but to have parterres in a revived Le Nôtre sort of style which echoed, outside the windows, the carpets and patterned curtains inside. Full of abrupt changes of direction, of curves suddenly sprouting from short straight lines, these patterns were boldly scaled and often bore reminiscences of late-Gothic or high-Renaissance forms;

---

[1] Reproduced in the Victoria and Albert Museum's *Guide to the Wellington Museum*.

[2] The remodelling of Scarisbrick and the building of Harlaxton both began in 1837. Scarisbrick included a good deal of transplanted Flemish fifteenth-century woodwork, and Harlaxton's anthology of interiors culminated in Baroque plaster draperies at the top of a great stair hall; these were by William Burn.

they were at their most splendid in the flock wallpapers which Pugin designed for the libraries and committee rooms of the Houses of Parliament, and in the French *brocatelles* which (sometimes for upholstery, sometimes even for dresses) the Lusso preferred to smaller-patterned English printed fabrics.[1]

Both from late seventeenth-century furniture of the Boulle sort and from the Louis XVI cabinet furniture which had outset corners, the Lusso taste drew a fondness for marked articulations which was rather at variance with its only slightly lesser fondness for the structure-concealing curves of Louis XV; and the second-Rococo objects created for this taste used much more abrupt transitions, more nearly horseshoe-shaped curves, and more deeply-cut carving than their eighteenth-century models. Consider the difference between the slow arcs of a Louis XV sofa-back and the roller-coaster-like profile of a second-Rococo sofa.

The blond woods which in the time of Charles X had spread from France to Germany and England (maple, birch, beech, sycamore) appealed less to the Lusso than to the Grec taste; the Lusso liked rosewood even more than the Grec did, but tended to inlay it or at least to use contrasting yellowish stringing close to the edges of the wood; and the Lusso continued to like those deep-toned complex veneers (thuya, burl elm) which the Empire favoured; it also revived walnut, which had hardly been used in England since George II. Walnut, thuya, and rosewood could stand the strong colours which both the Empire and the earlier eighteenth century had liked.

The Lusso taste, and the French and Italian forms which it favoured, were also in a sense a revolt against the intellectualism of the Grec.[2] Some very grand Lusso furniture even parodied the sort of fine early Empire made for Thomas Hope, by enlarging mere decorative elements so that they became in a sense the whole object. But by 1840 Grec was already elderly, and Lusso was set in its ways; the former was dying so far as outward forms went, and the Greek lines of the *klismos* had almost

---

[1] A fine French example in a self-assured Renaissance style is reproduced by Henri Clouzot in *Le Style Louis-Phillippe-Napoléon III*, 1939, pl. XXIII.

[2] One thinks of that grand anti-intellectual remark made by a Tory on hearing of Edward VII's institution of the Order of Merit: he preferred the Garter because there was 'no damned merit about it'.

vanished into the curves of the 'ribbon-back' or 'balloon-back' chair which almost everyone in the mid-century used, and which in its more expensive and Lusso examples might have second-Rococo carving. But a third taste was rising.

What John Steegman has already called the Olden-Time taste had its roots in literary romanticism. As far back as Alderman Boydell's *Shakespeare Gallery* (1802) the popularization of the British past, by prints reproducing paintings of *tableaux* from favourite plays, had been well begun. The Waverley novels helped, and so did the new augmented Gothic silhouette of Windsor Castle. The Napoleonic break in the long continuum of styles, already mentioned, created a sort of vacuum into which eclecticism rushed. Hence, the abundance which the nineteenth century admired was *expected* to include a wide choice of styles; freedom of choice without limit tended of course to encourage an anarchy of taste, against which in their ways Ruskin, Prince Albert, and the School-of-Design-*cum*-South-Kensington team all fought. But they did not fight the Olden-Time taste as such.

The people who did not recognize the law of the economy of experience – and there are always millions of them – welcomed a wide choice. The pattern books of the 1820s were already offering a box of delights, and by 1840 the confusion was enormous, and the nomenclature delightfully vague. Designers and manufacturers could call almost anything by any name: it would be impossible to predict, from our viewpoint of academic and archaeological knowledge, what 'Arabesque' or 'Cinque-Cento' would turn out to look like in their catalogues. Furthermore, rising population offered such a demand for manufactured goods that it was often easier to meet demand by continuing old models and adding just a few new ones annually than by 're-tooling' and built-in obsolescence in the twentieth-century way. Thus a tinned copper jelly-mould designed in Regency times might coldly furnish forth the catalogue which also contained high-Victorian brass bedsteads.

For those eclectic styles which looked to the British past there was scholarly sanction in such books as T. F. Hunt's *Exemplars of Tudor Architecture and Furniture* (1829–30) and Henry Shaw's *Specimens of Ancient Furniture* (1832–6); there were studies of the Elizabethan by John Shaw in 1839 and by C. J. Richardson in 1837. Pugin's books of 1835 and 1836 on furniture and metalwork in the style of the fifteenth century were crowned by his *Contrasts* (1836), in which he lambasted Georgian and Greek Revival architecture and helped to lay the foundations for Ruskin's later moral judgements in favour of Gothic (though Ruskin thought little of Pugin). At a more obvious and popular level, the Olden Time taste may be said to have 'jelled' with Joseph Nash's *Mansions of England in the Olden Time* (1838–49), whose chromolithographs showed fifty-odd late Gothic, Tudor, and Jacobean buildings. Architecturally these were by no means inaccurately reported, but Nash's scenes were populated by strolling figures in rather misunderstood seventeenth-century costume. Strangely, Thomas Shotter Boys's far better chromolithographs, *Picturesque Architecture in Paris, Ghent, Rouen, etc.* (1839), had less vogue than either Nash's work or Pugin's *Details of Ancient Timber Houses of 15th and 16th Centuries* (1836), which were from French sources. Perhaps Boys's failure to argue in Pugin's way or to put his *staffage* figures in fancy dress spoiled him with the public.[1] Joseph Nash's work whetted the appetites of travellers, who were now taken cross-country by the new railways, and of the new industrial class, conscious of their blessings and ready to have what money would buy. Prepared by Nash's lithographs, and perhaps by Rickman's older *Attempt to Discriminate the Styles of Architecture in England* (1817), they became connoisseurs of the Olden Time.

Their demand was promptly matched by a supply. From Mr Fair in Mortimer Street, London, they bought remodelled Elizabethan fragments; from Fair's neighbour Kensett some of the earliest careful reproductions; from Wilkinson in Oxford Street or Hanson in John Street they could get both real and false antique English furniture, while their Lusso contemporaries went to Nixon & Son of Great Portland Street or to the Leveson-Gowers' man Nias for Louis XIV [*sic*]; Wilkinson could make that, too, as he did for the Goldsmiths' Hall.

But the Lusso taste looked down on Olden Time. The Duchess of Sutherland, when she was still Countess Gower, writing of Blore's work at Lambeth Palace in 1830, called him 'the *cheap* architect' (her italics); the same lady was also very severe upon the late Georgian taste, for in 1827 when she went to look at furniture to be auctioned from

---

[1] Boys' *London As It Is*, 1842, gives in its admirable chromolithographs an excellent picture of the Regency and its early successors at their architectural work.

Attingham Park she found 'little that would suit us except a few plain things. It is singular what bad taste generally reigns in the second class of English country houses'.[1] As to the second rank, let us admit that Blore was of it; yet he was a decent performer who had learned much from his work at Abbotsford, Lambeth, Hinchingbrooke, and Westminster Abbey; he had built several Olden-Time houses before becoming surveyor to the Office of Woods and Works, but he was not the brilliant designer or *pasticheur* that Salvin was.

It is true that the itch for antiquity, in view of the short supply of those who could plausibly reproduce it, led to much that was bogus: Pugin's Gothic coal grates and fire-irons were bogus, too: and he was willing sometimes to use cast iron to simulate other material; but his best work put him, like Salvin, in the Lusso group. The Olden-Time taste did not, by and large, enlist many really distinguished architects. At worst it was a sort of aesthetic jingoism, at best a reaction which was ethically no more objectionable than Grecianism, and visually less satisfactory in its furniture. With the best will in the world, it is still hard to accept as anything but an oddity those 'Gothic' chairs in which a pierced and spindly back towers above a low and bulgingly-upholstered seat. In such special situations as Masonic halls, Victorian Gothic furniture can be both lively and rather charming, but as a domestic permanence it was and is hard to live with. Objects which did not need to be moved, such as clocks, cabinets, picture-frames, and of course wallpaper, were happier with Gothic ornament than were chairs; and some of the finest Gothic design went into bookbindings and stained glass. Pugin, it seems to me, was at his best in designing glass and other flat things such as tiles[2] and wallpaper; and the same could be said of his followers. For things in the round, when there was a precedent as with chalices, all went well; but only Pugin himself could get away with a Gothic silver teapot.

---

[1] Attingham Park, then about thirty years old, will have seemed small and upstart to a daughter of Castle Howard; the extraordinary Italian Empire gilt furniture which is now there might have suited her better. The quotation is from Leconfield and Gore, *Three Howard Sisters*, 1955, pp. 79–80.

[2] E.g., those for his own house, or those for St Augustine's, Ramsgate, reproduced by Hitchcock in *Early Victorian Architecture in Britain*, 1954, II, pl. III, 36.

By the same token, there were forms and styles out of the British past that became viable for the Olden-Time taste in different ways. Elizabethan or Jacobean strapwork, with lively silhouettes, was peculiarly adapted to printer's ornament and to door- and window-trim; the tall narrow Caroline chair, with caned or stuffed seat and back-panel, and with its frame almost entirely turned or carved, was comfortable enough and also ornamental enough to speak to the Victorian condition, and it provided the better part of the compromise with Gothic which the so-called Abbotsford chair presents. As is so often the case with romantic antiquarianism, the first impulse was satisfied by empirical adaptations, followed later by more grammatical forms. The search for real antique furniture is reflected in such careful and appreciative use by artists of old objects as we see in Stephens's good Caroline chair (with Victorian embroidery) in 1849 or Egley's good William and Mary caned chair in about 1855.[1]

Yet the period was rich in the invention of new types: the Davenport or lady's desk with side drawers, the Omnium or wheeled whatnot for the dining-room, the Sutherland drop-leaf small table.[2] Most of these were at their best in their most unmistakably Victorian forms, free of applied archaeology.

Olden Time was, then, the youngest of the tastes discernible about 1840, and it was lively, various, and pushy. Put together its search for the ancestral, patriotic, and solid with the supply of objects available through factory production, and you get an inorganic sort of design, in which almost interchangeable parts may be substituted without notice and without much improvement or even real change. Such elegance as the Olden Time had was one of oak, deep carving, bold embroidery, rather rugged colour; the best (except in the case of stained glass) was often the most fantastic. In building, with more dependable prototypes, the norm was closer to archaeological plausibility than in furniture. Church Gothic may certainly be considered a style for the Olden-Time taste, though Gothic had a head start for church use; domestically, the 'vicarage' style was more Tudor than Gothic, and was rather more

---

[1] The Stephens is reproduced in Robin Ironside, *Pre-Raphaelite Painters*, 1948, pl. 76; the Egley in Ralph Dutton, *The Victorian Home*, 1954, p. 75.

[2] Trollope, thinking of the Sutherlands, reversed the reference to create his Duke of Omnium.

widespread (in wood) in America than in Britain. Not until the Ruskinian sort of Gothic came to dress row-houses and, as Ruskin complained, public houses were dwellings heavily Gothicized. By that time the high Victorian synthesis had taken place in the generation of architects (Butterfield, Burgess, J. L. Pearson) who were of the age of the Queen and the Prince, and Ruskin himself.

All this categorizing is done by hindsight. Prince Albert may or may not have observed these varieties in 1840, but he was both inquisitive about British art and likely to pass judgement. However well prepared he was by reading, the facts of British painting and sculpture and collecting must have been rather surprising. Passavant had said almost nothing about the 'minor' arts except for printmaking (he liked Bewick but did not mention Lucas); on sculptors and painters he could give a young German visitor as much information and opinion as on architects (he thought highly of Barry and Lawrence, but Gibson seemed less good to him than Schadow).[1] Perhaps the Prince had read Pückler-Muskau on British social institutions as well as Passavant on art collections, but on his visits to England before marriage he had kept Court company entirely, and the only non-royal sightseeing he did was to look at Sion House in 1836. One of his most interesting surprises will have been the figure-painting; for from Runge to Schwind the human being in German paint, whether naked or dressed, tended to look rather like a group of rather glossy pillows and bolsters tightly packed with sand; only Genelli and a couple of Nazarenes could both articulate the body and paint its surfaces with delight, and it was not until Marées that a German would really be at ease as a figure-painter. British painters, despite the insipidity of much of their *genre*, could still give a human being a certain physical grace, even muscles when they were called for. The state of the representative arts has been so well set forth by Boase and Oppé[2] that I need hardly dwell upon it, except to suggest

---

[1] Waagen (in *Works of Art and Artists in England*, 1838) did not differ greatly in his judgements from Passavant.

[2] T. S. R. Boase, *English Art 1800-1870*, 1959; A. Paul Oppé, 'Art', in *Early Victorian England*, edited by G. M. Young, 1934, reprinted 1951. Boase reproduced (pl. 84a) Dyce's *Joash Shooting the Arrow of Deliverance*, which was bought by the Kunsthalle of Hamburg, and whose tough athletic nudes put those of most German painters to shame.

a few of the choices likely to be made on the lines of the varying tastes I have sketched.

It is hard to understand now why critics and collectors and artists themselves were so concerned over the fact that there was no history-painting (still generally considered about 1840 as the highest form of painting); Haydon thought he was the man to inherit the mantle of Benjamin West, but no one else thought so; John Martin painted a *sort* of history in his 'mad' biblical visions, but history had already turned to anecdote, while portrait-painting continued on its way and landscape flourished. The principal worriers were usually of the intellectual or Grec taste; they usually had small houses and regular but not large incomes, so they were likelier to buy watercolours than Haydon or Martin's big pictures. On the other hand, they were not worried by Turner in his mature years, when his stated subjects almost disappeared into pure paint and optical effulgence; and they liked Constable and the early pearly, modest, Wilkie.

The Lusso taste ran to old masters; its preferred portrait painter might have been Lawrence, but he was ten years dead in 1840, and there was really no one to take his place though Hayter, Martin Archer Shee, and Francis Grant were acceptable. If people of the Lusso taste cared for any modern painter, it was Delaroche and his British or French pupils. They were perhaps less likely than the Grec to fret about 'truth,' which was already a concern of some collectors long before the pre-Raphaelites, and much likelier to care about 'effect'; but like other nineteenth-century consumers they appreciated evidence of hard work, and as owners of older painting they were able to enjoy the bravura of Etty and the mature, almost Baroque, Wilkie.

The Olden-Time taste would obviously favour the genre painters who dressed their models in exotic or ancient costume; subject, which was important to all the readers of pictures in our period, was above all weighty with devotees of the Olden Time. Because they had great appetites but not always large budgets, they formed the public for engraved or lithographed repetitions of successful pictures. The Art Union and its provincial emulators, which were an unofficial and unexpected outgrowth of the Parliamentary enquiry of 1835-6, became great publishers and, by many of their lotteries, great promoters of medium-priced paintings;[1] *Punch* argued in September 1841, when Maclise's *Sleeping Beauty* was chosen by the winner of a £300 prize, that a painter who could do a picture priced at that sum did not need money.

By 1840 the steam had gone out of the Romantic movement;[2] the Eglinton Tournament of August 1839 was a last damp puff, and it is interesting that this wonderful mummery, organized by people whom I would suppose to have been of the Lusso taste, was observed by thousands of visitors whom I take to have been drawn by its Olden-Time attractions.[3] In the very same year, photography arrived. Prince Albert, newly married, saw it as an admirable tool, and patronized photographs from early in 1842. Photography was a sudden change, although – speaking again from hindsight – not unexpected in view of the demand for pictorial realism. In most other respects, change was slow in the early Victorian era. Nathaniel Hawthorne, who liked the Reform Club because it had a good library and because its marble columns were marble not scagliola, remarked in his *English Notes* that most of the Club servants, especially the waiters, still wore plush

---

[1] For an account of this enterprise see Anthony King, 'George Godwin and the Art Union of London 1837–1911' in *Victorian Studies* VIII/2, December 1964, 101–30. The London Art Union survived an attempt to outlaw its lottery; the New York equivalent did not. For an account of the Parliamentary inquiry see Quentin Bell, *The Schools of Design*, 1963, chapter IV. The Select Committee which conducted the inquiry was appointed originally as part of a campaign against the independence of the Royal Academy, but its writ ran much broader before it had finished; its minutes cover long hearings of testimony on the state of art and industry, art schools in Europe and Britain, methods of design, the neglect of British art at the National Gallery, and the varieties of museums.

[2] But Queen Victoria, as late as 9 October 1838, heard that Lord Lansdowne had had an offer from a man to become a hermit on his property.

[3] Ian Anstruther, *The Knight and the Umbrella/An Account of the Eglinton Tournament*, 1963. There had been a pseudo-medieval tournament at Potsdam in 1829 (the 'Fest der Weissen Rose') in honour of the Empress Alexandra; much of the armour made or bought for Eglinton was sold at auction on 17 and 18 July 1840 at fairly low prices; the Tower Armoury bought one suit. Queen Victoria commented on 2 September 1839 on the inundation of Eglinton, 'It served them right for their folly.' Landseer's *High Life*, one of a satirical pair of dog pictures, may refer to the Eglinton tournament: most of the apparatus is false-Gothic, a sword, helmet, breastplate, hawking gauntlet, and battlements.

breeches and white silk stockings; '. . . these English Reformers do not seem to include Republican simplicity of manners in their system. Neither, perhaps, is it anywhere essential'.[1] What would Emerson have thought?

---

[1] This was in the middle fifties. I quote from the Riverside Edition of 1902, *English Notes*, II, 229.

4

First Royal Commission

Much repetition has made familiar Prince Albert's complaint, early in his married life, that he was not master in his own house, as well as his later saying that in such a relationship as that of a male consort to a sovereign, the husband must lose his individuality in his wife's. The Queen was not perhaps as quick as she might have been to put the Prince's skill and knowledge to use. But she was almost besottedly in love with his person, and already caught up in that habit of emotional involvement that was to cause so much harm during her widowhood.[1] Also, she had established herself thoroughly in the routine of the sovereign's work, and shown a strong if debatably constitutional hand in the matter of the Bedchamber appointments in 1839. She was not a feminist, and had no suffragist ideas of the capacities of women; she resented having to do a sovereign's duty *and* a wife's. It has been said of her

---

[1] The long-preserved idyllic picture of a perfect love with never a harsh word, which the Queen herself created with her idolatry of 'that perfect being', is now almost effaced. What we can see emerging from behind alternate screens of debunking and reglorifying is the much more interesting picture of mutual modifications: the Queen's temperament firmed by her husband's correction, the Prince's confidence increased by his wife's applause and even by her power to put his ideas into execution. Lady Longford, in *Queen Victoria/Born to Succeed*, 1964, has contributed greatly to our understanding of the conduct, which was both formal and sensitive, of the Royal couple's arguments over decisions and behaviour. The Queen's habit of keeping everything at arm's length through the use of written memoranda on the least question (a habit abetted by her husband's interest in filing records properly) was useful when she and the Prince were disputing; for the memoranda somewhat sublimated her storms and gave him an outlet in which he could be franker than he was willing to be orally. Thus it was possible in the course of a day's exchanges, if the Queen was aroused over some governmental blunder, to get through the exchanges of rant, reproof, revision, response, and apology along with the rest of the day's business, so that the sun need not go down upon their wrath.

16. Sir Edwin Landseer: *Queen Victoria and Prince Albert in Costume* as Edward III and Queen Philippa for a fancy-dress ball; commissioned by the Queen, 1842

17. *Silver-gilt table centrepiece*, designed by Prince Albert and made by Garrards, 1842; 30 in. tall

18. *Silver statuette of Prince Albert* by Garrards; his gift to the Queen, Christmas 1843

19. *Silver-gilt baptismal font*, made by E. J. & W. Barnard for the christening of the Princess Royal, 1840–1; 17 in. tall

20. Gegenbaur: *Hercules and Omphale*; Fresco (in iron chassis), 6 ft 3½ in. tall, signed and dated Rome 1830; bought by the Prince, 1844

21. Friedrich Overbeck: *Triumph of Religion in the Arts*; pencil and black chalk on reddened paper, 4 ft 8⅝ in. × 3 ft 10¾ in.; bought by Gruner from Overbeck for Prince Albert, who gave it to Queen Victoria, Christmas 1847

22. Emil Wolff: *Prince Albert*, 1846; marble, 6 ft 3 in.; acquired 1849

23. Richard James Wyatt: *Penelope*; marble; commissioned by Queen Victoria, 1841

24. Joseph von Führich: *Saints Peter and John Confirming the Churches*; pencil, $13\frac{3}{8} \times 17\frac{3}{8}$ in., signed and dated 1850; gift of the Prince to the Queen, 24 May 1852

25. William Dyce: *Neptune Resigning the Empire of the Sea to Britannia*; academy board, $13\frac{1}{2} \times 20$ in.; 1846(?)

26. Lucas Cranach: *Apollo and Diana*; tempera on panel, 2 ft 9 in. × 1 ft 10¼ in.; bought for Prince Albert by Ludwig Gruner from Campe of Nürnberg, 1846

27. William Wyld: *Manchester*; watercolour, 14 × 20 in., 1852; commissioned by the Queen

28. George Cruikshank: *Disturbing the Congregation*; canvas, $17\frac{1}{2}$ × 22 in., bought by Prince Albert, 1850

husband that he could not resist duty; and although duty did not beckon to her so winsomely as to him, she did her duty firmly.

This duty had not been thrust upon her, she had been born and trained for it. The Crown was infinitely precious and, though not perhaps in the abstract *desirable,* it was in fact a thing to be cherished fiercely by the wearer. Anticipating a little the time when the Queen and Prince were to be in effect a sovereign partnership, one could say fairly that they both considered the Crown and their own persons in an almost medieval light.[1] The Crown must not be diminished: compared to its preservation the value of an individual's life, even a sovereign's, was small. On the several occasions of attempted assassination, both Queen and Prince acted with great calmness and bravery, and were invariably of opinion that the would-be assassins were poor unfortunate creatures of deranged mind, not beastly malefactors. A threat to the Crown was something else; anything that smelled of rebellion was to be *put down* at once and with little or no mercy. From the Queen's almost mystical attachment to the Crown, as well as from her attachment to persons, rose her attitude to all that flowed from the fountain of honour; one might almost pervert Blake's phrase, saying 'all the emanations of the giant Albion'. The Garter, for instance, was such an emanation; and anyone who had ever had the Garter became therefore a sort of member of glory. Similarly, anything that served the continuation of Crown and Throne in their full state was desirable.

When it became clear that what King Leopold, the Coburg grandmother, and Stockmar had had in mind was the creation of an admirable monarchy, and that Prince Albert's education and her own had been pointed to this end, then away with Lord Melbourne's devices for easy adaptation to the *status quo,* away with his 'the done thing', and up with Improvement. Yet something was to be learned even from the wicked Hanoverians, for George IV had known how to glorify the Crown through works of art.

Repetition has also made familiar the fact that Sir Robert Peel, a man with as good an eye for persons as for works of art, saw the qualities of the Prince and noticed that he was chafing under his comparative

---

[1] The Queen did not believe a sovereign's right came from the people alone; see page 19, note 3.

inactivity. The Prince was, to be sure, studying his wife, her court, the British land and landscape,[1] the Constitution,[2] and the royal possessions; and by May 1840 the Queen was occasionally showing him a Government paper – but Peel saw that the Prince could be immensely useful to the nation. A Select Committee 'to take into consideration the Promotion of the Fine Arts of this Country, in connexion with the Rebuilding of the Houses of Parliament', led to a Royal Commission, appointed in late October 1841, with the Prince as Chairman.[3] Not only did he insist to Peel that its membership must cross party lines, but he showed thus early his understanding of the work of trustees and managers by saying that he thought it wise to have no professional artist on the Commission; this in spite of his fondness for artists and his understanding of them. Indeed, he liked and understood professional men, specialists, and technicians; he felt that in technical matters Britain was pre-eminent, but he shared the uneasy feeling of C. R. Cockerell, Eastlake, John Martin, and many others that all was not well with the arts in Britain. Desiring the professional opinion and expert testimony of artists on which to base some decisions of the Royal Commission, he also wanted the trustee class to be free to discuss testimony as laymen and as the representatives of the public, which indeed they were. Eastlake, whom he chose as Secretary, was an artist and had testified before the Select Committee which preceded the Royal Commission, but Eastlake was at this time on his way out of the studio and into the picture-gallery (Steegman says he 'ceased to be a painter and became an authority').[4] Eastlake had once refused Peel, but the Prince in his turn, making one of his own first brilliant choices, insisted.

Uneasiness about the state of British art, already expressed by the

---

[1] The prince, from the early months of his marriage, used the railways and thus shared those novel views of British landscape which the level lines of track, different in their courses from the coaching roads, gave to the first generation of rail travellers. The Queen did not take a train until the summer of 1842.

[2] It now seems to be agreed that some of Stockmar's notions of a constitutional monarchy, which became articles of Victorian-cum-Albertine faith, were erroneous, unhistorical, even 'un-English'; the Queen nevertheless managed to make some of them prevail.

[3] The Royal Commission first met on 15 March 1842.

[4] *Consort of Taste*, p. 137.

witnesses before previous Select Committees, was endemic. One result of the Committees of 1835 and 1836 had been the creation of the School of Design, which received the quarters in Somerset House vacated by the Royal Academy upon its move to the National Gallery; the Art Union had been another and more surprising result. William Dyce became head of the School of Design in 1840; he later, like Eastlake, became one of Prince Albert's team. There was, then, a degree of readiness for governmental intervention in the arts; and the Royal Commission was to undertake, in the internal decoration of the new Houses of Parliament, a direct patronage of artists that would remain unique for a long time.

In the rebuilding of those Houses (correctly but seldom colloquially called the New Palace of Westminster), the 'Gothic or Elizabethan' style which the terms of the competition called for was perhaps a triumph of romanticism, or perhaps a remembrance of the college-chapel ancestry of the seating arrangement in the Commons, or perhaps a proper gesture to Westminster Hall, which survived the fire. At any rate, the Gothic dress which the well-informed and passionate antiquarian Pugin created for Barry's masses was not the romantic Gothic of Hafod or Coleorton but something more disciplined.[1] Yet so free was the eclectic air that it was apparently never suggested that the pictorial interior decoration should accord in any stylistic way with the exterior or with the inner architectural enframement (where Pugin was able to be bolder and richer than on the outer walls – so bold indeed that the Queen found the House of Lords a bit brassy).

Perhaps too much has been said about a 'battle of styles'; though certain conventional notions of suitability linked certain styles with given purposes, eclecticism was of a mind to accept, not to reject, and hardly to sort out. The last century's Rule of Taste had said in effect, 'It is written that this is Done, that is Not Done'; the new word was, 'It is given', and burgeoning production made it possible to take what was given, to take more and more, and to produce more and more.

---

[1] See page 9, note 3. The only way to use Gothic for secular buildings without making the interiors too dark was to push the style and design beyond the Perpendicular towards the Tudor use of great batteries of small lights which added up to a sufficient glass area.

Alternatively, we might say that to the old upper classes' 'I have it', the new classes answered, 'I want it'. And to the trifocal classification of taste in chapter 3 should certainly be added Hitchcock's judgement that, after all, every revival style yielded eventually to an unmistakably Victorian look.[1] Taste did not yield so much in matters of quality as in matters of quantity and of breadth of choice. Human beings are human, and abundance encourages all but a few of us to clutter.

Nor was there a bitter battle, really, over ancient and modern. Partisan critics and the partisan press (how partisan they could be in the 1840s!) might rant, but on the whole new composers, new architects, new painters were not sneered at for their mere newness. There was only one 'wild' modernist in the public eye, Turner, and he was an R.A. who never ceased to show at the Academy.

There were, however, real questions of scale, means, and technique. The early nineteenth century was as willing as any optimistic and expansionist period to equate greatness occasionally with bigness, and painters partook of this failing. Even Constable, whom we now love for his intimate Englishness and his direct sketches from nature, thought of his six-foot exhibition pictures – not his 'lanes and hedges' – as his real product. And although he and Turner, Etty and Haydon, Wilkie and Martin painted very large canvases, they *were* canvases, in frames, portable; the sense of great scale (rather than large dimensions) which had informed the architectural decorations of a Thornhill had petered out at the end of the eighteenth century in such dainty stuff as Stothard's murals at Burghley. Craftsmanship in the painter's studio, as in the cabinetmaker's or silversmith's shop, had tended to decline with the division of labour, and many a painter could not have told why he was using the materials he used, unless simply for the immediate 'effect'. His colours could now be bought ready-ground; was there a British painter who complained, as Delacroix did, that he had served no apprenticeship and possessed no real craft or *artisanat*?

In the years just before Prince Albert's Italian journey, the Nazarenes' chief men had turned from their fresco-painting in the Casa Bartholdy and the Villa Massimo to spreading the gospel in various German art academies. As men with the labels of idealism and the

---

[1] *Early Victorian Architecture in Britain*, 1954, preface and chapter XVII.

laurels of accomplishment upon them, they were much visited, both in Italy and in Germany, by such seekers as Ford Madox Brown and William Dyce who spread their fame further. All the good values were supposed to lie with them, so that their intentions and methods were often mentioned by witnesses before the Select Committees of 1835, 1836, and 1841 (whose inquiries by their very existence suggest a belief that standards had broken down). In February 1841 Henry Labouchere, President of the Board of Trade,[1] sought a grant of Parliament for experiments in fresco technique, and that year's Committee and the subsequent Royal Commission seem to have roots in his request. Peel had met Cornelius, Prince Albert had met Schnorr von Carolsfeld, Dyce knew several Nazarenes and had seen the fresco-painting campaign in progress in Munich; and Eastlake (though he was probably a party to Cornelius's visit to England later in that year) had had many contacts which had shown him that the substance of the Nazarenes' and Düsseldorfers' art was not of such importance as their technical integrity and their teaching. Cornelius's brains were picked but he was not hired.

Prince Albert, however convinced he may have been by testimony and by his own enthusiasm that fresco was the right sort of painting for the walls of capital structures, realized that most of the painters who would be called upon would be quite out of their depth.[2] So he ar-

---

[1] Labouchere, who was created Baron Taunton in 1859, was a collector shrewd enough to have bought for himself the unfinished Michelangelo panel of the *Virgin and Child with St John and Angels* which was then called Ghirlandaio, and which is now in the National Gallery. He is sometimes confused with his nephew, also Henry Labouchere, Member of Parliament, husband of the actress Henrietta Hodson, and owner of Pope's villa at Twickenham, whom Queen Victoria called a radical and refused to have in the Cabinet.

[2] To Keith Andrews' mention (*The Nazarenes*, 1964, 83) of Dyce and David Scott as almost the only men with any knowledge of fresco one more can be added, though he was so old as to be out of the running: Barker of Bath. In 1825 he had painted in his own house a remarkable fresco on a subject also used by Delacroix, the massacre of Scio. Archdeacon Fisher mentioned this to Constable in the same year, and 'E.M.' wrote about it from Bath to the *Art Union* under date of 22 March 1841; printed 15 April 1841. There may be some truth in Ford Madox Brown's story that Cornelius was actually asked by Prince Albert to paint at Westminster, and that Cornelius replied by recommending William Dyce (E. H. Hueffer, *Ford Madox Brown*, 1896, p. 36).

ranged a large-scale attack in stages, and also planned a private sort of trial by which the probable success of the public programme might be gauged. The Commissioners announced a competition for fresco decoration at Westminster, calling for cartoons or *cartoni* (big paper patterns) between ten and fifteen feet in the larger dimension, and with life-sized figures depicting scenes from British history or from Spenser, Shakespeare, or Milton. When the drawings began to be delivered in late May 1843, the Prince was surprised to find as many as 150 entries, and pleased that ten of them seemed really good. The exhibition of the cartoons in Westminster Hall, which opened on 1 July, was visited by throngs; an early appearance of the skill at popularization which always marked Prince Albert's team, and which was related to his own tendency to impart information at the drop of a hat, was a sixpenny explanatory pamphlet with all the pertinent quotations from the chosen authors; Eastlake abridged this to a penny pamphlet for 'the million', but found that the poorly-dressed often bought the sixpenny one.

It has frequently been said that our modern use of *cartoon* in the sense of a comic drawing dates from *Punch's* printing of some parodies in its early numbers of July 1843; but *Punch* must have begun the modern use with the announcement of the competition, or else its editors must have been aware during the hearings before the Select Committee in their own earliest days as a working group; for in a late number of volume I, on 11 December 1841, there is a caricature of Lord John Russell accompanied by a 'Cartoon of Mr Daniel O'Connell, taken from Raphael' (the Raphael cartoons for tapestry were still at Hampton Court); again in late January 1842 there is an 'inimitably comic cartoon' called *Prince Albert's Stock*. At least one caricature in volume I is signed *Fresco*.

The Prince realized that Parliamentary mills ground slowly, and he decided to make a private trial. Fresco was already in his mind when he first talked with Eastlake on 2 December 1841, as Eastlake's memorandum of the conversation shows,[1] and in July 1842 he was planning to make fresco experiments at Buckingham Palace in a small garden pavilion. On 5 November the Queen referred to it as a 'little cottage on

---

[1] Quoted by Martin, 1, 123–5; Princess Beatrice's brief extracts from her father's diary (*Archives*, Y/204) confirm this.

a mound' (dredged out of the Palace garden lake); by February 1843 the scheme was well in hand, and painting began in May. Prince Albert had seen *Comus*, perhaps for the first time, at Covent Garden on 9 March 1842, and it was from that charming and moral masque that he asked eight artists to choose subjects and paint frescoes in an octagonal room of the Pavilion. In one of the side rooms the younger Doyles, sons of the famous John ('H.B.') and brothers of Richard Doyle,[1] frescoed in 1844 some subjects from Sir Walter Scott, and in another room there were Pompeian arabesques by the decorators Rice and Morley. The building, which was surrounded by a terrace and urn-topped balustrades of the Prince's own design, may have owed something to the Pompeian frescoed circular temple in the *Englischer Garten* at Meiningen or to the frescoed room in honour of Goethe and Schiller in the *Schloss* at Weimar, decorated in 1836-44 by a pupil of Cornelius. In June 1843 an elderly Italian named Aglio, 'who understands about it [fresco]', stood by to help the artists, who were rather floundering, and he eventually painted the ceilings in encaustic in the last three months of 1843. The fact that Richard Doyle was already of the *Punch* circle may have facilitated *Punch's* acquaintance with cartoons, though it certainly did not mollify the magazine's savage treatment of Prince Albert, one of its favourite targets.

Miss Rigby (not yet married to Charles Eastlake, whom she met in 1846) saw the Pavilion in March 1844, called it 'a little Chinesey box', thought the octagon room 'overfinished' except for Eastlake's work and Etty's, and said Etty came 'the nearest to real fresco effect'.[2] The other painters, all R.A.s, were Clarkson Stanfield, C. R. Leslie, Landseer, Daniel Maclise, Sir William Ross (whose profile of Prince Albert at twenty remained one of the Queen's favourite icons), and Thomas Uwins (who in 1847 at the age of sixty-five succeeded Eastlake as Keeper of the National Gallery). Oddly enough Etty failed to please the Royal clients, disliked having to tackle an unfamiliar technique, was unhappy about the experience, and proposed through the Prince's secretary Anson to paint at home in his studio a substitute on canvas,

---

[1] Richard Doyle first appeared as a caricaturist at the age of fifteen, with jokes at the expense of the Eglinton tournament. The Queen was enthusiastic over his first *Punch* drawings in 1843.

[2] Lady Eastlake, *Letters and Journals*, 1895, I, 117-18.

which could be white-leaded to the Pavilion wall. His sketch for the substitute was 'only glanced at', and Dyce was called in to fill his place, but the Prince took the trouble at the Royal Academy dinner on 4 May 1844 to praise Etty for the *Comus* subject (*Hesperus and His Daughters*) which he showed at the Academy, perhaps partly in justification. Despite these stately mutual gestures, to which Dyce later added by writing Etty (8 July) a sort of apology, it seems clear that Miss Rigby's judgement was likelier to be right than the Prince's, who was not a man of flair but a man of justice. Again there was an epilogue: Etty showed at the Academy in 1846 another Comus subject, *Circe with the Sirens Three*.[1] In the same year, the pavilion was published by Ludwig Gruner in one of his agreeable lithographed picture-books; he had had an advisory share in the enterprise and would bear a larger share at Osborne. The little building itself is no more.[2]

From this and other practical experiences Eastlake wrote *Styles and Methods of Painting Suited to the Decoration of Public Buildings*, printed as an appendix to the second and fifth reports of the Royal Commission in 1843 and 1846.[3] That essay is another early example of Prince Albert's good managerial device of the printed follow-up. The Pavilion, though not a brilliant success as a trial balloon, nevertheless indicated that some old balloonists could learn new tricks. The Royal Commission, having chosen Maclise, Dyce, Edward Armitage, the young G. F. Watts, C. W. Cope, E. M. Ward, John Tenniel, J. C. Horsley, and J. R. Herbert for the decorations of the Houses of Parliament, asked for definitive compositions in 1844 and eventually held another exhibition. In 1845 when the House of Lords was beginning to take form, the

---

[1] Alexander Gilchrist: *Life of William Etty, R.A.*, 2 vols., 1855. Gilchrist (also the biographer of Blake) reveals that each painter was paid forty pounds for his work on the Pavilion.

[2] None other than Mrs Jameson of *Sacred and Legendary Art* and *Legends of the Madonna* wrote the preface to Gruner's work *Her Majesty's Pavilion in Buckingham Palace Gardens*, 1846. Some have blamed the late Queen Mary for the destruction of the pavilion, but one inclines to accept her explanation (quoted by Steegman in *Consort of Taste*, 203) that previous neglect and weather had already seriously compromised its condition before she herself had any responsibility.

[3] Reprinted in Eastlake's *Contributions to the Literature of the Fine Arts*, 1848.

Commission asked each artist for a cartoon, a small colour sketch, and a sample actually executed in fresco. Parliament, however, did not approve the total decorative scheme until 1847, or appropriate money for it until 1850; part of the reason for the delay was the delay in the building itself, but more important perhaps was a coolness between the Commission and Barry, who felt that a good deal had been taken out from under his control (and who in any case was paid his architect's percentage only on the original estimates for the building, not on the actual cost which was roughly triple the estimate). Pugin, though there was later some dispute as to what was his and what was Barry's share in the great Westminster work, provided admirable settings for the sculpture and painted decoration, as well as some of his richest carved ornament in panelling.

Though the decoration was not completed until after Prince Albert's death, it may be well to complete our account of it here. Much of the fresco has perished, and the only paintings which have come down to us in reasonably sound condition and with some deserved reputation are Maclise's, Cope's, and Dyce's. Cope's scenes from seventeenth-century history in the Lords' Corridor are not painted on the wall but on slate panels and in water-glass, which the Prince recommended as a result of some of his technical inquiries and Eastlake's; they are in good condition.[1] The Prince liked Cope's direct style; this and his fairly good understanding of seventeenth-century costume give his work a far more plausible air than that of most Olden-Time performances, and

---

[1] During Schnorr's work on the frescoes of the *Residenz* in Munich there were experiments with encaustic and other old techniques (Andrews, *The Nazarenes*, 1964, 62–64). Karl Rottmann (1798–1850) seems to have painted on slate the series of Italian landscapes with which he decorated the arcades around the *Hofgarten* in the late twenties, and to have used encaustic for a series of Greek landscapes with which in the second half of the thirties he painted a room in the Neue Pinakothek. It must have been because of his knowledge of these doings that Prince Albert sent the painters Horsley and Cope to Italy in 1845 to examine the technicalities of fresco at the source whence Dyce had also gotten his knowledge. He also sent Maclise to Berlin in 1859 to learn the water-glass method. The Prince never saw Cope's water-glass work, which was done in 1862–3 on the basis of Maclise's reports to the Royal Commission; and Cope's frescoes elsewhere in the Houses of Parliament have all perished.

his colour is kept (like Puvis de Chavannes's later) within a controlled range suitable to architectural enrichment. In the Queen's Robing Room, Dyce's work seems rather heavily dependent on Raphael via Overbeck.[1] Maclise's superb *Death of Nelson* and *Meeting of Wellington and Blücher* in the Royal Gallery[2] are packed figure compositions, with some of the intricacy and over-all decorative density of fifteenth-century foliage tapestry; they have a virile quality that makes one think of derring-do and the roast beef of old England, but also a sympathetic (or as we now say, *empathic*,) sensitivity to human bodies in motion, stress, or distress.

Of the sculpture for which the Royal Commission in the Prince's time had some responsibility, the seated figure of the Queen between *Justice* and *Mercy*, commissioned in 1854 of the dependable Gibson, and carved as usual by himself in Italy, is perhaps most satisfactory. Despite its solemnity, it has a certain shock value in the contrast of its Italianate character with the Gothic quatrefoil frame. Barry is said to have thought it out of scale; the side figures have recently been removed.[3] Among the designers and suppliers of smaller elements in the Westminster complex were many who came later into the Prince's orbit when it enlarged in 1851 and thereafter. The Birmingham firm of Hardman, who made ironwork of Pugin's designs as well as very sound stained glass, and Minton of Stoke-on-Trent, for whom Pugin and Owen Jones designed tiles and mosaic, both had entries in the 1844 show of decorative work intended for the Houses; Jones's book on the Alhambra was then appearing, and he too in 1851 became one of the Prince's team. A contemporary judgement and a recent one may close these references. The recent one says of Pugin's Gothic that 'what had until then been a game became suddenly deadly serious . . . Pugin's intransigence and

---

[1] A corner of the Robing Room is reproduced by T. S. R. Boase in *English Art 1800–1870*, 1959, pl. 78b.

[2] A detail of each is reproduced by Boase, pl. 79a, b. The cartoon for *Wellington and Blücher* (now in the Royal Academy) was completed and approved by Prince Albert in July 1859; the painting (in water-glass; see note 1 p. 55) was completed just as the Prince was dying. Maclise seems to have been treated badly by the remaining Royal Commissioners, but persisted and finished the *Death of Nelson* in 1865, in which year the Art Union issued tremendous reproductive prints of both compositions.

[3] Boase, op. cit., p. 220, note 2.

his sense of urgency achieved its objective'.[1] Nathaniel Hawthorne in 1855 thought the exterior ornament at Westminster mechanical: it had a 'weariness in the effect' and 'a deficiency of invention'; the House of Lords he found magnificent and 'gravely gorgeous' but supposed some of the ornament must be done by machinery; and in the Commons he remarked that the Speaker's chair was 'loftier and statelier' than the Throne.[2]

But let us return to the *jeune ménage*. In the first four or five years of their married life, Queen Victoria's diary often mentions the Prince's fencing, dancing, swimming or skating in season; drawing, painting, or etching; riding, shooting, or tennis (this of course was court tennis, usually played at Hampton Court); card games, of which the Prince was always teaching his wife new versions, and tactical games (which the Duke of Wellington found boring). The reputation of the connoisseur of music grew rapidly as he continued to assist at and choose programmes for the Ancient Concerts. By June 1840 the organ which he had used in Florence arrived at Buckingham Palace, and in October a larger organ had been set in the music room at Windsor. The Prince also turned the Queen's Band, which had been one of wind instruments, into a real orchestra.

His managerial faculties were soon exercised, even if not immediately in government; by the middle of April 1840 he had had the Duchess of Kent removed with her household to Clarence House, and two summers later managed to get her into a separate Windsor establishment at Frogmore (at about the same moment, and not without vacillation, he broke the news to the Queen that Lehzen would soon be leaving).

In the summer of 1841 the couple made the first of their rounds of country-house visits, all fairly close to London: Chiswick House, Panshanger, Brocket Park, Woburn Abbey, Hatfield, Nuneham (whence the Prince went alone to Blenheim), and the Oxford colleges. The almost photographic memory undoubtedly retained useful impressions from Chiswick, Blenheim, and Hatfield; while the Queen only recorded that Nuneham was 'like Claremont but grander' and that Melbourne's

---

[1] Dutton, *The Victorian Home*, 1954, p. 36.
[2] The quotations are from the Riverside edition of 1902, *English Notebooks* II, pp. 105, 147–9.

Brocket needed 'furnishing and being lived in'. The Cowper Raphaels were still at Panshanger and would not have escaped the Prince's eye; nor would Capability Brown's work at Nuneham.

In 1842, besides the early visit to Brighton and some local excursions to Cliveden and Kew, they made one to Walmer Castle in Kent, which the Duke of Wellington had as a perquisite in his capacity as Lord Warden of the Cinque Ports; again they were looking for a seaside place for the children. But the great expedition was the autumnal one to Scotland, their first; the sharp air, the healthy barefooted people, the mountains,[1] and the feudal, kilted private armies of the great landlords delighted them both, as the institutions of Edinburgh delighted the Prince; but they did not stay at Holyrood until 1850.

1843 was the year of a State visit to Cambridge, an informal visit to the family of Louis Philippe (a mixture of business and pleasure nevertheless, and a great success), and a trip to Belgium. In Antwerp the Prince explained to his wife the development of Rubens's style, but what fascinated her more than Rubens was the variety of costumes of the orders of nuns. They both rather liked the modern Belgian painters, and then or soon afterwards made purchases of Verboeckhoven, Leys, and Wappers; Gallait they liked so much as to repeat. Later in the year there was a northern expedition to Chatsworth where the house, the landscape, Paxton's conservatory, and the model village of Edensor all made their mark. The marvellous seventeenth-century state rooms were not then furnished, but Wyatville's Italianate sculpture gallery (finished just before his death in 1840) was full of statues by such admired modern hands as Thorwaldsen and Canova; and Edensor with its picturesque stone cottages (each with running water) seemed to the Queen 'the prettiest thing imaginable' and impressed the Prince, who was already in contact with Lord Ashley and the problem of housing the poor. Haddon Hall, then uninhabited, was to the Queen merely 'most gloomy'; Belvoir, like Chatsworth, she had seen before, and here too there was work in progress or barely finished, as well as a private mausoleum. They also visited Peel at Drayton Manor, whence the Prince

---

[1] The Prince was reminded of Thuringia, but when his unromantic brother Ernest II came to Balmoral, Ernest said this was all nonsense, the Thuringian crags were of quite a different shape.

almost on the spur of the moment made a quick run to Birmingham; he had been advised not to do this, for the mayor of Birmingham was a Chartist, and riots and indignities were feared by the Cabinet. The Prince, curious to see a great industrial city and willing to see what good there might be in the adversary, met the mayor and was well received. He also saw King Edward's School in its fairly new Gothic buildings by Barry, and there met its headmaster the Rev. James Prince Lee, who would later be Bishop of Manchester (one of his pupils at Birmingham was E. W. Benson, whom the Prince was to choose many years later as first headmaster of Wellington College).

In 1844 the schedule of visits made and received became the crowded one standard for all the rest of Victoria and Albert's life together. The French royal family returned a compliment by coming to Windsor; the King of Saxony and the Emperor of All the Russias both came to Buckingham Palace in the season; and all these monarchs noticed that the British court was not only splendid but efficiently and 'effortlessly' catered for. Then the Queen and Prince made a second expedition to the Highlands, this time to Blair Castle, lent by Lord Glenlyon, where the royal couple were in effect householders, taking their eldest daughter with them. In November there was a visit to Burghley, where the admirable paintings held the Prince's attention; the Queen (who had been there alone in 1835) remarked that there was 'a Chapel room, not a real Chapel'. Between these two forays there was a happy week in the small house and estate of Osborne in the Isle of Wight, which was leased after several discussions with Peel, two visits by the Prince in March and August, and an inspection by Stockmar and Anson in May. There, in a delightful association of land and water, they saw the chance for a family life with the maximum of privacy permissible to a ruler who was inseparable from some amount of court life. The old house was too small for the growing family and its attendance; plans for a new one and negotiations for more land were well advanced before the end of the year.

Throughout 1844, the Royal Commission had met a great deal, quite as much as in the two previous years. The Prince had also become interested in the Royal Society of Arts, which had been founded in 1754 as the Society of Arts and Manufactures but which, at his first exposure to it in May 1840, had been almost moribund. Its original purpose, 'the

Encouragement of the Arts, Manufactures, and Commerce of the Country', appealed to him as lying between the scientific purposes of the Royal Society and the aesthetic and didactic ones of the Royal Academy. It offered annual prizes, and as soon as Prince Albert became its President (1843), the list of prize competitions grew more interesting; for example, in 1850 he offered personally prizes for improved methods of cultivating sugar cane and (doubtless looking toward the Exhibition Building of 1851) for a 'cement for uniting glass', especially glass pipes or glass roofing.

The Prince went as faithfully to the Academy dinner (about the first of May) as to the Waterloo dinner (18 June) at Apsley House, and in the early forties he was in demand for livery company dinners. One would suppose, if one had only the pages of *Punch* to judge by, that he was doing nothing but father children, criticize British tailors (perhaps he had one of those wonderful Hungarian tailors), and buy birds for the Palace aviary. He was also buying horses, buying or leasing land close to Windsor Great Park (Bagshot and Rapley), seeing the Dulwich Gallery, Peel's collection, and others, beginning the Windsor illustrated albums and the resurrection of neglected works of art from Hampton Court, reorganizing the wasteful Household, reinvesting the Prince of Wales's revenues from Cornwall, ordering a royal railway-carriage, and straightening out the affairs of his father, who died early in 1844. The necessary trip to Coburg at Easter was his first absence from the Queen; his organization of the royal messenger service allowed rapid communication, and the correspondence that issued from him during the journey was enormous; on each of his several stops he managed to kill two or more birds with each stone. The following year he took the Queen to Coburg.

The death of one's father always calls for a taking of stock, a growing up if one has not yet grown up. It was practically certain that Ernest II would not have an heir; as the Queen and Prince Albert now had two sons and two daughters, there were long looks into the future. Meanwhile, at home, there were public works and private.

5

Osborne House

As a girl, Queen Victoria had visited the Isle of Wight and had seen John Nash's Gothic retreat, East Cowes Castle, and Norris Castle; she talked to Melbourne in August 1839 about the possibility of acquiring Norris Castle, and this notion was revived in October 1843. The Queen and Prince had taken a quick look at the castle in August on their way by ship to France. So Peel began to look into possibilities for them, because of their desire for a seaside house where they and their children could have the privacy lacking at Brighton. By December 1843 Peel was recommending Osborne; through the early months of 1844 he continued to discuss methods of financing with the Prince, and in late March of that year they closed with Lady Isabella Blachford for several hundred acres. The royal family spent a week in October 1844 and much of the summer of 1845 in the old Osborne House, which the Prince engaged Thomas Cubitt to revise slightly (and for which the two men together chose new wallpapers). The clearing of land for the new house began in the middle of May, and there was a ceremonious cornerstone-laying on 23 June 1845.

In his comings and goings in London Prince Albert had admired the urbane and well-built groups of houses of the Cubitt developments in Bloomsbury, Belgravia, and Pimlico. Thomas Cubitt was not only an honest builder and a really great entrepreneur but also a man who understood the new sort of city life and its needs. His brother Lewis was an architectural designer and his brother William a sound engineer, alderman, and eventually Lord Mayor. Over the shoulders of the Cubitts, so to speak, and in particularly close relations with Thomas Cubitt, Prince Albert designed Osborne House. Hitchcock has compared it to Cubitt's mansions at Albert Gate, and suggested the influence upon the 1845–6 building of the Duchess of Sutherland's private wing at Trentham, and the influence upon the later blocks of the Trentham arcades and of the *Orangerieschloss* at Potsdam.[1] These are apt and just comparisons, and there may have been influence through published designs; but I do not believe the Prince ever saw Trentham (he was touchy about Barry, but he did later employ Nesfield, the landscape collaborator at Trentham and other Barry sites, and he of course knew how much the Queen admired everything of the Sutherlands). Chiswick House must have had some influence, and there were memories of the relation of house to garden in many Italian constructions which the Prince had visited, especially the Pitti-Boboli, the Villa Madama, and the Villa di Papa Giulio.

There were obvious reasons for choosing an Italianate style for Osborne. The Cornish Riviera would have seemed too far from London but the Isle of Wight had almost as temperate a climate; from later Cornish travels by yacht, the Queen and Prince brought back plants for Osborne, where almost anything short of the palms acclimatized in Cornwall would grow. 'We drove between rows of laurel and myrtle, as in Italy', wrote Baron Bunsen in July 1847 about a visit to Osborne.[2] It might have been equally obvious to employ Barry, the prime architect of the Lusso taste and the Italian style. But Barry had already proved resistant to certain proposals in Westminster, and the Prince found him difficult.[3] Perhaps Barry was too brilliant for royalty: there was the danger that the whole project might run away and become Barry's and not one's own. Something a little more domestic, perhaps a little more

---

[1] *Early Victorian Architecture in Britain*, 1954, I, 181 ff. The *Orangerie-schloss* was executed after the death in 1845 of its designer Persius, says Hitchcock in *Architecture, Nineteenth and Twentieth Centuries*, 1958, p. 35; so it is even conceivable that there was mutual influence; the orangery below the Osborne clock tower was not installed until 1849.

[2] Frances Baroness Bunsen, *Memoir of Baron Bunsen*, II, p. 84. Bunsen, long the Prussian ambassador, had the *petites entrées* to the Prince, and was friendly with both religious and scientific worlds in England; his wife was British. By a curious chance he entered Rome as a young man on foot in the company of Eastlake on 24 November 1816. As a diplomat Bunsen was rather a lightweight. He did draw from Prince Albert in conversation at Osborne in July 1849 the ironical comment that 'every German knows all and every thing better than all others' (*Memoir*, II, p. 152).

[3] Grey to Cole, 16 December 1853 (Cole Papers, Victoria and Albert Museum, box 1), quoted the Prince as saying that 'every step Sir Charles takes requires careful watching'.

visibly organic than Barry's splendid piles, was wanted – even if the detail was not to be original or exquisitely worked.

Edward Lear, during the short period when he was giving drawing lessons to the Queen in 1846 (July and August at Osborne), reported seeing a model of the whole Osborne complex; that would have been typical of the Prince's and Cubitt's thoroughness, as well as wise because of the complexity of the scheme, which involved an amount of earth-moving that would now be done in a few days with bulldozers, but which then required a small army of Cubitt's labourers. Osborne was meant from the beginning as a grand composition of wooded hillside, clumps of nearer trees, lawns, terraces, building, sculpture, flowers, sunlight, and the glorious view of the Solent. The building, admittedly dry in detail, is admirably related to its site and intelligent in plan, with a rather striking silhouette which became influential across the boundaries of style; its visibility from every Cunarder approaching or leaving Southampton increased its influence. Internally it is fine in colour, and it was at first severe in the arrangement of its furniture. Above all, it was practical: it was one of the first nearly fireproof domestic buildings intentionally so designed, and the flat roof made possible by the iron-and-brick flat-arch construction was a delightful promenade; this roof was double, with a large insulating inner space corresponding with the depth of the cornice.

The site plan called originally for a principal mass in nine bays, of which the central one had a Venetian window in each of the three storeys; at each end an advancing two-storey feature of three bays would end in a tower, but one tower in turn became the pivot for a cubical mass attached at one corner and enriched on two adjacent sides by a three-storey bay window and a three-storey bow window reminiscent of the Regency row-house bows of Brighton; this cube, containing the Queen's and Prince's rooms, was built first and was called by them the Pavilion. Beyond the other tower stood an extra-tall chapel- or hall-like mass,[1] behind which service buildings on a lower level were partly masked by trees. From the central mass, and full width from tower to

---

[1] The tall mass was later made by the Queen into a Prayer Room, in which she installed some of her post-Albertine purchases of religious pictures (Sir Noel Paton, for instance) and the altar which Edward VII set up in his parents' bedroom after the Queen's death.

tower, an almost empty terrace gave on to broad double flights of steps which led down to a second terrace, more protected, more gardened; several ingenious and rather sensitive devices for maintaining a semblance of symmetry mask the actually diagonal contours of the sloping site; and these formalities lead by way of lawns with Reptonian clusters of trees to dense woods. Exact symmetry is avoided by the salience of the Pavilion and by the two towers, which are different in weight and pattern. The stucco would be dull if it were not for strong quoins and the rustication of the ground-floor walls in many places; and the central mass would be hopelessly dull without the accents at the ends and the clusters of chimneys at the centres of the roofs.[1] The larger tower (which the Queen on 25 November 1845 called 'not at all too high') served as water-tower and flagstaff for the Royal standard; the clock tower (slighter and more archaeological, suggesting Santa Maria in Cosmedin) was finished in 1848.

From then on, the influence of Osborne was vast, far beyond that of any Barry buildings except the clubs. Suburban villas in Britain and Canada and the United States, and even some in France and Germany, had to have a tower or two; the larger houses of A. J. Downing, his successor the English-born Calvert Vaux, and McMurtry were strongly influenced; small American college buildings in Ohio, Indiana, and westwards borrowed freely from Osborne, and the Smithsonian Institution in Washington, though in a Lombard dress revised from the first Gothic intention (by James Renwick 1847-55), had a remarkably Osborne-like silhouette. A posthumous (1856) edition of one of Minard Lafever's American books, *The Architectural Instructor*, included among the 'modern English and United States' examples nothing by Bulfinch or Strickland or Soane or Barry, but the White House, the Capitol (as it then was), Robert Mills's Patent Office in Washington, Osborne, Balmoral, and (rather surprisingly) Kedleston.[2] In other words, the examples were viable rather than brilliant.

---

[1] Barry liked to emphasize the ends of his façades, but he usually put chimneys in outside walls and disguised their tops as elements of a parapet or balustrade; the Osborne chimneys are in the inside walls, but are made much of where they issue from the roof.

[2] Dr Johnson once said that Kedleston would have done very well for a town hall. Osborne also appeared as frontispiece to the 1852 edition of Nicholson's perennial *Encyclopaedia of Architecture*.

The Pavilion, completed in mid-September 1846, is differentiated from the rest of Osborne by having no arcuated forms, by a somewhat expanded horizontal scale, and by its projecting bays. The scale throughout the complex, though by no means that of a palace, is ample, with broad communications such as Sir Edwin Lutyens would have approved of sixty years later. The chief corridor in the *piano nobile*, having penetrated the main block of the building, emerges as an open loggia of Venetian or Palladian-window form, with Ionic columns; it turns the corner at the Pavilion tower, and continues along the entrance-yard face of the main block. Outdoors, the stairs, niches, and varying balustrades were adorned with a repertory of electrotype copies by Elkingtons of familiar classical sculpture, plus a few restored originals shipped from Italy by Gruner. Fountains in metal or terracotta, a summer-house, and vases (sometimes of coloured terracotta) characterized the several terraces. The servants' barracks (built 1849–50) and the service courts look more Soane-ish than Italianate. Long after Prince Albert's death the Queen built the Durbar wing for her Indian trophies; it stands behind the Pavilion, facing the two-storey corridor-colonnade that connects the front and back sections of the main block.

The fairly strong light of summer in the Isle of Wight, and the brilliant colour of Victorian bedding plants on the lower terrace and in the vases of the balustrades, were brought into the house by large windows and by strong colours used on an ample white ground. The paving of the open colonnades and the inner corridors which extended them was of excellent Minton tiles on which the arms of Great Britain and Saxony appeared in their blue, red, gold, and green on a ground of starch-blue scrollwork and white. This tough, clean, saturated colour, picked up in the porcelain doorknobs and finger-plates of porcelain painted with flowers, again on a white ground, was extended to the ceilings in a more muted fashion, but in the chief rooms the ceilings were accented with gilding.

These principal rooms on the ground floor and new furniture, much of it designed by Henry Whitaker and made by Hollands, which had elements of the palace or royal style developed for Buckingham Palace in the twenties; some of it was gilded and might also be described as post-Hope or faintly Neapolitan Empire in style. It was large in scale and was not meant to be freely moved about; lighter portable pieces were more up-to-date.[1] The colour was rich; the drawing-room originally had yellow satin-damask curtains and furniture-covers, while its specially woven Aubusson carpet was made to fit around the bases of the scagliola columns (with white Corinthian capitals) which divided the room nominally into three sections. Though it is smaller by far than the Ehrenburg's *Riesensaal*, this room in its sub-division suggests that older one, but there is an ingenious change. The gentlemen of the Household were required to stand in the Queen's presence; but one end bay of the three-part room was extended by another bay which was effectively an L around the corner, so that anyone in the L would be out of sight of the central section; thus men could sit or play billiards at a table designed (like its hanging lamps)[2] by the Prince.

The decorating scheme was based upon the presence of works of art. In the ground-floor rooms the pictures were almost all large: Winterhalter's family group of 1846 was painted for the dining-room, where Belli's copy of it was hung after the original went to Buckingham Palace in 1901. Pictures were expected, and sculpture, too. The pedestals, often of yellow Siena marble or porphyry, added to the strong colour just as the white marble figures cooled it. Mary Thornycroft's life-size statues of the four eldest children as the Seasons, on red Cornish marble pedestals, were intended for the drawing-room. The high wall above the half-landing of the main stair, lit from above, was occupied by one of the best (and now the best-preserved) of Dyce's frescoes, *Neptune Resigning the Empire of the Seas to Britannia*, which has neither the obvious Raphaelesque character of the Westminster frescoes nor the sanctimonious look of many of Dyce's easel paintings; the cheerful mermaids are bifurcated as in Renaissance bronzes.[3] Facing this fresco from the top landing is Wolff's marble portrait of the Prince,

---

[1] Peter Floud, 'Furniture', in *Connoisseur Period Guide No. 6, The Early Victorian Period 1830–1860*, 1958. Much of the Osborne furniture was put in store by Edward VII in St James's Palace and served various temporary uses, as when York House was fitted up in 1903 to receive President Loubet of France; the Osborne furniture often proved too big in scale for older rooms.

[2] The Queen's diary reports these in use by 3 March 1847.

[3] Rather better than the fresco, completed in the autumn of 1847, is the oil sketch for it, now the property of Lady Patricia Ramsay.

standing barefoot in Roman armour.[1] Built into the walls of the council room in a less private quarter of Osborne House are figures in relief by another favoured sculptor, William Theed, and large portraits of the Queen and Prince enamelled on Sèvres porcelain; but many of the personal, rather than semi-official, pictures went into the Pavilion; one of these was Winterhalter's *Florinda*, a huge composition of nudes derived from a forgotten narrative poem of Southey's (see my chapter *Collecting*).

The broad corridors were intended, like those at Windsor, as places where he who ran might read; they had niches for sculpture and, in the indoor sections, vitrines for the endless gifts of porcelain, 'Parian' figurines, silver trowels from cornerstone-layings, and objects in polished granite or ormolu. Thus did the Prince keep clutter under control, and not until after his death did it overflow the house to such an extent that Edward VII wanted none of it. The Prince kept in his dressing-room at Osborne many of his Italian and German 'primitive' paintings, and began in 1849 a catalogue of all the Osborne works of art. When Edward VII turned the house over to the nation in 1902, he removed the best objects to Sandringham or one of the palaces, leaving the private rooms in the Pavilion untouched and firmly closed, the state rooms downstairs visible to the public but not in their original condition; the private rooms were opened in 1955, and the rest of the House is a convalescent hospital.

Those private rooms have come down as Queen Victoria left them except for some minor and pious Edwardian accretions. If we imagine away the dozens of framed photographs which the Queen required, we see the early and middle Victorian taste bang on centre: the many pictures hung symmetrically, the close carpeting in rather loose patterns a bit too large, the excellent balloon-back or modified Regency chairs, the plain woods, the chintz, the upholstery. When we look at the state rooms below, we see that 'the taste of the Court tended to be some ten years or so behind that of London society generally';[2] that is, I think,

---

[1] This statue had been intended for Buckingham Palace as companion to a Gibson statue of the Queen, but was thought a little too 'undressed'; the one now in Buckingham Palace is carefully shod.

[2] Floud, *op. cit.*

so far as what was meant to be visibly *of* the Court is concerned. However much he laboured for the dignity of the Crown, Prince Albert cared little for typical Court people: one can imagine his thinking, 'Let the Court be the Court'. Osborne itself, though it was a large country house such as people of sound taste might have been building at the time, was not meant to be judged by the Lusso taste, nor was it meant for public consumption as the Westminster frescoes were; and its influence may perhaps be credited as much to its freedom from didactic intent as to its visibility.

The private rooms were largely furnished from Dowbiggins with plain rosewood and mahogany. A few special pieces closer to the Grec than to the Lusso taste were designed, like the grand gilt Lusso furniture, by Henry Whitaker, notably some hall chairs entirely of mahogany, with sidewise curule supports and vigorous escutcheon-shaped back carved with the V and A in monogram;[1] they have tremendous style, and no one else could have done them at the time except perhaps Alfred Stevens.

The top floor of the Pavilion was devoted to nurseries; the older children in time had their own rooms in the main block. From the top of the first tower Prince Albert directed the great planting and grading operations by means of signal flags. He was also a passionate drainer of soggy places, and caused the laying of hundreds of thousands of drain tile yearly for five or six years. When he could spare a whole day he would gladly spend it staking out new plantations, thinning old timber stands, remodelling the shape of a valley, or improving the line of roads and paths. He began a tree nursery as early as March 1846, and in December 1847 his wife accused him of being too fond of transplanting – one of the few times when she found fault with him in her diary. She was as usual slow to accept some novelties, and did not at first like the tall mound, planted with evergreens, which insulated the ice-storage well; but the doorway to the ice-house pleased her; an arch of huge voussoirs, flanked by down-swooping scrolls and topped by an eagle, it was almost Vanbrugh-like, perhaps a memory of Vanbrugh's garden

---

[1] Various Whitaker pieces are reproduced in Elizabeth Aslin, 'Early Victorian Furniture', in *The Antique Dealer and Collector's Guide*, October 1962, pp. 37–39; Floud, *op. cit;* Floud, 'Victorian Furniture', in *Concise Encyclopaedia of Antiques*, vol. 3, pp. 17–29; Barbara Jones, *English Furniture at a Glance.*

gates at Claremont; the motive was used again for the vault door at the Duchess of Kent's mausoleum.

The Osborne estate was also a working farm, with productive orchards, its own piggeries, hayfields, and dairy. The Royal children were taught gardening and brick-making and tent-pitching; for them in 1853 a Swiss Chalet, prefabricated and shipped to England in sections, was set up; it contains some of the most advanced kitchen fittings of the period or indeed of any period before plastics and aluminium. There were also swimming lessons; and one of the Prince's latest works was a sort of sun-trap close to the water, shaped like a band-shell and lined with more of the brilliant tiles that he liked. Over the years he built farm cottages and gate lodges, several more spacious cottages for equerries and visitors, an orangery below the clock tower, new farmhouses for the adjacent Barton and Alverstone estates, a new chancel (1855–6) for Whippingham Church, and in 1860–1 even a new nave, all in more or less Norman style, which has not been generally admired; the architect was Albert Jenkins Humbert.[1] The Prince and William Cubitt not only introduced a steam engine for some of the farm work such as wood-sawing, but even experimented with a sewage-treatment plant which seems to have been on the 'activated sludge' principle but was a little too far ahead of its time. They do not seem to have tried central heating; but a most practical move of Thomas Cubitt and the Prince's was to build early in 1845, before the Pavilion began, a kitchen and scullery and kilns for making brick and tile; presumably all that was needed was made on the spot, using locally felled wood for fuel.

Some of the larger outlying buildings had each a special room, independently entered, for Royal stop-overs during walks or rides around the Osborne property; the same provision was made in some of the buildings in Windsor Great Park.

In December 1859 Sir Howard Elphinstone complained to his diary that 'Osborne is *not* a winter residence. Everything is calculated for summer enjoyment.'[2] And although the Queen herself complained

---

[1] Humbert found favour at Whippingham and eventually was commissioned to design two Royal mausoleums and the Prince of Wales's house at Sandringham.

[2] *Archives*, Victorian Additional MSS. A. 25/819. Elphinstone was tutor to Prince Arthur.

twice during her married life that when the north-east wind blew they could not keep warm at Osborne in spite of enormous fires, she chose after the Prince's death to spend six weeks there in December and January as well as six summer weeks every year. In the 1890s, when the Queen's bedroom was hung with a Dyce *Madonna*, a Winterhalter portrait of herself and a favourite cousin, van Eycken's *Abondance* (which she had given to her husband in 1848), and two recent religious paintings, the Prince's dressing room still contained ten or eleven of his early Italian pictures, including the Gozzoli *Simon Magus* (one of his best purchases), a good Raffaelino del Garbo (then thought to be a Verrocchio), a Cima which the Queen had given him in 1847, and one surprise. This was the rather startling *Hercules and Omphale* signed A. Gegenbaur, Romae 1830, which the Prince bought in 1844. The big Mabuse-like nudes, astonishing when glimpsed through the door, are in fresco – thick plaster in an iron frame. One wonders whether this purchase was simply a footnote to one of the great interests of 1844, or whether the man who was 'not the master in his own house' bought this subject-piece for the story of the hero in servitude to a woman. Again, one is thankful that a few mysteries remain.[1]

Like the several Barry-cum-Nesfield house-and-garden compositions, Osborne gave notice that the older European scheme of *parterres* as part of an architectural whole, long eclipsed by the informal 'picturesque' and naturalistic setting, was again to be taken seriously and, indeed, had returned. The England of the second and third Georges, propagandized by Edmund Burke and served by Lancelot Brown and Humphrey Repton, had liked to bring lawns to the very walls of the house, and to keep flowers in a garden elsewhere; but the interrelation of indoors and outdoors made possible by increasingly large windows, conservatories, and (for the rich) orangeries, called for those patterned bits of garden seen through Regency windows to echo the carpet on the floor inside. At Osborne the formal *parterre* and the subtly remodelled natural landscape lived well together, while the colour of the flower garden was greatly enriched by novelties brought in by both exploration and breeding. The resident 'planter' at Osborne, Mr Toward, like

---

[1] Robert Graves, *The Greek Myths*, 1955, II, pp. 162–8, gives the Omphale story in several variants.

Ingram, his opposite number at Windsor, often helped in other projects of Prince Albert's; for example, in April 1856 they were both called on to plan plantations around the Royal Pavilion at Aldershot. And on his birthday in the same year, when Balmoral had succeeded Osborne as the scene of great campaigns, the Prince was enjoying gladioli, the corms of which had come from Fontainebleau, and which now glowed against the myrtle and magnolia leaves.

6

Buckingham Palace

Almost before it was completed in its original form, Buckingham Palace began to be neglected, and indeed some parts of its interior were not finished at William IV's death. It was not much of a dwelling, but primarily a place for Court entertainment, a replacement of George IV's Carlton House on a grander scale, a bringing up-to-date of St James's. Its virtues were due to Nash and to his patron, George IV, but Nash retired at the King's death, and his work was carried on by Edward Blore under a sort of committee of taste which was no concern of William IV's.

When Queen Victoria entered upon her inheritance, she was at first uncritical; 'my collection' was there to be enjoyed, and so were the White Drawing Room, the Music Room with its marvellous violet-blue scagliola columns (Creevey called them 'raspberry-coloured'),[1] and the spacious and very private grounds. After a ball at the Palace on 10 May 1838 Lady Stanhope said that 'Devonshire House looked quite dingy' in comparison, or so the Queen heard three days later.[2] The

---

[1] Creevey visited the Palace in 1835 when William IV was thinking of moving in: 'wicked, vulgar profusion' he called it. It must be admitted that it is not Nash's best work and that, in spite of the fine execution of most of the detail, the inorganic nature of the design makes the interiors look more 'profuse' than they are. The ornament of the deep coves in the state rooms is in many cases a mere assembly. *The Creevey Papers*, edited by Sir Herbert Maxwell, 1903, II, p. 224.

[2] Devonshire House, demolished in the 1920s, was one of the few London houses, in effect private palaces, built in the eighteenth century on a scale comparable to that of Paris *hôtels particuliers*. It was by William Kent, who wrapped it around a great forecourt on the north side of Piccadilly, over which it looked straight down the Queen's walk past Spencer House (one of its few rivals still in existence) and the old pre-Barry Bridgewater House to the former York House, then recently renamed Stafford House and being enlarged for the Sutherlands.

piano nobile of the western block of the Palace consisted almost entirely of great reception rooms in two parallel ranges separated by a top-lighted picture gallery. The complicated façade of this block was visible only from the garden, which was so protected that flowers came out there earlier than in the country; in the Queen's opinion, therefore, spring was the 'nicest moment for staying in London'.[1] Four conservatories, attached at their corners to the corners of this great parade block, brought it down to earth; and from its north and south ends long narrow wings pushed eastward, enclosing a forecourt. Though all this was in three storeys, the only consistent horizontal communication was an open passage around the courtyard, its roof carried on cast-iron columns; from it the separate staircase entries could be reached. The grille that enclosed the east side of the court was centred by the Marble Arch, which stood there until 1851. Between the two south conservatories was a small octagon, originally intended as an armoury but ordered in August 1837 to be fitted up as a chapel; it was no bigger than an oratory, and proved inadequate. The north-east conservatory, useless because overshadowed, had been removed in 1836 to Kew Gardens.

Although the Palace was substantially new, it was already subject to the same wasteful bureaucracies and vested interests as Windsor; to the reform of these Prince Albert addressed himself. The savings in household expense produced by his consolidations helped his wife to pay for Osborne. The Palace, however, was not private property, and the Commissioners of Woods and Forests were almost like landlords. The Prince's first building effort there was the conversion of the south-west conservatory into a chapel, on which, of course, he worked with Blore, Surveyor to the Commissioners. There was, however, one rather mysterious earlier change. A semi-popular print of 1841[2] shows a deputation from Oxford presenting to the Queen the University's address on her marriage. This event of 1840 takes place in the Throne Room, where figurehead-like nymphs carrying garlands flank George IV's monogram under the beam which sets off the throne bay from the three other bays of that room (they are still in place). But in the lithograph a pseudo-Gothic canopy and a series of tracery-topped panels bearing

---

[1] Diary, 20 April 1843.
[2] Reproduced in Gernsheim, *Victoria R.*, 1959, fig. 50.

heraldic achievements surround the throne, looking thin and papery amid the robust Palace-style splendours. Less than a year later we see the baptism of the Princess Royal (10 February 1841, her parents first wedding anniversary) taking place in the same room, in C. R. Leslie's painting.[1] An altar has been improvised in place of the throne, and a Regency table on a circular dais carries the portable silver font, but the walls are now in their full Palace-style trim. Was the Gothic stage-setting a hasty temporary one, made because the room was unfinished early in 1840, or was it a polite gesture of Prince Albert's or Blore's to the antiquities of Oxford? The octagonal chapel might have served for the baptism but was probably too small; it would not have served for receiving a congratulatory address.

The conservatory to be transformed into a chapel had, like all of them, glass walls and roof, the latter carried on cast-iron trusses in a pattern of tangent open circles of graduated diameters.[2] There were intermediate cast-iron columns, on the axes of which a clerestory might have been raised higher if it had not been disfiguring on the outside; high side-lighting was managed. The new chapel, consecrated by the Archbishop of Canterbury on 25 March 1843, was broader than the Chapel Royal of St James's and larger in all dimensions than the charming chapel (originally Catherine of Braganza's) attached to Marlborough House; a few days later the Bishop of London remarked that it was the first time the royal servants had had a regular place of worship. There, perhaps in part prompted by Stockmar's views of right conduct, the Queen and Prince went to prayers every morning when they were in London, before the daily walk in the garden.

The artificial lighting of this otherwise uninteresting chapel (now converted into a public gallery for objects from the Royal collection) was one of Prince Albert's early science-and-art undertakings. In time for the christening of Princess Helena in 1846, gas light 'on Faraday's ventilating principle'[3] was installed in eight large ceiling fixtures and ten ormolu candelabra; down the hollow shafts of the latter the carbon

---

[1] Gernsheim, *op. cit.*, fig. 53.

[2] Cf. those of Repton's design for a Carlton House conservatory (never executed), reproduced in Dorothy Stroud, *Humphrey Repton*, 1962, 116. But the pattern was pretty much in the public domain.

[3] *The Times*, 27 July 1846.

dioxide was exhausted; each gas jet was surrounded by a glass globe cut with the monogram IHS and radiating stars.

But long before Princess Helena, her fifth child, the Queen was complaining of the lack of space for her children at the Palace. When she and her husband were discussing the possibility of buying Osborne, they were also asking Sir Robert Peel to approach Parliament about enlargement of the Palace. On 10 February 1845 they composed a formal letter for him; the outside of the building, the Queen felt, was 'a dis- grace to the country'. It is hard to tell what she meant by this – her annoyance was really with the accommodation, and the annoyance had been aggravated in June 1844 when she had had to receive the King of Saxony and the Tsar in London at the same time. Peel was 'quite willing to bring forward the plan', and it was he who suggested selling the Brighton Pavilion in order to use the money either for a quiet sea- side place or for the Palace; the quiet seaside place turned out to be Osborne and, being privately financed, it moved much faster than Palace affairs. The Prince had made designs of a sort as early as March 1844, but the outlook for building did not look hopeful until a year and a half later (the Queen noted on 15 September 1845 that 'he has a wonderful turn for architecture').[1] Parliament finally voted £20,000 for the addition to the Palace on 15 August 1846, with the understanding that most of the cost would be found by the sale of the Pavilion to the Corporation of Brighton. Much furniture and even some of the 'Chinese' chimneypieces of the Pavilion were brought to London for incorpora- tion into the Palace; one such was the famous marble and ormolu example executed by Westmacott and Vulliamy to a design by Robert Jones, who worked at Brighton for the decorator Crace and invented much of the detail. It has recently been said that some other Palace chimney- pieces are of marble that the Queen ordered sawn from George IV's bathing pool at Brighton,[2] but I cannot discover a source for this claim.

---

[1] This is one of the Queen's few uses of the adjective *wonderful* in the sense of *admirable;* she usually meant something pejorative or at least ironical when she said *wonderful:* the 'wonderful tartan' that the Duke of Leeds (no Scotsman he) had designed, or the 'wonderful Departments' of Government that would not let one call one's soul one's own.

[2] *New York Times Book Review*, 24 April 1960, p. 32, in review by Samuel T. Williamson of Lawrence Wright, *Clean and Decent*, 1960.

Cubitts were contractors for the new wing and the necessary connecting links. From January 1847 until the middle of 1858 there were
building operations going on at the Palace, and the later ones from
Pennethorne's designs were certainly more distinguished than the new
east front by Blore. Blore had had much practical experience of large-
scale construction, but had built almost entirely in Gothic or Jacobethan,
as at Abbotsford, Worsley, and Hinchingbrooke. By enclosing Nash's
colonnade around the Palace courtyard and creating a corresponding
corridor in the new wing, he succeeded in giving the house greatly
improved circulation; but he was never an imaginative designer. His
nominally Italianate façade not only flattened out the projections and
withdrawals of Nash's court but managed to look pinched itself, perhaps
because of his or his clients' insistence on ordering it in twenty-three
bays[1] when nineteen would probably have given it a nobler scale. The
Atlas newspaper, always contemptuous of Prince Albert and his works,
called it on 3 May 1856 'the public-house-looking front of Buckingham
Palace'. Indeed it had a faintly odd look with its skyline animated by
ornaments which were reminiscent of Jacobean printers' devices, even
a little of Heidelberg.

The many windows of this new east wing did make it possible to
work numerous rooms into the upper floors (the ground floor was
pierced by three arches opening to the now completely surrounded
courtyard). On the *piano nobile*, each of the projecting blocks was given
a large drawing room (the famous balcony opening of course from the
central one); the seven bays between these blocks on each side accounted
for a suite of bedroom, sitting or writing room, and two dressing rooms.
The materials brought from the Brighton Pavilion gave to the interiors
a certain direction which has never been lost: a dragon was promptly
painted on the ceiling of the room which received the Regent's best
pseudo-Chinese furniture; and Queen Mary brought real or Regency
Chinese into further play when she redecorated these rooms after 1910.

There is little more to say about the east wing, except that the new
corridors again gave space for hanging many paintings that had been
forgotten but rediscovered by the Prince at Hampton Court and in

---

[1] Twenty-five if we count the narrow windows at each end of the central
section, which were later suppressed by Sir Aston Webb.

other half-neglected places of storage. He was able, so to speak, to see through layers of neglect and even sometimes through layers of varnish on more 'established' pictures. Towards the end of the first half of the Palace campaign, early in 1851, the long picture-gallery in the middle of the western block was refurbished, the walls painted dove-colour, the floor newly carpeted, and numerous paintings reframed in a uniform 'gallery' frame – a simple cyma overlain by a honeycomb pattern over all, and with second-rococo corner cartouches.[1]

Whether because Blore was growing old or because Prince Albert was not as pleased with the east wing as the Queen was, the second half of the Palace campaign was entrusted to James Pennethorne, the mysterious cousin and adopted son to whom Nash turned over his practice in 1834. Ludwig Gruner, who had served so faithfully on the stage-managing of the frescoes in the Palace garden pavilion, and who was buying sculpture for Osborne, was made a sort of adviser to Pennethorne because the programme for the Ball Room was Raphael-esque, and among Gruner's several great tasks of engraving for picture-books had been much reproduction of Raphael compositions; he may, with Passavant's *Raffael* of 1839, have helped fire the Prince's enthusiasm for Raphael, originally kindled by his sight of the *Logge* and *Stanze* of the Vatican. The Prince began early in 1853 to arrange the Raphael drawings in the Royal collection according to Passavant, and thenceforth he and his librarian Ruland compiled the great photographic corpus of Raphael's works which is one of the pioneer undertakings of modern art-history. Gruner must have begun the designs for the decoration of the Ball Room at about the same time, for the outer walls were completed by 1 March 1853.

A ballroom of real scope had been wanted by the Queen ever since she talked with Lord Melbourne (17 June 1839) about 'making the

---

[1] The Prince may have been influenced in this rather unhappy undertaking by the nearly uniform Pitti Palace frames, the simpler standard frames of Augustus the Strong at Dresden, or even Napoleon's at the Louvre. But such 'consistent' framing was being done also at the National Gallery. It was said in London about 1950 that the National Gallery was slowly buying back many original frames from the descendants of the frame-makers who had replaced them with uniform 'gallery' models and who had had the good sense to keep the originals for a hundred years rather than burn them to salvage the gold.

Throne room one of the Ball rooms'. Though the state rooms of Buckingham Palace were long, their narrower dimension was at most thirty-four feet. The dances of the eighteenth and early nineteenth centuries were danced in sets of figures, largely double rows, small circles, or squares (such as the quadrille), which fell into place perfectly well in comparatively narrow rooms. The appearance of the waltz changed the requirements of rooms for dancing, and the increasing size of women's skirts, from the forties onwards, aggravated the change. As each waltzing couple was independent of all others, and needed space for whirling, the pattern of a party of many couples became centrifugal, needing ideally a circular room. So Pennethorne was asked to create a room of real breadth (there had been an earlier scheme by Blore, never executed).

The Ball Room itself, about sixty feet wide and over a hundred feet long, stands well south of the south-west corner of the Palace on the *piano nobile;* the complex of kitchens, sculleries, larders, and servants' hall on the ground floor was enlarged and renewed before the Ball Room was built on top. The new galleries connected it to the Nash west block, the east gallery (over a hundred feet long) leading to the Grand Stair; and the top-lighted gallery between these connectors allowed still more space for large assemblies.

The Ball Room had reminiscences of the Villa Madama. Under a great arch at one end (with a concentric and smaller but free-standing archivolt within it to reduce the scale) was a throne-alcove. On the long sides, above continuous tiered platforms for seated spectators, the walls were covered with stretched silk damask to well above door-height; then came a deep frieze in which seven windows alternated with six panels. As the room is forty-five feet high, these windows easily cleared the roofs of the connecting galleries; above them a cove led to the coffered ceiling. The windows had two sets of glazing, between which were gas-jets, well vented, 'the lighting most original and beautiful', said Lady Eastlake.[1] There seems to have been a change in the execution from Gruner's original scheme, which in his own published perspective shows the walls in panels below the frieze, and a series of gas-brackets (the light diffused by inverted umbrellas of glass) projecting just below

---

[1] Letter dated 8 May 1856 reprinted in her *Letters and Journals*, 1895.

29. John Gibson: *Queen Victoria*; marble, 1850–5

30. Louis Gallait: *Le Sentiment de la Maternité*; 18 ×
16⅝ in.; gift of the Queen
to the Prince, Christmas 1846

31. William Dyce: *Virgin and Child*;
canvas, 31½ × 23¼ in.; signed and dated
1845; commissioned by Prince Albert

32. C. W. Cope: *Embarkation of the Pilgrim Fathers*; waterglass on slate, signed and dated 1856

33. Franz Xaver Winterhalter: *Florinda*; canvas, 5 ft 11 in. × 8 ft 2⅞ in.; gift from the Queen to the Prince, 26 August 1852

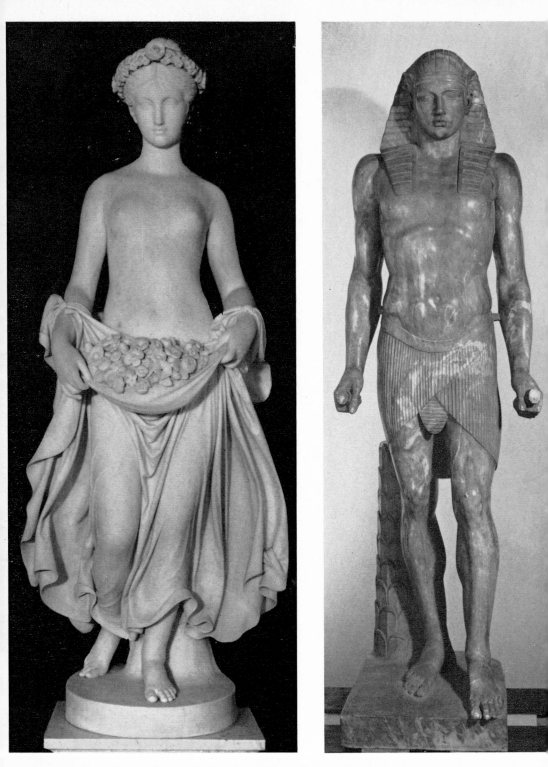

34. Pietro Tenerani; *Flora*; marble, 5 ft 4 in., signed and dated 1849; bought by Prince Albert, 1849

35. *Antinous*; grey marble, 5 ft 7 in.; Egypto-Roman, late 2nd Century A.D.; bought by the Queen from the Ward Collection, 1850

36. Pesellino (Francesco di Stefano Ginochi): *The Trinity with Four Saints*;
lower left, St James the Great and St Mammas; panel, 4 ft 7¾ in.; gift of the
Queen to the Prince, 26 August 1846

37. Bohemian or Moravian: *The Virgin and Child*, tempera on panel, $23\frac{1}{2} \times 19\frac{1}{2}$ in. ex coll. Oettingen-Wallerstein

38. Benozzo Gozzoli: *Fall and Judgment of Simon Magus*; tempera on panel $9\frac{1}{2} \times 14$ in.; bought by Prince Albert from Warner Ottley, 1846

IOÀNIS BELLINI OP.

39. Giovanni Bellini: *Saint Dominic*; canvas, signed and dated 1515; ex coll.
Soulages

40. Justus van Ghent (?) *Federigo da Montefeltro and his Son Guidobaldo Hearing a Humanist Lecture*; chestnut panel, $51\frac{1}{8} \times 83\frac{1}{2}$ in.; bought by the Queen at the Woodburn sale, 1853

41. Duccio di Buoninsegna: *Triptych*; tempera on panel, the chief subject $12\frac{1}{2}$ in. wide; bought by Prince Albert through Gruner from Metzger of Florence, 1845

the windows. In Louis Haghe's watercolour of the Ball Room as it was in June 1856, these umbrella-like forms appear only in the lighting fixtures which centre the coffers of the ceiling; while the lower lighting is provided only by twelve great standing candelabra of high-Renaissance form: these were of ormolu by the eminent French Barbedienne foundry,[1] from Gruner's design.

The colour scheme was as strong as Osborne's: the cove and coffers had alternating green and red grounds, with ornament in relief in white, and some details gilded; the twelve panels alternating with the windows were painted with Raphaelesque figures of the Hours by Nicola Consoni (1814-84), chiefly in crimson and white on a bright blue ground; the doorways were framed in rather flat broad bands, sculptured and painted but without orders. All this was swept away in 1902 by Edward VII, who found the throne alcove sufficiently grand but took away all the small detail, provided the doorways with enormous aedicular frames, and suppressed the colour.

The contractors were again Cubitts: William Cubitt's estimates dated 3 September 1851 (he was knighted six weeks later for his services to the Exhibition of that great year) total £45,000 plus extras.[2] In spite of his great organization, he could not move any faster on this than on the previous Office of Works job on the east front of the Palace, and the Ball Room could not be used until more than two years after the outside walls were finished; admittedly the Crimean War made a difference.

The south-east conservatory of the Palace had also necessarily vanished, and approximately above its location Pennethorne built a Supper Room, completed in 1858, as part of the Ball Room scheme. Its walls, divided much like those of the Ball Room so as to allow space in the lower range for side tables with great arrays of plate and for fireplaces, were panelled, but with imitation marble rather than silk or

---

[1] The candelabra have a family resemblance to those designed by Richard Redgrave for use in St Paul's at the Duke of Wellington's funeral, and actually made only in bronzed plaster. Ferdinand Barbedienne was a self-made creator of 'art manufactures' after Henry Cole's own heart, and a great promoter of Renaissance forms. The ormolu branches of the Ball Room candelabra were removed during Edward VII's remodelling and used in chandeliers for the principal corridor of the east front of the Palace.

[2] *Archives*, vol. C. 81, No. 157.

Raphaelesque motifs. One of the chimneypieces, with busts of George IV and William IV, came from the old octagonal Armoury, and a second, with busts of Victoria and Albert, was made to match it. This sort of conservatism was rather typical of both the Prince's attitude to the Palace and the Works' approach to its charges; yet in the Supper Room and in one of the connecting galleries new high-relief sculpture by Gibson and by the younger William Theed was installed above the doorways. And despite the rather domestic scale of the Raphaelesque ornament, the bigness of the two rooms was a real contribution to Royal entertainment.

The ground-floor rooms on the west or garden side of Nash's block, and some rooms on the north side which led towards the new wing, were gradually put to the Queen's and Prince's new uses. The Prince took as his library the room under the White Drawing Room,[1] though in 1844 it was temporarily turned over to hospitality when the Tsar and the King of Saxony were both guests (it has since been called the 1844 Room). In 1853 the Queen's large purchases from the auction of Louis Philippe's Spanish paintings turned some of the rooms almost into picture-galleries. In 1855 the rooms arranged for the visit of Napoléon III and Eugénie were carefully recorded in watercolour for the Windsor albums;[2] these and several other Buckingham Palace watercolours show throughout a fondness for strong colours: in the later rooms violet begins to triumph over red and green, and the trick of draping a mantel-shelf with a lambrequin creeps in. There is invariably a hearth-rug on top of the carpet; in the Queen's and Prince's own room (1849) there

---

[1] Queen Victoria's diary mentions on 27 December 1851 'the great Austrian library which has been put up in Albert's room' at the Palace. The rapid purge of the Prince's books, about which Sir Lionel Cust was the least bit shamefaced, cleared the way in 1901 and 1902 for uses of King Edward VII's. No Austrian library survived; the Queen was probably thinking both of the great Gothic bookcase (*bibliothèque* in French) given her by Kaiser Franz Josef and shown at the Great Exhibition, as well as of its contents, which seem to have included albums of views and other drawings by Austrian artists, and books about Austria, enough to constitute a library (*Bibliothek* in German). The bookcase was given by George V to the University of Edinburgh.

[2] There is a fairly well-authenticated story about Eugénie's being taken to see these rooms when she was old and dotty; she was heard murmuring to herself, 'Toujours ces affreux rideaux.'

is not only a canopy over the bed but another canopy over a sofa along the window wall. Carpet is universal, but almost never in such realistic flower designs as to cause dismay to Owen Jones (we shall hear later of the great design controversy in the Society of Arts, in which pictorial realism in carpets became a high moral question). The carpets ordered by the Prince for the state rooms of the Palace and of Windsor Castle were invariably of an architectural formality; they are quite unlike the repeating-patterned carpet-by-the-yard of private rooms, and much more like those carpets ordered by Robert Adam for some of his greatest interiors, where the ceiling pattern was echoed on the floor. The Ball Room and Supper Room, especially the shallow oval dome of the latter, which was treated as one vast patera or velarium, were also rather Adamesque but for their strong colours.

At Buckingham Palace the Queen and Prince seldom mixed their acquisitions of painting and sculpture intimately with inherited objects. A few old masters of some size were hung in the Palace, notably Cranach; almost nothing modern came there unless it was very large, as for instance John Martin's *The Eve of the Deluge* and Leighton's *Cimabue* picture; but Frith's *Ramsgate Sands*, which though large was *genre*, went to Osborne with smaller modern work. The *Cimabue* was later banished to St James's, but *Ramsgate Sands* came to Buckingham Palace.

For better for worse, most of what Prince Albert did at the Palace has been altered, and his chief legacy there is good housekeeping, the ample planning of the Ball Room and its dependencies, and the famous east balcony.

7

Second Royal Commission

Everyone knows something about the Great Exhibition of 1851 and about the contrast between the unprecedented beauties of the Crystal Palace and the fussy elaboration of many of the exhibits. I shall not repeat the more usual elements of the story, especially as the affair was not intended to have anything to do with 'High Art' as it was then thought of. Painting was specifically omitted because the Exhibition was of 'the Industry of All Nations'. Sculpture rushed in because foundry work and pointing and carving with mechanical devices were involved. Indeed the whole enterprise could be called an epiphany of early Victorian technology. What is most interesting for my purpose is the method of organization and 'sale' of the idea long before the opening on 1 May 1851; so is the popular effect of the Exhibition on high (rather than early) Victorian taste; not to mention the conclusions drawn from the Palace and its contents by the men who became Prince Albert's team in South Kensington.

There will always be some mystery (happily, I think) as to the priority of invention between the Prince and Henry Cole. The former was of course better acquainted than a boy born in Bath with the great old European trade fairs which had had an internationalizing effect for generations. The Prince will also have known, through the reading of quantities of consular and other government reports, about certain national industrial exhibitions which had grown up separately from the trade fairs and more recently. His presidency of the Society of Arts (since 1843) had acquainted him with its encouragement to 'manufactures' and had greatly strengthened the programme. It was within the framework of the Society of Arts that Cole proposed to the Prince in January 1848 a series of national industrial exhibitions; but when the Prince put the proposition informally to some members of the Cabinet early in February he could rouse no interest. More preparation of the ground was needed; and both men were very good at such preparation – we might call it propaganda, public relations, or salesmanship. The two men seem to have been exposed to each other first in March 1842 when the Prince was pursuing the Carlton House furniture, which he found stored along with George IV's collection of armour in the former riding-school in Carlton Terrace; there the Public Record Office had installed a branch, and there Cole worked. The Prince admired his storage and classification methods and his use of a small hand press on the spot for printing docket-tickets;[1] and they met later on Society of Arts business. Cole, as 'Felix Summerly', had already written small unofficial guide-books to such collections as that of Hampton Court, before he won the Society's prize in 1846 for a good simple 'nursery' tea set.[2] From then on his 'art manufactures' from his own and others' designs were successful and probably profitable. So were his books for children. In 1848 Cole was active in promoting Grimsby Docks, for which he composed advertisements in French and German and saw them through the press in suitable types; when, in April, Prince Albert went by rail to lay a sort of cornerstone at the Docks, Cole arranged in the royal railway carriage a special topical library, other briefing apparatus, and decoration, which included notes on Lincolnshire, geological maps, charts, a portfolio of unspecified drawings, and even a Dürer print on the wall. The Prince's secretary Phipps reported him as '*very much* pleased with his expedition to Grimsby'.[3] In March 1849 Cole had begun *The Journal of Design* and had prodded Milner Gibson[4] into securing a Select Committee of Parliament to investigate the Schools of Design,

---

[1] Cole seems to have printed his branch's letterheads on the same press; he understood the Caslon typefaces almost as well as the Chiswick Press did. Indeed, his 'Felix Summerly' series of small square octavo children's stories were printed by the younger Charles Whittingham at Chiswick from 1843, using Caslon types, occasional dotted-manner woodcut ornaments, and some-times laid paper of prominently ribbed texture; but the illustrations (by Horsley, Cope, Redgrave, and others) were wood-engravings (some by E. Dalziel) and had to be printed on a smoother wove paper.

[2] Queen Victoria often used one for breakfast at Balmoral; so General Biddulph, Master of the Household, once told Cole.

[3] Phipps to Cole (Cole papers, Victoria and Albert Museum, box 6).

[4] Thomas Milner Gibson (1806–84), free trader and friend of Cobden, had been vice-president of the Board of Trade 1846–8.

which later came under his and the Prince's wing at Marlborough House. There seems little doubt that Cole rather wanted to lay hands on the Schools from the beginning.

Cole had, then, the skills of the industrial designer, the promoter, the general manager, as well as some of the skills of the courtier and the good host or hostess. Dickens satirized him in *Hard Times* (1854) as Gradgrind's anonymous companion, 'always in training, always with a system to force down the general throat like a bolus. . . .'[1] He was resourceful and he learned quickly.

A first big step followed a good deal of probing (the Prince and Cole both became adept at putting out feelers and sending up trial balloons). The step was a proposal for quadrennial select shows of the best things from the Society of Arts' annual competitions; this was discussed by the Prince, Cole, Thomas Cubitt, and John Scott Russell on 29 June 1849; though Martin says an international exhibition was a 'project long thought over',[2] Cole claimed that at this meeting he got Prince Albert to agree, 'International, certainly'; and from this moment on the plan may be considered complete in principle and in its main lines. For example, Phipps on 4 July 1849 wrote to Cole that the Prince wanted plenty of room for building, and wished to use the space 'between the carriage drive to Kensington and Rotten Row'.[3] On 30 July the same four men, plus Francis Fuller, met at Buckingham Palace and agreed to ask for the use of a Hyde Park site and to take opinions in manufacturing quarters and elsewhere; Cole, Fuller, and Digby Wyatt did this, though Cole had to be reprimanded for hinting that 'Prince Albert is back of this'. The Prince, who had been under great strain for over a year as a result of the European revolutions of 1848 and subsequent diplomatic difficulties, began to see the Exhibition as a peacemaking and economy-bettering device; but he was not yet free to come into the open because royalty could not afford to be associated with anything of which the success was not reasonably assured.

Cole and Digby Wyatt went to see the French national industrial fair early in the same summer (1849), and were told by the French Minister

---

[1] K. J. Fielding, 'Charles Dickens and the Department of Practical Art', in *Modern Language Review*, xlviii, 1953, pp. 272–7.

[2] Martin, ii, 202.

[3] Cole papers, Victoria and Albert Museum, box 6.

of Agriculture and Commerce that Louis Napoleon would give French support to an international fair. Francis Fuller, who also went along, later claimed that on the way home he met Cubitt, who was on his way to Osborne, in Southampton railway station, and that the two then and there proposed to inoculate the Prince with the international idea. Fuller, who was of the trustee class and useful at fund-raising, later took a dislike to Cole and to Sir Charles Dilke, and was not included in later stages of the work.[1]

The result of much further spadework was the appointment on 3 January 1850 of a Royal Commission, which first met on the eleventh with the Prince as chairman; the membership included Gladstone, the capitalist Lloyd, Lord John Russell, Peel, Eastlake, Sir Charles Lyell, Lyon Playfair, Labouchere and Lord Granville (president and vice-president of the Board of Trade), Stafford Northcote (who with Granville and Labouchere was on the Committee of Management of the School of Design in London), George Wallis (formerly head of the Manchester School of Design), Dilke, Pusey the agriculturist, and Richard Cobden. Some of these appointments were of course honorific; but Granville (whom the Prince called 'the only working man on the Commission')[2] thought Dilke and Cole tremendous workers; and Cobden, despite the Prince's dislike of 'agitators', was brought in because of his own devotion to work, his knowledge of public feeling, and his experience in raising money for the Anti-Corn-Law League.[3] Although the Royal Commission had to retrace many of the steps

---

[1] Fuller, *The Omitted Chapter*, 1876, 52 ff.

[2] Memorandum quoted in *Letters of Queen Victoria*, series I, vol. 2, 311.

[3] Cole (in his autobiographical *Fifty Years of Public Work*, completed by his children and published 1884 after his death) quoted John Morley as having said that Cobden was the most laboriously conscientious man he had ever known, and that, 'allowing for differences in grasp and experience, the Prince Consort was in this respect of the same type'. At one of the exhibition-preparing meetings, held in Marylebone 2 May 1850, Cobden described Prince Albert as a 'working man', and said that only with the Prince presiding could he, Cobden, have sat on the same board with Lord Stanley, Sir Robert Peel, and Gladstone 'in perfect harmony of action'. It must have been Conservatives, not aristocrats, that he objected to, for he and Lord Morpeth (before the latter succeeded his father as Earl of Carlisle) sat together in Parliament for the West Riding. The Prince after this same meeting described Cobden to his wife as 'a little dark man, very much put out' (by which the Queen meant 'ill at ease').

taken by the Society of Arts, especially in regard to raising guarantees, it took over intact from the Society an Executive Committee, only adding Sir William Reid as President; Cole was one of this Executive though not on the Royal Commission.

A series of public meetings all over the country was begun with one held in London on 21 February 1850, at which Belgium, France, Prussia, the United States, and other nations were represented by their ministers or ambassadors; some of these men by pre-arrangement put motions or seconded them, or otherwise indicated the willingness of their home governments to encourage participation by their people in the Exhibition. Through them and through British consuls, a ramifying national or regional committee was set up in each quarter to which invitations were sent.[1] There were greater difficulties at home than abroad; the more picayune and amusing complaints and prophecies of doom are well known. 'Prince Albert's scheme is so unpopular', wrote Effie Gray (who was then still Mrs John Ruskin).[2] Subscriptions did not come in very well, and worst of all was the problem of the building.

A committee on design had been appointed soon after the naming of the Royal Commission, but the designs it received were all so unsatisfactory that committee and Commission together sponsored a compromise scheme, which required so many millions of bricks that the estimates were discouraging. The public may well have felt a wrongness in the published design. When Joseph Paxton found the solution, his means of making sure that it would be adopted were as shrewd as the Prince's and Cole's propaganda. Paxton, using his already large connexions, got the engineer Stephenson's assurance of the feasibility of the plan, and then had his project published in the *Illustrated London News*.[3] A letter from Prince Albert's secretary Grey dated 9 June

---

[1] Some of the regions were rather oddly assorted; cf. the list at the beginning of the official catalogue (*Great Exhibition of Industry of All Nations/1851/Official Descriptive and Illustrated Guides;* 3 vols., 1851. The *Art Journal* also issued a smaller guide.

[2] Letter to Rawdon Brown, quoted in James, *The Order of Release*, 1947, p. 161.

[3] His granddaughter, V. R. Markham, C.H., in *Paxton and the Bachelor Duke*, 1935, 162–3, gives a puzzling quotation from a letter that Paxton wrote his wife from Paris in the autumn of 1848: he had attended a concert at the 'Jardin de Verre' – 'nearly as big as Chatsworth Conservatory' – 'they have

1850 shows that space allotments were already a grave concern of the Prince's; the foreign acceptances were such that he feared for home representation, which in principle was to have the same number of hundreds of thousands of square feet as the rest of the world put together. Paxton was taken to Cole at the Board of Trade with his design on 11 June; but despite the Prince's immediate recognition of the virtues of Paxton's scheme, it was not until after the *Illustrated London News* publication of 6 July that the Royal Commission was persuaded to approve; the Commission met on the sixth, the eleventh, and the fifteenth, and voted acceptance on the last day.

The extraordinary completion within a few months of an unprecedented building using unprecedented fabrication and assembly methods, the raising of the guarantee fund, and the wild success of the Exhibition from its opening, are old and good stories. The construction was fascinating to Londoners long before 1 May 1851, and they were admitted (for a fee) to watch the glazing and painting crews at work. An interesting feature of the building itself, aside from its being made of modular and interchangeable parts, was[1] its 'functional' colour, which like all the rest was overseen by Prince Albert; he owned the book on the Alhambra by Owen Jones, who thought up the colour scheme, and he consulted with Jones and Cubitt about it. When I describe the colour scheme as 'functional' I am thinking of its relation to the colouring of those beautiful early nineteenth-century mechanical drawings, whose lines were as sharp as ruler and compass and pen would make them, but which had sensitive pale washes of watercolour, partly abstract or schematic, partly illusionistic (as where the wash is shaded to show concavity). Jones used warm white for the glazing bars seen against the

---

constant balls and fêtes in it'. Can *Jardin de Verre* be his version of *Jardin d'Hiver?* But Hittorf's Cirque d'Hiver was not built until 1852. Paxton may not have been very good at French; like Henry Cole he had trouble with his H's; Queen Victoria once quoted him as speaking of 'the hextinct hanimals'; Diary, 1 November 1853.

[1] Hitchcock's account in *Early Victorian Architecture in Britain* (1954, Chapter XVI) is admirable. A possible source for the great arched 'herringbones' of glass (already used by Paxton at Chatsworth) might have been the arrangement of prisms in certain Regency chandeliers to suggest the palm fronds which are generally taken to have been the direct inspiration of the 'herringbones', J. B. Papworth is said to have invented these prisms.

sky, light blue for the girders; the underside of each girder was striped in red;[1] the diagonal faces of the uprights were light yellow, and so were some moulded details; and besides the brilliant colour of many of the exhibits there were translucent free-hanging streamers of turkey red. Joseph Nash's watercolours of the interior (Windsor souvenir albums), which were well published in lithographs by others, gave an excellent idea of the festive colour of the Exhibition. When it closed, Queen Victoria, with her usual reluctance to part with anything around which her affections clustered, mourned over the fading of these red banners; and Labouchere was so sentimental about the Crystal Palace that he added to his house at Stoke, near Windsor, a glass room in memory of it.[2]

The Exhibition did not produce world-wide understanding and peace; it did make geography books come alive for many people. China and Russia temporarily were real. Pugin's famous exhibit propagated Gothicism, and the whole fair created an increased appetite for ornament. The visitors of 1851 admired, as we do, the carriages, theodolites, fine balance-scales, and turbines, the 'dioptric revolving light-house', and the prototypes of many machines now taken for granted; but they also marvelled at the show-pieces which the more ambitious manufacturers of furniture created as climaxes to their normal lines, and which, reproduced in the official catalogue of the Exhibition, have been mistaken as typical by most readers ever since.[3] Unhappily, however, the presence of these complicated hand-made objects under the same roof as machines which could imitate hand work offered temptations which were soon accepted. Designers of machinery could create machines to reproduce any pattern, even three-dimensional wood-carvings, but they could not vary the output as even nominally 'uniform' products of a human hand are varied; nor did designers of things to be

---

[1] Owen Jones had evidently not yet received the Law according to Ruskin, who said in *The Seven Lamps of Architecture*, 1849, ch. IV, para. 36, that such stripes should be crosswise, not lengthwise.

[2] This charming gesture was renewed at the Festival on South Bank in 1951 with a Crystal-Palace-like canopy to a bus shelter.

[3] 'Freak furniture' before 1851 'had been made only to a client's order', says Barbara Jones in *English Furniture at a Glance*, 1954, p. 64. 'The average home was not the over-upholstered den of burgeois vulgarity Georgian revivalists would have us believe.' *Ibid.*, p. 84.

produced by machine as yet understand this pitfall, of which Ruskin had uttered warnings in *The Seven Lamps of Architecture* (1849). Machine-made ornament was not in itself wicked; in ceramics and textiles it had an honourable history in England and elsewhere. The problem was to find out what sort of ornament, producible by machine, was aesthetically possible or acceptable. This was not, and never is, a problem that the large public can solve in the short run, however rightly the public may in the long run judge. We may well lay some blame on the Great Exhibition for having led an abundance-demanding public into tempting, false paths. Innocence and ignorance, with the best will in the world, often do great mischief; and it would be fair to say that few designers for industry in the 1840s, using the equipment of artists, quite understood their position even if they understood their tasks.

It is impossible to dispose of mid-Victorian design as merely bad taste and eclecticism; we are barely beginning to look clearly at the huge body of evidence. The objects used in evidence in 1851 led William Morris to violent reaction, Ruskin to an unusually eloquent silence, Cole and Jones and Redgrave and Digby Watt to works of correction.

The more special, untypical, and menacing articles shown in the Crystal Palace greatly impressed the unwary and ill-prepared, who in due course helped them, so to speak, to come true to the extent to which, on a lower budget, they could become new, typical objects. With expanded markets for mass-produced articles, the real arbiter of the general taste became now neither the designer nor the manufacturer who chose designs that he believed would sell, but the salesman or agent.[1]

Let us take silver as an example of one field of industrial design. It is symptomatic of the slow change in taste during the early Victorian years that some silver in the simplest Empire style was shown along with gobbeted objects having mechanically irritated surfaces. There

---

[1] Francis D. Klingender, *Art and the Industrial Revolution*, 1947, p. 41. It may be worth mentioning that before and even after the American Revolution the plantation economy of southern colonies and later states put tremendous power of choice in the hands of the London representative or cotton-factor, who was asked to send 'fashionable' things.

were a few silver things of Pugin's design in which, almost in spite of his *Drang nach Gotik,* the problem was resolved, in that they looked and felt like silver, and still seem now rather fine; but they were not mass-produced. In true mass-production, the division of labour and the assembly methods long practised by the makers of Sheffield plated wares infected even the makers of solid silver, who turned out vessels built up from polygonal flat or even concave 'facets', joined by thick mouldings or clusters of second-Rococo ornament over actual joints in solder. The testimonial centrepieces shown by the grandest silver-smiths were no worse than such things had been since about 1780,[1] but there was little relief from them, and one designed by Prince Albert was, like its kind, an assembly of animal, vegetable, and architectural forms loaded with ideas but lacking in *flair*; or we might say rich in vocabulary but poor in syntax. It is fair to add that the centrepiece itself, seen in fact and in the round, is better than the wood-engraved illustration in the 1851 catalogue would cause one to suppose. Likewise it is fair to say that some patterns of table silver, especially those in which there were really intelligent variations in the design of handles between knives, teaspoons, tablespoons, and forks, were better than merely decent, as their continuing use suggests.[2]

The Prince exhibited in 1851 grain, wool, and coal from his own or Crown lands; two rather fine table-tops designed by Ludwig Gruner and executed in Derbyshire stones in the manner of Florentine mosaic; a *Theseus and the Amazons* in marble by Joseph Engel (an Hungarian-born pupil of the Royal Academy school, working in Rome); and of

---

[1] Gottfried Semper said he had never seen such a rich display of silver, but that it left much to be desired, and that 'most of these silver monuments had been ordered for some special festivity and did not belong to the category of standard wares for the market' (*Wissenschaft, Industrie, und Kunst,* 1852; my free translation). *Punch*, vol. II, 1842, p. 30, mentioned a gift of silver to the Duke of Buckingham from the farmers of Buckinghamshire: a column, supported on lions, and topped by a wheatsheaf for which a candelabrum could be substituted. Late eighteenth-century regimental trophies were of much the same sort of inorganic assembly. Paul Storr made in 1814 for presentation to the Marquess of Huntley a candelabrum in which double lion paws support grey-hounds who in turn support a trio of Highland soldiers (*The Prince Regent's Style*, Cooper Union, New York, 1953, fig. 15).

[2] Some of the best are by Tiffany of New York. The *Illustrated London News* abounds in such gifts of plate, shown in woodcuts.

course the famous garden seat in coal designed by Gruner. The Queen's exhibits included the excellent Axminster carpets designed by Gruner in rather severely plain fashion for the Red and Green Drawing Rooms at Windsor Castle, and made by different manufacturers, Scottish and English; a table designed by a student at the Birmingham School of Design and made in gold and silver electroplate by Elkingtons; the same manufacturer's jewel-case designed by Gruner, of bronze electrolytically gilt and silvered, and set with portraits of the Royal family; the rather splendid glass candelabra, eight feet tall, by Osler of Birmingham, which came from and returned to Osborne; and a carpet embroidered by a hundred and fifty British ladies to a 'geometrical, heraldic, and floral design' by one of the younger Papworths.

An interesting exhibit of Messrs Holland, the cabinet-makers who supplied much of the Osborne furniture, was described as a 'Cabinet made for her Majesty',[1] which was what we should now call a storage wall designed as a unit, having a Jacobethan chimneypiece flanked by arched and inlaid doors between carved pilasters, all united by a sort of parapet of shell niches; it is called in the text of the catalogue a 'book-case in British woods and marbles designed by Macquoid'. This might serve as a counterblast to the monumental sideboards shown by some other makers. Though in a different style, it is rather suggestive of the small Audience Room done later in Windsor under the Prince's influence, especially in its suggestion of useful but formal treatment for the reachable lower part of a very high room. This cabinet or bookcase can no longer be traced.

In 1851, the sewing-machine, the power bandsaw, and other labour-saving devices were ready or almost ready; but it is characteristic of the human craving for *more* that at first they were not used to reduce labour but to increase needlessly the quantities of ornament. The sewing-machine would make possible the immense load of fringes and braids borne by the already voluminous clothing of women in the mid-fifties; the bandsaw and mechanical carving devices facilitated the manifold elaboration of brackets, drawer-pulls, and minor balustrades that began to irritate house and furniture. Further, the early-Victorian interest

---

[1] Official catalogue, volume II, reproduced opposite p. 645. Half is reproduced in *The Art-Journal Illustrated Catalogue*, 1851, p. 22.

in 'effect'[1] which had produced experimental mixtures of material (e.g., precious and semi-precious stones and lava in the same jewellery) led to outright shams, dangerous adulterations, and the grand repertory of aniline dyes with which the high Victorians would be free to go wild. Even Pugin occasionally allowed cast iron to simulate stone.

Though they naturally enjoyed the afflatus of the Exhibition, the group which I call the Prince's team – a group really formed by the Exhibition itself – almost unanimously took alarm over the details. They saw the exhibits repeatedly, and were in a position to make informed choices and comparisons. Even Cole, who was more inclined than the others to give manufacturers the benefit of the doubt, saw the dangers of profusion: 'We are the richest people in the world and, I fear, the most pugnacious, partly in consequence of our superior wealth'.[2] From his experience in evaluating the Schools of Design he concluded that it was better to educate the great public to its needs in design than to educate artisans who might never be employed by an uneducated public. From this conclusion, implicit in all Cole's writing, springs in large part the museum-education feature of the work in South Kensington which I shall mention in a later chapter; against it rose Ruskin's growing conviction that the artisan was the man to educate, that the human being who had to execute a bad design or even part in a division of labour was degraded by his work. Just as Cole's thought had an element of *pis aller,* of choosing the lesser evil, so Ruskin's had an element of unrealism and of refusal to come to any terms with modern life. In another field there was also a basic variance between the South Kensington team and Ruskin: he, though willing to admit that there was always an abstract element in design, mistook difference in degree for difference of kind and would not grant that flat pattern of the Oriental sort had any basis in life. For Cole and his associates, the stylized ornament of several Oriental cultures was a splendid discovery. Without actually smiting the occidental designer and manufacturer, Cole said, 'It was from the East that the most im-

---

[1] 'Effect' might be called the child of 'the picturesque' and the parent of that 'character' which the high and late Victorians wanted in their buildings.

[2] Cole, lecture 'On the International Results of the Exhibition of 1851', reprinted in *Fifty Years of Public Work,* II, 233 ff.

pressive lesson was to be learnt. Here was revealed a fresh well of art'. The fertile invention, sinuous space-filling, and avoidance of illusionism in much Oriental work were not only beautiful and memorably novel; they acquired a sort of moral significance when the team (and other wise observers) compared them to the over-representational ornament of European ceramics and textiles. And there was Ruskin with his glittering moral structures and crashing strictures; so the battle was joined; and of it we shall hear more.

Richard Redgrave's *Report on Design,* published as soon as possible after the Exhibition, shows (although with some official circumlocution) a bit of this tendency to moral judgement; and his *On the Necessity of Principles in Teaching Design* (1853) even has a 'loaded' title. The approach to design which was to become the sound preachment (or party line, depending upon one's preference) of progressive art schools thereafter was, in other words, already formulated in the early 1850s as a direct outcome of the Exhibition and more particularly of the reaction to its exhibits, good and bad, among the men who looked hardest and most regularly at them. The prejudices in which they may be thought to have encouraged one another were not brought to the Exhibition but drawn from it; and the several books by members of the team formed a base for the methods followed in two or three generations by most British art instruction.

Digby Wyatt's *Industrial Arts of the Nineteenth Century* (2 volumes, 1851) was another official outcome of the exhibition; Owen Jones's *Grammar of Ornament* (folio edition, 1856), though not official, owed much to the author's experience with Semper on the Crystal Palace and to his own travel experience as well as to much that he saw in the Exhibition itself; it was enormously influential and is still useful in spite of some mysterious omissions.[1] Gottfried Semper himself, a refugee in England 1851-5, designed the Canadian, Danish, Swedish, and Egyptian displays in the Crystal Palace; he published at Braunschweig in 1852 a pamphlet called *Wissenschaft, Industrie, und Kunst,* which may have been inspired by Prince Albert (Semper speaks in his first page of a *Privataufforderung* to write it) and which draws con-

---

[1] He seems to have disliked the Rococo. Steegman, *Consort of Taste,* p. 306; Giedion, *Mechanization Takes Command,* 1948, p. 356.

clusions from the Exhibition (notably the British and American sections) with the intention of inspiring an improvement in German sensitivity to art.[1] This pamphlet contains a few rather Ruskinian expressions ('Art has now stood long in the market place, not to speak to the People, but to seek employment'); yet on the whole Semper has much the same approach as the English members of the Cole group to the mishandling of materials – it is bad, but we are at the threshold of new possibilities, which we must help to use properly. The most important section of *Wissenschaft, Industrie, und Kunst* for us is that in which Semper said, 'Public monuments and collections are the true teachers of a free people', and went on to speak of the application to all art-instruction and taste-formation of collections of the two most widely-practised arts of mankind, ceramics and textiles. I believe we must count this section among the important influences upon the whole South Kensington development after 1851.

Semper, though he was warned that Prince Albert was careful not to show favouritism to Germans, secured employment under Cole as soon as the Department of Practical Art (later Department of Science and Art) was set up; his class in 'Practical Construction, Architecture, and Plastic Decoration', given at Marlborough House 1852-5, included furniture design, and its very title breathes the spirit of *Bauhaus* as does Semper's later saying: 'Every technical product [should be] a resultant of use and material. Style is the conformity of an art object with the circumstances of its origin and the conditions and circumstances of its development'.[2]

The whole South Kensington team, then, was much of one mind. By 1854, so rapidly was its doctrine spread by the official and semi-official publications deriving from the 1851 show, and by the programmes of the Society of Arts, that Gradgrind had absorbed its ideas, and in *Hard Times* Dickens caused him to say that flowers were not suitable for carpets, nor 'foreign' insects for wallpapers. Cole planned for Marlborough House a 'Chamber of Horrors' which the Prince approved in

---

[1] L. D. Ettlinger, 'On Science, Industry, and Art: Some Theories of Gottfried Semper', in *Archtectural Review*, vol. 136, July 1964, pp. 57–60.

[2] Semper, *Der Stil in den Technischen und Tektonischen Künsten*, 2 vols., Munich, 1860–3; my free translation from a repeated *Leitmotif*.

principle and which was actually opened;[1] but in his installations Cole indiscreetly named the manufacturers, who made such outcries that the exhibit had to be dismantled. Such efforts usually backfire, as Edward Bok was to learn during his own moral endeavours with the *Ladies' Home Journal* early in the twentieth century.

As one example of the degree to which the Prince's team was exercised over problems of design, we may take the great controversy in the Society of Arts, which came grandly to a head in 1856 with a well-managed Cole circus which might be called 'Carpets and Conscience'. At a meeting which is reported in the Society's *Journal* for 22 February 1856, Alexander Whytock, a carpet-manufacturer, gave a long paper in which he discussed flatness of pattern, the illusionism of woven bouquets which appeared to cast shadows, and the like. George Wallis, now back in the Schools of Design under the wing of the Department of Science and Art as head of the School at Birmingham, spoke to the same point, as did J. G. Crace the grand decorator and others; it looks as if the speech had been circulated in advance, for comment on it is printed in letters from distant correspondents. Wallis was evidently asked to come and speak formally, which he did on 12 March (text in the *Journal* for 14 March 1856). He expressed his disapproval of the ultra-imitation of natural objects, saying that one reason for this 'horror of stamping, electro-depositing, power-loom-weaving, printing, etc., lies' in the fact 'that almost exclusive possession of a work becomes impossible'. It does not matter whether he meant to deplore endless multiplication, or the escape of a really original design from the designer's control, or the lack of patent protection; there is doubtless some of each in his plaint.[2] He added that the Exhibition of 1851 had exercised strong influence on high-class furniture, and said he feared British and United States wallpapers of whatever class were 'super-ugly'.

Cole, who was in the chair, saw Ruskin in the audience (by invitation?) and asked him to speak. Ruskin said great art could not be

---

[1] The approval in a letter of Phipps to Cole, 10 September 1852 (Cole Papers, box 6); actual showing of the Chamber confirmed orally by Mrs Shirley Bury of the Victoria and Albert Museum.

[2] Only designs containing human figures, animals, or 'any subject being matter of invention in sculpture' seem to have had adequate patent protection, according to testimony before the Select Committee of 1835.

cheap: 'When art was too common it would fail to excite attention'. He agreed with Wallis's principles, but if it was wrong to represent flowers on carpets why had Wallis, a few minutes later, praised Palissy wares, which of all dishes were most useless, though he (Ruskin) admired the wares? Wallis rebutted that Palissy ware was never meant to be useful, but merely ornament. Ruskin went on to say, 'Great art ought to be accessible, but not to be multiplied in a way which would diminish the power of attention'; he had heard a good deal about consumers and manufacturers; what was the effect on the workman of these works? He agreed that material and use were first considerations in design, as for instance in stained glass; he for one always directed artists and workmen to nature.

Crace and Redgrave, also present at this session, both spoke, Redgrave pointing out that Ruskin talked 'fine art' and Crace talked 'manufactured art', which latter *might* be both good and cheap. Cole asked his chief speaker to sum up; Wallis sympathized with Ruskin's desire that the workman should take an interest in his work; the more a man understood 'the why and wherefore', the greater the interest he would take. Ruskin was obviously warming up for *Unto This Last,* in which he would say in effect that a workman might understand his work but if he found it to be bad work of bad design, how could he be interested? This, however, he did not say on the spot. The lectures later published as *The Two Paths* were to be largely counterblasts, made oddly enough at Cole's request and on South Kensington's pitch, to the School-of-Design approach to art instruction. 'Carpets and Conscience' was protracted[1] by further correspondence in the *Journal* of the Society of Arts, and Wallis was given a last word in the number for 21 March 1856, saying in part: 'Our furniture wants less wood and better construction, more taste and less turnery, . . . better carved work, put in more convenient and less obtrusive places'; his last phrase – the assumption is that ornament is to be expected – could never be taken as prophetic of the *Bauhaus* or even Louis Sullivan; it is pure Victorian.

---

[1] One of its earliest signs of life was in an article in the *Art-Union Illustrated Catalogue* of 1851 by Mrs Merrifield, the translator of Cennino Cennini. Her title was 'The Harmony of Colours as Exemplified in the Exhibition', and though she was rather sound when writing of colour in general, she grew rather funny on the subject of carpets.

It is amusing to be able to add that no less an authority than Viollet-le-Duc at least once designed for the Gobelins factory a carpet in which bouquets seem to float in air, casting shadows on a complicated ground of interlaced patterns.[1]

The Royal Commission had been incorporated on 15 August 1850 when it became clear that the show was really going to take place; when it was sure in the late summer of 1851 that there would be a surplus after repayment of guarantees, the plans in the minds of Prince Albert and his colleagues grew more splendid. Sir William Reid, president of the Executive Committee, had to hold down enthusiasms lest the public should form too positive an idea and be disappointed. Cole and Dilke, who had seen the Conservatoire des Arts et Métiers in Paris, were already clearly thinking of a public collection which would lead to the Victoria and Albert Museum; Playfair, the scientist, wanted to endow professorships (he eventually became secretary for Science in the Department of Science and Art). The Prince saw a chance to bring all the learned societies into close communion in a series of buildings to be erected for their headquarters[2] – a scheme which later came to fruition not in South Kensington but at Burlington House, when the Royal Academy moved there from the National Gallery after the Prince's death; there was, however, a time when there was a serious plan to move both Gallery and Academy to Kensington. One of the German biographical dictionaries reports a design for a 'National Museum in London' about 1854 by Leo von Klenze, the architect and city-planner of Munich; but of this I can find no trace.[3]

Perhaps on account against the coming surplus, and surely on the Prince's recommendation, the Treasury allowed the Board of Trade £5,000 shortly before the Exhibition closed; the President, Labouchere,

---

[1] It is reproduced in Henri Clouzot, *Le Style Louis-Philippe-Napoléon-III*, Paris 1939, pl. XX; the design is in the Musée des Arts Decoratifs. There is an equally anaesthetic cartoon by Virolet for a carpet, dated 1848, in the Cooper Union Museum, New York, repro. in *Chronicle*, vol. 2, No. 8, June 1956, fig. 13.

[2] Minutes of the Royal Commission's meeting of 13 August 1851, in Commissioners' file, VIII, numbers 9, 9a, 10, 13, and 14. These establish not only the first sketching of the Burlington House idea but also the accuracy of the prognostication of a surplus, almost two months before closing.

[3] His latest biographer Oswald Hederer (*Leo von Klenze, Persönlichkeit und Werk*, Munich, 1964) mentions the project in his lists, but names no source.

appointed Cole, the painter Herbert, Redgrave, Pugin, and Jones as a committee to spend this sum on suitable objects from the Crystal Palace; their choices became the kernel of the modern collections in South Kensington (the 'museum' of the School of Design had not amounted to much though it, too, was moved from Somerset House to South Kensington). The committee (it must have been one of Pugin's last appearances) bought Tunisian and Asiatic work, Belgian gold-smiths' and silversmiths' exhibits, Elkington electrotypes after Cellini, Turkish and other Eastern arms and armour, Minton and Sèvres china, English carpets, some furniture, and even several of Pugin's chalices. When their choices were shown at Marlborough House in May 1852, Queen Victoria noticed that there was only one piece of fine lace in the lot, and at once sent some laces as a loan, also sending the 'Cellini' shield from Windsor.[1]

Although decisions about what to build were deferred, the decision to spend much of the Exhibition surplus on land opposite the Crystal Palace was quickly taken. There were temptations (and many outside requests) to keep the building where it was and use it; but the Royal Commission had agreed with the Government to move it; its resettling in Sydenham was done by a private company which later asked Cole to come and manage its exhibits; he declined. With the land-purchase in sight, it seemed wise to charter the Royal Commission in perpetuity; and the Royal Commissioners for the Exhibition of 1851 are still the ground landlords for the great group of institutions from the Royal Geographical Society, the Albert Hall, and the Royal College of Music, down the hill to the Imperial Institute, the Science Museum, the Natural History Museum, and the Victoria and Albert. Some interesting private buildings were also built on the land by lessees; the Royal Geographical Society occupies one. The development of the Victoria and Albert Museum is another chapter.

The truly great experience of the Exhibition united the responsible participants, as shared work and pleasure or even military service or other durance will unite men; and they wanted to build a memorial to the Exhibition itself.[2] Prince Albert took the programme in charge but

[1] It is not by Cellini, but of French sixteenth-century origin.
[2] They all received something in the next Honours List after the end of the

refused to allow any portrait of himself to be included, and would not subscribe until he was promised by his colleagues that there would be none; this promise had to be broken after his death, by the Queen's insistence. Though neither the Prince nor Henry Cole thought very well of competitions,[1] there was a limited competition for this monument, a competition which may have been one of Alfred Stevens's first disappointments in this line, for his entry (the *maquette* of 1857 still exists in the Victoria and Albert Museum) was not successful, though it contains certain elements which appear in the Wellington monument. It is a wonder that the memorial to the Exhibition turned out anywhere near as good as it is, for the eventual designer, Joseph Durham, was subject to many pressures (Cole once tried to put Smirke over him). The Memorial was first intended as a fountain, to stand in the gardens of the Royal Horticultural Society, a site in Hyde Park itself having been refused; the death of the Prince and the building-up of the Gardens changed all plans, and the Memorial settled at last on the terrace south of the Albert Hall, and now has steps where water was to have flowed down, and the music comes from open windows in practice-rooms of the Royal College.

The scheme of the monument is rather eighteenth-century in style, like much of the work bearing some impress of the Prince in his late years: a base with low segmental arches in its concave faces bears at its corners figures of the four quarters of the earth, each backed by a pedestal carrying twin granite columns; in the cage of columns a granite drum gives space for inscriptions; on top, where originally a Britannia was intended, stands the Prince himself in Garter robes, booted and cloaked. It is possible that his own memories of Donner's fountain in

---

Exhibition, except Scott Russell, whom Granville called 'rude' and a 'bad secretary'; he was a shipbuilder and engineer, and was secretary jointly with Stafford Northcote; also secretary 1845–50 of the Society of Arts.

[1] Grey to Cole, 9 January 1862 (Cole Papers, box 2), wrote that the Prince had been opposed to competition in general (this sounds surprisingly Ruskinian) and to competitions in particular 'as invariably leading to the exclusion of the *best* artists'. Cole himself in a memorandum of 22 October 1859 (Cole Papers, box 1) lists 'competitions which proved nothing not known before – Ho. of Parliament; Stamps for Penny Postage; Plans for Exhibition of 1851; Wellington Monument; Barracks; Foreign Office; Memorial of '51'.

the Neuer Markt in Vienna, or even of Fischer von Erlach's *Josephbrunnen* in the Hoher Markt, have something to do with the design; Fischer's fountain has a similar high drum with pedestals and volutes instead of twinned columns, but with a canopy of columns higher up. The Memorial as it stands is almost the only remaining part of the South Kensington that Prince Albert knew; some of the early galleries of what is now the Victoria and Albert Museum still stand, but the remnants of the Prince's Arcades, which articulated the Gardens, and which were long hidden in the two pavilions at the ends of the Imperial Institute, have vanished recently.

To this epilogue I must add a note characteristic of the Prince himself. When the model of the Memorial was to be tried in the Gardens in the last year of his life, he seems to have realized, sensibly, that it would be thrown out of scale by the vast building for the Exhibition of 1862 which was going up all around, so the model was set up in the grounds of the South Kensington Museum, near 'Brompton Boilers' and the new Sheepshanks Gallery, and the Prince had a ditch dug in which he and others might stand in order to have their eyes at the right level for the reduced model. This was recorded in a rather amusing watercolour by A. C. Stannus.

What the Prince would have thought of the Memorial to himself on the other side of the Albert Hall (and actually in Hyde Park) I can only guess. When Mark Twain saw it in 1872 he greatly admired it, and thought only Shakespeare could deserve anything so fine; he professed surprise that it was indeed the *Albert* Memorial: '. . . a most excellent foreign gentleman who was a happy type of the Good, and the Kind, the Well-Meaning, the Mediocre, the Commonplace – and who did no more for his country than five hundred tradesmen did in his own time, whose works are forgotten, . . . [he] gave a notable impulse to industry by admiring it'.[1] This judgement of course contains a large element of reaction against the idolatry in the Queen's *Leaves from the Journal of Our Life in the Highlands* (1868). We have seen the Memorial fall in esteem as the Prince rose.

---

[1] 'From an English Notebook', 1872, in *Letters from the Earth*, edited by Bernard de Voto, 1962, pp. 171–4.

8

Balmoral Castle

Like Osborne, Balmoral in its original form was tried out by rental. The house which the Queen and Prince first occupied for three weeks in September 1844 had been built in the thirties for Sir Robert Gordon by John Smith of Aberdeen; Sir Robert's surviving elder brother, Lord Aberdeen, sold the remaining lease of twenty-seven years in 1848, and soon afterwards there were negotiations with Sir Alexander Duff, who owned the land and who, the Queen wrote in January 1849, was 'asking such an enormous price'. When they reached agreement, the land was acquired in 1852 for the Prince of Wales, but his father complemented the large Balmoral shootings by buying or taking long leases of such adjacent properties as Abergeldie, Birkhall, and Invergelder.

Balmoral I, as Henry-Russell Hitchcock calls it,[1] was not much larger than the original Osborne, it had one remarkable feature, a conservatory in a re-entrant angle of the Jacobethan house; the outer glass wall undulated in plan as a sort of Cupid's bow, and the wall of the house, which was elsewhere granite or harled brick, was revetted under the conservatory roof with blue and white tiles. This handsome installation was not repeated in the new house, but it may have had some effect on the arcades and greenhouses of the Horticultural Society's gardens in South Kensington.

After 1848 a number of additions were made to the house, sufficient to warrant calling it Balmoral II; but as this was completely removed after Balmoral III was finished in 1856, there is little to say about it. Balmoral III, however, took much of its character from Balmoral I, its crow-stepped gables, its association of sixteenth- or seventeenth-century window-clusters with so medieval a mass as that of the square

---

[1] *Early Victorian Architecture in Britain*, 1954, I, p. 245.

tower; but these features were returned, in the much larger Balmoral III, to a more plausible relationship of scale; the Prince did not forget the numerous genuinely ancient Scottish buildings he had seen.

William Smith, who designed Balmoral over the Prince's shoulder as Cubitt had designed Osborne, was John's son and city architect of Aberdeen; he may have regretted having to tear down his father's work. The previous owner seems to have felt regret, for Lord Granville on 24 September 1857 wrote to Canning: 'Aberdeen very *piano,* but probably affected by the disappearance of the old house'.[1] The two buildings were temporarily connected by a covered passage during the season of 1855, when the Royal family wanted to use part of the new, though unfinished, house. Another building was a prefabricated iron ballroom from Manchester, in use 1851-5, of much the same construction as the buildings that were shipped disassembled to Australia and San Francisco.

Like Osborne, the Balmoral estate was designed as an entity by the Prince, who had the advantage in this case of having stalked deer for several seasons from the mountain-sides all about, whence fine bird's-eye views were to be had. There is an account in the Queen's diary of his modelling earth-masses in sand in 1854 to instruct his workmen. To the north the river Dee is close to the Castle, and on the side commonly called north (but more nearly north-west) the ground was made to descend by two terraces from the principal ground-floor level to the riverbank; at the north-east end of the terraces a ballroom wing projects from the mass of the Castle at basement level. The interior ballroom stair comes up into a low wing which forms a sort of valve between the tower and the mass of the house, which lies at an angle to the compass-points. The tower, a hundred feet tall, is otherwise detached; at its own north corner, farthest from the house, is a stair turret; at its other corners (as on too many other corners of the main building) are pepper-box turrets. The Castle itself is almost square, with a small enclosed court which is little more than a light-well. The entrance is by a Windsorish *porte-cochère* which projects from the south corner. Little more is made of the two southern faces of the building than of the others; but the Highlands were expected to be cold, though Balmoral was consid-

---

[1] Fitzmaurice, *The Life of Lord Granville,* 1905, I, p. 259.

ered to be unusually dry;[1] and neither the Queen nor the Prince seems to have been sensitive to cold in middle life. The Queen loved cold weather.

The Castle must have been intended to have a random character and even perhaps a look of having been built at different times; the north-west or river front has a central feature marked by a slight raising of the roof and a carrying of stepped walls above the roof-line (possibly as a fireproofing device); the south-west façade is also basically symmetrical, but its elements are marked at all the articulations with pepper-box turrets which, far from masking the symmetry, only confuse the composition. The south-east front, presumably always intended for the Household, has three storeys in the height of the two storeys of the other façades, and has a rather nice alternatation of projecting bays of triplets with pairs of windows in a decisive Tudorish rhythm; this front and the tower have a real liveliness of spirit which the turrets and chimneys cannot give to the rest of the Castle.

The granite (from Kemnay) is almost white; William Smith's chief mason, James Beaton, had the Aberdonian respect for granite, but all concerned in the building had the nineteenth-century respect for 'finish', and the stone is therefore dressed to a surface not actually sleek but terribly regular; only in the castellated ballroom wing and in the battering terrace walls was Beaton allowed a more rugged surface. There was, to be sure, as good psychological reason for this as for the rustication or vermiculation of the ground-floor and terrace walls at Osborne; but the Victorians did not, in the middle of the century, enjoy 'natural' textures as we do, and the Industrial Revolution had given them sufficient tools for control of almost everything, so that there was little left of the Romantics' surrender to Nature.[2] One could almost say that 'machine-made' was a good word then, as 'hand-made' is now. I have not seen Balmoral, but it seems to me that only in some of Carl Haag's brilliant watercolours does the crystalline granite have any visible character. The outside walls, however, were enlivened in some

---

[1] Though larches had been introduced into the region before the Royal family came there, some of the neighbours complained that the Prince's tremendous plantations had somehow caused an increase in the rainfall.

[2] Gottfried Semper (in *Wissenschaft, Industrie, und Kunst,* 1852) remarked that granite could now be cut like chalk and polished like wax.

places with partly-gilded coats of arms and with reliefs of Saints Andrew, George, and Hubert by John Thomas, who had done so much architectural sculpture on the Houses of Parliament and many other public monuments.

There were also, as at Osborne, many outbuildings, cottages, a carpenter's shop, pony stables, coach-house, greenhouses, a distillery, a venison larder, lodges, a dairy, a telegraph office, and miles of paths and drives with their bridges. Farther away were three or four shiels or modest hunting-lodges where the Queen could even spend a night on those 'expeditions' into privacy which she loved; they were plainly furnished and wallpapered, but one was wittily treated in the style of a rather Regency-looking tent.[1]

Balmoral is always supposed to have been devastatingly horrible inside; although the Queen was already complaining of tourists and sightseers in 1860, its remoteness and legendary privacy never lost in the telling, and much of the telling must have been done by the legions of German royalties who got themselves into the kilt for a visit. Again we must remember that the clutter began *after* the Prince Consort's death. Despite the well-known tartan carpets in the various Stuart setts, the white 'Victoria' tartan or thistle-pattern furniture-covers,[2] and the many candelabra with ormolu hunting-horns held up by bisque Highlanders, the furniture was simple and rather severely arranged: maple and other blond woods, stuffed sofas and armchairs, very light and rather fanciful cane-seated portable chairs. The pictures were mostly black-and-white, the walls were mostly in plain cool colours except for the Queen's own rooms, and the woodwork was originally ash and pitchpine, left in its natural state but for planing; Queen

---

[1] The only non-funereal construction undertaken by the Queen during her long widowhood was a new shiel, suitably inscribed in Gaelic.

[2] Lord Clarendon was heard (perhaps not quite *heard*) as a dissenting voice early on: he said the thistles 'would rejoice the heart of a donkey if they happened to *look like* his favourite repast, which they don't'. This is quoted by Lady Longford in *Queen Victoria, Born to Succeed*, 1964, p. 237. On the other hand, Balmoral seems to have been highly acceptable to the Duchess of Sutherland, the Queen's impeccable model of taste. The Queen wrote to her on 10 September 1858: 'My beloved Prince desires me to say that *he* considers it the greatest praise which *can* be bestowed on his Creation (wh. Balmoral so entirely is) to hear that you admired it'. *Archives*, Vict. Add'l. MSS. A/24, 66.

Victoria in later years had a marmalade-coloured varnish applied. The 'Balmoral' tartan designed by Prince Albert was very subfusc: grey, black, lavender, and dark red; but it *was* one more tartan; and the stags' heads did accumulate on the walls.

There are certain violent contrasts and oddnesses of scale at Balmoral which are unhappy. The entrance hall, for instance, had a stalactitic sort of chimneypiece whose complication makes antlers seem simple; and the deerskins with scalloped felt borders on the stone floor contrasted as strongly as the sleek marbleized walls with the interlaced plaster profiles of the Jacobethan ceiling. In the ballroom (arranged by Grieve, the impresario of plays at Windsor) the walls were hung, to about twelve feet of their total height of perhaps twenty, with green-and-yellow silk from rather ecclesiastical-looking crisscrossed cords, nice enough; but then tartan curtains faced them at five huge windows. Four generous, rather swooping, Puginian Gothic chandeliers hung from the timbered ceiling; a Gothic-detailed and much-mirrored small stage gave room for musicians. Altogether, it looked more like Viollet-le-Duc than like Pugin.

There were small flower-gardens in sheltered places, and the eagle fountain which Frederick William IV of Prussia had given the Queen and Prince was removed from Windsor to Balmoral during the later campaigns of the Prince. His tremendous plantings of trees suffered from a hazard not existing at Osborne, namely the deer; therefore they had to be protected by dikes or stout fencing until established.

The influence of Balmoral, though not quite so wide as that of Osborne, was strong; since its external features were largely plantations, the influence was not so specific as Osborne's influence on terraces, balustrades, and the fitting of house to ground. The romantic silhouette, steep roofs, occasional castellations, above all the splendid granite, left their marks on large free-standing houses in Britain, America, and even the European continent: stone became the right material for an important seat, and Gothic or Jacobean the desirable style. The suburban mansions of Philadelphia after the Civil War, and of Chicagoans after the Fire, tended to emulate Balmoral, as they had tended towards Osborne half a generation earlier. Indeed, the Olden-Time taste may be said to have moved up (or down, as you please) by a notch or two; but by the late fifties the idiosyncratic style of Butterfield was making itself felt widely. A late example of the influence of Balmoral, practically without a trace of the intervening High Victorian of Butterfield and Street, is Friedrichshof, the house which the Princess Royal built for herself as Empress Dowager at Kronberg near Frankfurt; a work of the early nineties, it has reflections of Balmoral in its massing, though the detail is more archaeologically consistent with sixteenth-century precedent in Germany.

Travelling to and from Balmoral, the Queen and Prince seldom tarried in Edinburgh, for the vested interest of the hereditary Keeper of the Palaces of Holyrood made it almost impossible for them to establish a foothold; even Edward VII would have great difficulty. The water-colours made for the Windsor souvenir albums to record the State visit of 1857 show temporary and mixed installations of furniture, old and new, in the fine seventeenth-century rooms, with splendid moulded plaster ceilings and almost bare walls. The only thing of special interest to us is one interior in which Prince Albert's portable shower-bath sits like a striped toy tent on the floor of his dressing room.

There was a common sense in the Royal couple that let them understand, almost from their first visit, that the Scot was not prepared to tolerate grand, courtly behaviour, but was prepared to respect privacy. The people of Balmoral reminded the Prince of Coburgers; mountain people are universally known for independence. As he and the Queen became acquainted with the land and with the sports of the great landholders, as well as with the life and work of villagers and countrymen, they began to see themselves as enjoying the best of both worlds. The flavour of their life in the Balmoral retreat was like that of the small Germanic kingdom of old fairy-stories, in which a king and queen, their sovereignty always recognized, are nonetheless on a carpet-slipper basis with their subjects.

9

Windsor Castle

Wyatville having made Windsor one of the most splendid and, in its day, most convenient royal dwellings in the world, there was not much wanting there; the last of Wyatville's works, the stables just outside the Castle walls, came to completion only in 1842, when *Punch* (with its usual sneers and horrendous puns) said it had cost £30,000, which made Prince Albert a 'patron of the Mews' (the sum in fact was additional to £70,000 committed before the Queen's marriage).[1] The building included a riding-school; it is an example of Wyatville's contrasting associations of 'heath-stone' masonry with yellow freestone carved trim.

The Queen's typical reaction, after the first delightful years of frank enjoyment under Melbourne's tutelage, was to dislike the public access at almost all hours to many parts of her domain. Windsor Great Park was primarily a Chace, a preserve of woodland and wild creatures, with various private enclaves and lodges occupied by minor royalties, rangers, and lame ducks, extending to the Georgian frivolities of Virginia Water at one end and to the town of Windsor at the other. The Home Park and the Lower Ward of the Castle had long been semi-public, parts of the Park being quite trampled by trespassers; and George III had never been able to carry out his intent of clearing away the houses built against the walls of the Castle on the north and west.

Prince Albert set himself to increase the Queen's freedom of motion in the privacy which she needed and wanted, and to heighten the amenities of her nearer grounds and the usefulness of the working farms and forest. By judicious exchanges but not without protests, he succeeded in closing two roads across the Home Park (one *quid pro quo* was a recreation ground which the Queen gave to the Royal Borough of Windsor), so that the Queen could walk or ride considerable distances

---

[1] Claire Jerrold, *The Married Life of Queen Victoria*, 1913, p. 118.

unobserved. 'Only three years ago', she wrote on 5 June 1843, 'there was high grass up to the very walls of the Castle, then in the summer and autumn of 40, Albert laid out these new walks, . . . he has made it quite another place.' He planted the Slopes; built better cottages and barns for the Flemish, Norfolk, and Shaw Farms, an aviary, a new school (1845) for children of employees in the Great Park; created a beautiful garden at Frogmore House where the Duchess of Kent lived, and which she finally made her burial-place. He bred horses, cattle, and pheasants, even angora goats; removed (by 1851) the houses built against the Castle walls; improved George IV's sunken garden on the East Terrace; re-roofed the Curfew Tower and rebuilt the Hundred Steps (these last works, designed by Salvin, are not very successful). Very little of all this is visible; therefore its influence was not vast; but a fair example of that influence is Matthew Vassar's 'Springside' at Poughkeepsie, New York, laid out in 1852 (the last year of his life) by that diligent improver and crusader A. J. Downing who was well acquainted with English precedent old and new; the buildings included an aviary and an apiary (with tall bee weathervane) of a distinctly Albertine design.

By 12 February 1850 the Queen, who never really loved Windsor, was writing, 'I have become so much fonder of Windsor since all the improvements have taken place. It is so much more private and it is a nice feeling that it will be something of *our creation.*' One result of the improvements was that the Prince could swim in the Thames without too much of a gallery. He also bought land or leased it for shooting near Bagshot, and thus came to know the country towards Aldershot, with which he was later concerned for military uses and for Wellington College.

The useful buildings in the Great Park are almost all in a sort of 'vicarage' Tudor, brick with picturesque barge-boards and ornamental cut-brick chimneys. At Frogmore a tea-house, often used also for summer breakfasts, was built: a wooden bungalow with conical red tile roof, echoed in a smaller form for the kitchen; the two were connected by a covered passage.[1] The various farms and the aviary had

---

[1] Though the evidence is not conclusive for influence, there had been a similar scheme (two cones as lodges) in J. M. Gandy's *Designs for Cottages, Cottage Farms, and Other Rural Buildings*, 1805, pl. XLI. Gandy did have connexions with the Surveyors to the Woods and Forests.

each, as in the outlying buildings of Osborne, a room or two for the Royal family's use during walks or rides. The aviary (complete by 1845) has a particularly cottagey and 'old-world' look,[1] with dovecotes in the gables, ventilating cupolas and heating arrangements for tropical birds, and Gothic-arched doors in the trellises and cages. Another Tudorish construction, the brick terrace in the Ascot Road, stands at the very beginning of the town as one comes from the Great Park. The design for the attached but somewhat varied row-houses was shown at the Royal Academy in 1849 by the architect, S. S. Teulon; and Hitchcock is right in saying, 'For this project . . . the exalted sponsorship of Prince Albert may perhaps be assumed'.[2] The group is now called Queen's Terrace and separately numbered; the houses, well back from the road and with decent gardens behind them, were intended for the families of ladies-in-waiting and other Court people who needed some of the same escape that the Queen craved. The scale is small and the interiors are unpretentious but well planned for their day and still comfortable.

The Prince was also at work in 1848-9 with Ingram, the Windsor superintendent who was the opposite number of Osborne's Toward, on the relocation of roads and walks caused by changes in the railway lines. To the 'Windsor and Eton' station of the old London and South-western at the foot of the hill was now added the new Gothic station of the Great Western, with a Royal entrance, opposite the Castle near the top of Thames Street.

The dairy, like the aviary a part of the Frogmore compound, was a later work (1858–59) of wonderful complexity as well as admirable engineering; John Thomas, the sculptor who worked at Balmoral and the Houses of Parliament, was concerned in the plan of what is really just one room at the end of a building of other farm uses, whose exterior is marked by very prominent slab-like stone surrounds to the doors and windows. There are stained-glass windows on three sides of the dairy. Inside, six chamfered piers support a hopper roof; around the walls, and in two lines down the middle of the room, are marble tables whose marble legs stand in shallow troughs of cold running water, separated

---

[1] I am using the word in the sense in which the cosier real-estate agents use it.

[2] *Early Victorian Architecture in Britain*, 1954, I, p. 440.

by dry gangways. On these tables the great pannikins of milk stood while the cream rose. The walls are entirely tiled, in white below, but with polychrome borders above, and the higher the scheme rises, the more high-Victorian does it become. At the narrow ends of the room the borders include yellow-and-white ceramic bas-reliefs of children as the Seasons; and all around the room there is a frieze of Renaissance ornament punctuated by medallion heads of the Royal children which seem to derive from William Wyon's somewhat earlier silver medallions. Above the frieze a pierced tile cornice forms part of the ventilating system. The tent-like soffit of the roof, painted in scale pattern, is connected with braces of Ruskinian Gothic style to the piers, which in their upper stages become twisted colonnettes bearing trusses and finally the flat, central part of the ceiling. The two compartments of the ceiling, surrounded by a carved and pierced wooden moulding of the same pattern as the cornice but to a larger scale, are in turn coffered. The coffers being each a pierced blue-green tile, the whole ceiling forms an exhaust grille. This all sounds like a 'folly', and it is the usual fate of follies to fall into decay; but this one is so well ventilated that, after a hundred years of cold water and milk, the only visible deterioration is a slight one at the base of the piers, which seem to be of iron sheathed in wood.

At each end of the dairy stands a small terracotta fountain, and one of the long walls is centred by a sort of lavabo with a marble statuette, doubtless by Thomas; and there are square-headed niches, bordered and diapered with still other tile patterns, for shelves of jugs and ewers. The whole might have served as a sample-room for Herbert Minton; but there is an interesting difference. The ceiling coffers of pierced tile are of a favourite Chinese colour, and they almost certainly derive from Chinese use; the Chinese exhibit at the Great Exhibition had included platforms supported on just such tiles, standing on edge. Furthermore, southern Chinese temples for many centuries had had central pierced panels in their ceilings called *t'ien-ching* (Heaven-well) through which light from above might filter down. Little could be more likely than that the Prince, who always asked questions and remembered the answers, knew about the Heaven-well.

His last Windsor construction before his own death was the Duchess of Kent's mausoleum which, nevertheless, had been some time in

42. Franz Xaver Winterhalter: *The First of May*; canvas, 3 ft 6 in. × 4 ft 3 in.;
1851

43. Eugène Lami: *Baptism of Prince Arthur*; watercolour, 22 June 1850

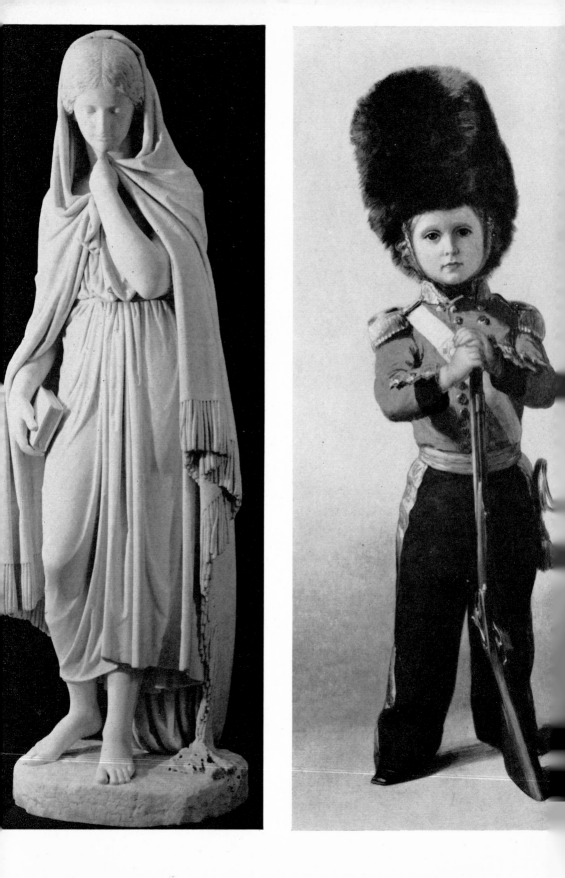

46. Eugène Lami: *State Ball at Buckingham Palace*, 5 July 1848; watercolour

opposite
44. Benjamin Edward Spence: *Highland Mary*; marble, gift of the Prince to the Queen, 24 May 1843

45. Franz Xaver Winterhalter: *Prince Arthur*, 1853; canvas, gift of the Queen to the Prince, 26 August 1853 (detail)

47. Louis Haghe: *Ball Room, Buckingham Palace*; watercolour, 17 June 1856

48. *Buckingham Palace*, East front by Edward Blore, 1846–7; photograph taken about 1888 (*Radio Times Hulton Picture Library*)

49. Eugène Lami: *Opening of the Great Exhibition*, 1851; watercolour, $24\frac{3}{4} \times 19\frac{1}{2}$ in., signed and dated

50. Edward Matthew Ward, R.A.: *Queen Victoria at the Tomb of Napoleon*, 1855; canvas, 3 ft 3 in. × 5 ft 10 in., commissioned by the Queen but not completed until 1861

51. George Housman Thomas: *Prince Albert and Napoleon III at Boulogne*, 1854; misdated 1853, watercolour over pen drawing

52. William Powell Frith: *Life at the Seaside* or *Ramsgate Sands*; canvas, 2 ft 6 in. × 5 ft 10¼ in.; bought by the Queen, 1854

53. Augustus Egg: *L'Amante*; canvas, 3 ft 4 in. × 4 ft 2 in.; bought by Prince Albert

54. Queen's Dressing-glass and toilet service, porcelain and ormolu, commissioned by Prince Albert from Mintons and given to the Queen, Christmas 1853

55. *Oak Cabinet* by Leistler of Vienna; carved by Anton Ritter von Fernkorn; gift of Kaiser Franz Josef to the Queen, 1851

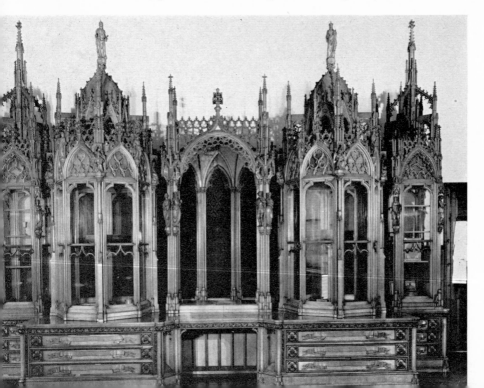

preparation. The old lady (who gave her nephew and son-in-law a fancy waistcoat every year) cared no more for the wicked Hanoverians than he did, and was determined not to be buried among them at St George's. In March 1859, after having settled the question in conversation, she wrote the Prince a formal request in German, and he added a memorandum; these papers[1] confirmed her desire for a mausoleum at Frogmore, on the mound which had been made of the earth dredged out of an artificial pond for Queen Charlotte in the 1790s. In this was to be dug a shaft with a sarcophagus at the bottom, and on top there was to be a circular temple which could serve as a summer-house until the Duchess's death. The architect Humbert, who had worked at Osborne and Whippingham, was engaged to work up Ludwig Gruner's designs for the builders;[2] work must have begun soon, for when the Duchess of Kent died on 16 March 1861 the mausoleum was almost completed, and it was possible to consecrate it on 29 July.

The entrance to the vault is an arch in a great rusticated composition of down-sweeping walls and grand piers, which probably comes from a common source with the ice-house portal at Osborne (perhaps Vignola by way of Vanbrugh, whose similar gate at Claremont must have been well known to Prince Albert). The temple on top of the mound, reached by a zigzag of stairs, is of Portland stone with sixteen granite Ionic columns around a cella, which rises to a dome pierced by an oculus. The terrace on which the temple stands is only sixty feet across: a large enough monument, a large enough summer-house, to be sure, but daintily scaled. With its balustrades, and the urns and swags in a rather Louis XVI style carved on the drum, it is a pleasant companion to the eighteenth-century Frogmore House. It seems likely that the form goes back to the Prince's memory of the *temple d'Amour* at Laeken, but there were more recent influences. The Queen (who was always, as her husband told their eldest daughter, living in the past and future) had

---

[1] *Archives*, M. 10/72 and 73.

[2] One of the few sheets of paper from Gruner's hand preserved at Windsor is a sketch plan of the mausoleum, inserted in the volume containing the documents cited in note 1. That there was much correspondence between him and the Prince is suggested by a notebook in which Col. Phipps recorded incoming letters in 1847 (*Archives*, Vic. Add'l. MSS, I, 309), and in which Gruner appears often, twice with notes of his questions and Prince Albert's answers.

begun talking about their own burial during a visit to Princess Charlotte's mausoleum (by J. B. Papworth) at Claremont (also intended as a
summer-house but completed in wedding-cake Gothic); later the same
year(1843) the subject recurred on the day of Queen Adelaide's funeral.
But the most powerful image in the Queen's mind was that of Hawksmoor's mausoleum at Castle Howard, which she saw at least twice. On
28 August 1850, in a long report to her diary on a visit to the Earl of
Carlisle, she mentions this circular building: 'a very pretty little Chapel,
with an extremely airy vault, – not at all dreary, – beneath. . . . It is
just the sort of thing, I wish one day to build for ourselves.' But it was
undoubtedly the Prince who turned the actually rather austere character
of the Hawksmoor building towards the lighter and more delicate
character of the Frogmore one; and he who thought of combining the
belvedere function of Vanbrugh's Rotunda, also at Castle Howard, with
the mausoleum function.[1]

When, all too soon, a mausoleum had to be designed for the Prince
and herself, the Queen again chose Gruner and Humbert; but here
there was some influence from the Coburg mausoleum which the Prince
had helped to work out. Once more Frogmore is the site, but the
cruciform building has Romanesque exterior detail and an octagonal
lantern, while inside there is a high-Renaissance marble revetment of
almost Petrine splendour, with effigies by Baron Marochetti.

In Windsor Castle itself, Prince Albert's only outwardly visible contributions are the Hundred Steps and the new roof to the Curfew Tower,
both designed by Salvin in the course of much repair work over the
years 1858–63. The steps from Canons' Cloister down to Thames Street
may or may not have numbered just a hundred, but as Salvin rebuilt
them with 122,[2] they are an uncomfortable convenience at best, having
as wrong a pitch as the long (and far older) flight going up into the
Round Tower. Sir Owen Morshead has demonstrated[3] that the roof of

---

[1] The Prince's memorandum (*Archives*, M. 10/73) says in part, 'The temple
to be erected over a vault . . . should be so constructed as to be capable of
being used by her as a summer house in the garden, if the other purpose was
given up. Mama was much pleased with this arrangement and the works were
begun forthwith'.

[2] The Queen's diary speaks of them as new on 28 October 1860.

[3] Morshead, *Windsor Castle*, revised edition, 1957, pp. 56–58.

the Curfew Tower was cribbed from a tower at Carcassonne which was of course itself a crib by Viollet-le-Duc, and he suggests the influence of Napoleon III, who visited Windsor in 1855. Salvin, in other words, did not do so well at Windsor as at Harlaxton; he may have been chosen because he understood Tudor and because Blore in 1858 had passed seventy.

An invisible contribution of the Prince's is an underground passage across the Quadrangle, burrowed in 1855, which was for the convenience of the Castle servants and (indirectly) of everyone else. Within doors his work is scattered. As at Buckingham Palace, he created a private chapel in the north-east corner of the Quadrangle, installing between it and St George's Hall a fine organ which could be played from either Hall or Chapel. The Chapel is rather plain, brown, oaken Gothic, with galleries for the Royal family, some strong-coloured but simple windows, and a shallow sanctuary; this was consecrated on 19 December 1843 but soon proved too small, and in 1852 the sanctuary was deepened and a lantern raised for better light. The organ console was carved with interlacing figures which suggest the Morning Stars singing together in one of Blake's illustrations to the Book of Job.

At the north-west corner of the Upper Ward, William IV had formed a library in the long gallery built by Elizabeth I for indoor exercise; under it was the room where the aged George III had lived so long in darkness of mind and eye. The two storeys, from the Norman gate east to Charles II's Star Building, were taken as space for a Royal Library by Prince Albert, who introduced his own German librarian, Praetorius, as adjunct to the librarian Glover, who was there by William IV's appointment and remained until his death in 1860 (Praetorius was later succeeded by Becker and Ruland). Not only did the Prince as an intellectual love a library, but as a man of great affairs he needed much reference material; he also collected some books for their own sake, but of these there is little trace, for rigorous house-cleanings at Buckingham Palace and Windsor dispersed most of them at the accession of Edward VII.[1] What remains is of the first importance: the Royal Archives are based upon the Prince's system, the marvellous pre-Victorian collection of

[1] Sir Lionel Cust, *King Edward and His Court*, 1930, pp. 12–13.

drawings began in his day to be properly mounted and cared for, and here he and Ruland did the great pioneer work of the *corpus* of Raphael. He may have chosen these rooms because they were, except for the upper gallery, in bad repair, or he may have liked the view over Eton. His, at any rate, are the cabinets for boxes and albums of drawings, the rather sympathetic Jacobethan plaster ceilings (where again John Thomas was helpful), and the nice domestic fire-places.

In St George's Chapel, what little there was to do was the Dean's business, but the Prince may have had a connexion with the restoration of some glass in 1842; he bought old stained glass at the Strawberry Hill sales in that year.[1] His chief interest there was musical; the choir was of a scope for the performance of the *Te Deum* and the hymns which he composed.

Typical of his endless concern with the Windsor continuum is, for instance, the record of some changes in the White Drawing Room. In December 1842 he caused Winterhalter's first large Royal portraits to be let into the walls; in April 1847 the Queen reports a fine new carpet, presumably one of the English Savonnerie carpets already mentioned; the Prince began the concentration of George IV's best French furniture in this room. The great rooms of the Windsor Private Apartments are much as he left them, except that the rather small Victorian chandeliers have been gradually replaced by the superb eighteenth-century and Regency examples which Sir Lionel Cust and later Queen Mary were able to acquire. Besides the carpets, some of the floors date from Prince Albert's time, as for instance the beautiful inlaid ones, dated 1854, in the Green and the Crimson Drawing Rooms. What we might call the ecology of most of the groupings of paintings is his.

As surprising in its way as the high-Victorian Dairy or the rather un-Victorian Mausoleum is the Prince's latest work, the Queen's Audience Chamber (1860–1), a small jewel of workmanship. The Queen wanted a small but dignified room in which to receive her Prime Minister or other important visitors one or two at a time; the Prince took an almost cubical space, about twenty feet on a side, in the Private Apartments,

---

[1] The Queen's diary on 27 October 1842 speaks of the 'new window . . . which has only lately been restored, & quite beautifully at St. George's'.

and adorned it with a most monarchical ceiling and a strange and beautiful reminiscence of the Raphael *Logge* in miniature. He and Gruner had learned a lesson from the garden pavilion at Buckingham Palace: don't use fresco for small and delicate effects.

This room is decorated, to the height of the door architraves, in satinwood, marble, enamel, porcelain, and scagliola, with the door-panels integrated into a scheme of three zones. The lowest zone, to the chair-rail, has arabesques and badges in the panels, and further Raphael-esque arabesques enrich the Corinthian pilasters and architraves of the doorways. Above the chair-rail the middle tier of panels is really a series of shallow glazed cupboards with ormolu frames for the display of groups of miniatures and cameos, which are hung in a sort of tree-of-Jesse also of ormolu; the upper tier originally contained the fifteen portraits by Gainsborough, in feigned ovals, of George III's family. The Gainsboroughs have been replaced in part by Winterhalter's small circular portrait canvases of Victoria and Albert's children, which look perfectly right (Gainsborough's letter to George III, with a diagram showing how to hang the oval pictures in a solid group, was found in our century, and the paintings were therefore re-hung elsewhere in their old assembly).

The only obviously 'dated' part of the room below the ceiling is the chimneypiece, in white marble with child caryatids, and an arched gilt-framed glass above; these have certain unmistakably Victorian cartouches. The colour is subtle: lavender, cream-white, grey-blue, rose, with tiny touches of stronger colour in the miniatures and the heraldry. The surfaces are hard and glossy. Far above this smooth and golden wall treatment, and separated from it by a rather neutral height of wall dimly diapered with Garter emblems, hangs or hovers a coved ceiling bordered by crowned heads (the Queen and her predecessors) and centred by a sort of dome with Saints George, Andrew, Patrick, and David in medallions; the programme must be the Prince's, the hand probably Thomas's. The ceiling is almost Garnieresque in its richness, and only its regularity of rhythm saves it from being oppressive. The more elegant wall decoration suggests a possible acquaintance with the 'glass room' of Northumberland House in Trafalgar Square (not destroyed until 1854), where one of Adam's decorators contrived a rich, rather Pompeian, ornament in distemper, cut paper, and silk, protected by glass held down by gilt paterae.[1] This Audience Chamber, a *tour de force* that even the Duchess of Sutherland must have admired, is one of the rare examples of flair rather than justice in Prince Albert's taste; it ranks with his employment of Eugène Lami as costume-designer for a fancy-dress ball.

---

[1] There were similar rooms decorated by the Scottish architect Charles Cameron at Tsarskoe Selo; one of the handsomest uses purple felt under glass.

10

South Kensington, Trafalgar Square and Burlington House

On his return from a meeting of the Commissioners for the Exhibition of 1851 held on 26 January 1852, Prince Albert was able to announce to his wife that the land had been bought which is now the site of so many institutions in South Kensington. The Commissioners, their Exhibition over, became chiefly landlords, and the new Department of Practical Art took initiative under Henry Cole. Despite the existence of Gore House and a few other buildings on the property, it was decided to make the headquarters at Marlborough House, which had forty or more rooms under one roof, and which had not been neglected as Gore House had been (the last tenant, Soyer the Reform Club cook, lost £7,000 running it as a restaurant during the Exhibition).[1] Besides, South Kensington was still almost suburban, and Marlborough House was in St James's.

Cole, preparing for his new work, took a busman's holiday in Berlin, Dresden, and Vienna; and reported on the last day of 1851 to the Prince's secretary Grey that, having seen some Continental institutions, he doubted that the surplus from the Great Exhibition would build as much of an establishment 'as the Prince has shaddowed [*sic*] forth'. That shadowing was of course the proposal to bring the learned societies together in new quarters where lectures, exhibitions, and 'conversazioni' could be held. An amusing sidelight on Cole and the Prince may be seen in the two sets of questions and answers about uses for the surplus which are preserved, the original in Cole's papers at the Victoria and Albert Museum, the copy in the vast file of Exhibition material prepared by the

---

[1] Alexis Benoît Soyer had been cook to a Polignac, to the Queen's Uncle Cambridge, and to the Sutherlands before he went to the Reform in 1837.

Prince and later transferred from Windsor to the Commissioners' present offices. The original, ruled down the centre of the paper by Cole, has his questions in the right-hand column so that the Royal answers should come before the questions; while the copy made by the Prince commonsensibly puts the questions first and the answers after them. Cole, without much 'background', but a great organizer and a rapid learner, moved fast. He and Richard Redgrave filed on 10 March 1852 with the new President of the Board of Trade their estimates for 1852–3 and their general plans for an undertaking not rich in precedent but well formed in Cole's mind. One job for the new Department was very clear: to take over the Schools of Design as a network which eventually would improve commercial art and train art-teachers for board schools all over the country. Quentin Bell in his *The Schools of Design* (1963) leaves little doubt that Cole deliberately set out to capture the Schools, but Bell is rather anti-Cole, and speaks of his 'cast-iron system'. Yet Cole and his South Kensington group were not, after all, taking over the Royal Academy schools or private ones; the Schools of Design had been founded by the Government with a special intent which was to be served. The often stultifying methods by which they later carried out the principles deduced by Cole, Digby Wyatt, Owen Jones, and others from the good and bad lessons of the Crystal Palace, were methods varying from the spirit of principles no more than B. R. Haydon's methods might have varied from *his* principles if he had ever been entrusted with the task of the Schools of Design.[1] What is more interesting than the endless tale of wrong teaching methods in the studio is the new tale of the art museum as a general educational

---

[1] Bell, *op. cit.*, shows by many quotations from Haydon that his ideas for art-instruction were sound, however difficult he was to get along with. One of Bell's appendices reprints a letter from Pugin to J. R. Herbert in which Pugin sketches out 'a work on vegetable floral ornament'; this is neatly paralleled by two pages, reproduced elsewhere in *The Schools of Design*, from Redgrave's *Manual of Design* (1876), which might well have illustrated the letter. Yet Pugin in this confrontation is made out to be somehow good, and Redgrave to be somehow wrong. And it seems to me unreasonable to say (footnote p.247) that Lyon Playfair, more than anyone, was the founder of the Museum and School at South Kensington. Cole is Bell's villain. Bell's book is admirably written and well indexed; but he makes Ludwig Gruner's Christian name Wilhelm.

instrument. Prince Albert, Cole, and their team created that instrument in less than a decade.

The Schools of Design had had a 'museum' of sorts, intended by Dyce when he headed them in the early forties as a great collection of British ornamental art; but Heath Wilson, who succeeded Dyce as Director, went with some colleagues to the exposition of French manufactures in Paris in 1844, and brought back purchases which were added to the Schools museum; on this material and the purchases from the Crystal Palace, Cole and his group based a museum which was first briefly called a Museum of Manufactures; but, just as the title of the Department soon changed to Department of Science and Art (with Lyon Playfair as secretary for science), so the Museum's title changed more than once. Cole's purpose was primarily to instruct students by example, as we shall see; but the frequent special exhibitions at Marlborough House were open to the public, and both the Schools of Design and the Society of Arts had circulated exhibitions to the provinces.[1] It is entirely possible that the Prince or Cole knew before 1851 something about the pioneer work of Alexander von Minutoli in Liegnitz, Silesia (see my Appendix on Minutoli), but I cannot prove this.[2] Cole at any rate, in preparing the Department estimates for 1852-3, wrote:

'It is to the development of the third or highest division of the new Department that the most careful attention will have to be turned. This consists of the practical application of the artistic powers which the pupil already had acquired to the exigencies of manufacture; to use the words of a Report of the School of Design in 1842, often repeated afterwards, in "the study of the various processes of manufacture and the practice of design for individual branches of industry". . . . We

---

[1] The Society of Arts, for instance, held in its Adelphi rooms in December 1852 and January 1853 a show of photographs which was sent out as a travelling exhibition the next summer. The School of Design sent some of the French purchases of 1844 on the road to provincial Schools in 1845.

[2] There is no reference to Minutoli in any of Prince Albert's papers, so far as I can discover. If there ever was any, it may have shared the fate of the Gruner correspondence. Minutoli certainly made himself annoying by claiming on two of his title-pages to be an honorary vice-president of an imaginary 'Universal-Society for the Encouragement of Art and Industry in London'.

submit that the first step to be taken to accomplish this, is to place before the student fine examples of what has already been accomplished in the specialty in which he seeks to be proficient. An educated designer for ceramic manufacture should at least have an adequate knowledge of what Japan, Meissen, Sèvres, and even Chelsea, have already done, and he should aim to acquire a power of execution as high as that which his predecessors have possessed'.[1]

The Marlborough House exhibitions, beginning in 1852, were such a public success that the Prince found new hope for the perfectibility of the public taste, or at least for improvement; he encouraged Cole and the rest of the team in every possible way, and he had of course the Queen's cooperation. Early in 1853 Cole was allowed to search Buckingham Palace for Sèvres, and found many of George IV's pieces in housemaids' cupboards, just as the Prince had found neglected paintings at Hampton Court. Later, when Cole was recommending Redgrave to succeed Thomas Uwins, R.A., as Keeper of the Queen's Pictures, he wrote to Grey (29 August 1857) rather smugly: '. . . seeing how much more care has been bestowed on general work of ornamental art in the Royal Palaces since H. Majesty has allowed us to borrow such works. . . .' By July 1853 the Department had in its library two thousand volumes, which were available on weekdays from ten in the morning to nine in the evening;[2] Cole cleverly asked Ralph Wornum, who in the days of Cole's *Journal of Design* had battled him from the pages of the *Art Journal*, to become librarian at Marlborough House. S. C. Hall's *Art Journal* became more and more friendly to the Queen and Prince and to the South Kensington team. Fourteen annual volumes in succession were dedicated to the Prince.

Early in 1853, having exorcized the ghosts of Lady Blessington, d'Orsay, and Soyer with a thorough coat of whitewash, Cole moved some of his classes to Gore House. Though unfriendly newspapers were calling the region 'Albertopolis', the Prince referred to it as 'our sanctuary' in a letter to Gladstone, then Chancellor of the Exchequer (17 November 1853), in which further enlargement of the site is

---

[1] There is a draft of this 'budget message' in Cole's papers at the Victoria and Albert Museum.

[2] *Journal* of the Society of Arts, 8 July 1853.

sketched: Kensington Barracks were to be transferred to Burlington House and their space added to the Commissioners' estate.[1] Gladstone's *No* by return of post was perhaps the first of his onslaughts upon South Kensington (years later when Cole retired he described himself as worn out by Gladstone's discouragements).

Exhibitions whetted everyone's appetite for novelty; but doubtless the work of preparing them also soon brought out in those responsible that familiar museum attitude: 'better spend the money on something we can *keep*'. So collecting went merrily forward. In 1853 the Prince and Cole somehow found £1,705 for more than seven hundred pieces of ceramics from the Bandinel collection. Then the Gherardini collection of sculptors' models came on the market – £3,000 asked – and Gladstone had to be appealed to. He agreed to sanction Government purchase if a trial show at Marlborough House disclosed real public interest; oddly, Dyce and Herbert, who were asked to report, were not as enthusiastic as the public (they thought not more than a dozen of the thirty objects really desirable) or the Queen and Prince, who saw the exhibit on 24 March 1854; the price finally paid (£2,110) was a bargain in view of the fact that a wax model by Michelangelo was included.[2] An interesting feature of this trial show was a penny pamphlet catalogue by Signora Gherardini, with a commendatory introduction by the young J. C. Robinson, who was to become Director of the Museum (he produced the first catalogue of the 'Museum of Ornamental Art' in 1855).

Even after the Crimean War broke out in 1854, demanding most of the Prince's attention, he took part in moves for important acquisitions. The Bernal collection, formed by an M.P. of Sephardic extraction and West Indies fortune, was the most tempting of all; his son, who called himself Bernal Osborne, approached the Prince after his father's death. Grey, writing to Cole (of course for the Prince) on 4 December 1854, suggested inviting Bernal Osborne to show the collection at Gore House or even in a temporary building. In January 1855 the executors offered the collection at a large price to the Commissioners after preliminary skirmishes in which Lord Granville was also active; but the

---

[1] Commissioners' file, XII, 34 and 35.

[2] Sir Eric Maclagan: 'The Wax Models by Michelangelo in the Victoria and Albert Museum', in *Burlington Magazine*, xliv, January 1924, p. 4; but more recent scholarship reduces the autograph Michelangelo work to one.

price was too great. Prince Albert, presiding at a meeting of the Commissioners on 28 February 1855, drafted a proposal to the Government for a grant to buy part of the huge gathering (he particularly wanted the glass, porcelain, and Limoges enamels); after much difficulty an agreement was come to for a limit within which the Department might buy at auction. The Society of Arts was prompted to petition the Commons to buy *en bloc*;[1] its message reminded Members of Parliament that the Government in the past had often turned down opportunities to buy *en bloc*, and had then bought a remnant for more money. When the Bernal sale took place, Marlborough House bought the first lot, 'a very curious plate, pencilled with oriental characters in gold, alternately with red lines', and went on to spend £8,283 for 725 lots out of a total of about 4,300, which brought over £60,000. The marked catalogue is enchanting reading as to prices, terminology, and names of bidders. John Webb, who did most of the bidding for the Department, had to compete with the Rothschilds, Lord Hertford, other peers, Mr Holford of Dorchester House (whose taste was as fine as his fortune), the Tower Armoury, the dealer Durlacher, Rousselle and Beurdeley of Paris, Colonel Sibthorpe who had so hated the Crystal Palace, Chaffers the compiler of potters' marks, and the British Museum (with which at least one lot was divided; the British Museum's bidding was done by A. W. Franks, later Director but then a young assistant in the department of antiquities). Among the Urbino and other Italian Renaissance pottery which Cole's Department bought was the famous Caffagiolo piece on which a painter is watched by a couple as he decorates a plate; it had been bought at the Stowe sale in 1848 (a distress sale) and Bernal had then bought it privately for £5; now Marlborough House had to pay £120. The arms, medals, jewellery, ivories, and furniture bought, along with the classifications which the Prince had especially wanted, were shown at Marlborough House in 1856, and became some of the prime glories of South Kensington.

Later in the same year, Herbert Minton brought to Cole's attention the Soulages collection in Toulouse; the Prince started the ball rolling

---

[1] *Journal* of the Society of Arts, 23 February 1855. Talleyrand's famous remark about the failure of the Government to buy Sir Thomas Lawrence's collection of drawings was part of the ammunition.

by guaranteeing a thousand pounds towards the purchase price, Cole raised another ten thousand in guarantees, and John Webb went to France and packed up the collection for shipment; but there was so much medieval material that Palmerston, who by this time was Prime Minister and who liked only classic or Renaissance forms,[1] balked at a Treasury grant, and Cole had to persuade the Committee for the Art Treasures Exhibition of 1857 to buy the whole for exhibition in Manchester. 'In the end, the [South Kensington] Museum got round the Treasury and acquired the collection from the Manchester Committee piece by piece over a period of years'.[2]

Before continuing with South Kensington, I must turn to Trafalgar Square, which in 1852 had its column but not yet its lions. The National Gallery had less than half the space it now possesses, and half of what it had was occupied by the Royal Academy. The Gallery in 1847 had received from Robert Vernon his carefully chosen collection of recent British painting, for very little of which it had room; and late in 1851 Turner died, leaving his many remaining pictures, a sum of money which was frittered away in lawsuits, and thousands of drawings and watercolours, to the Gallery, which now had a major problem. Happily, Charles Eastlake had become President of the Royal Academy upon Archer-Shee's death in 1850; Landseer was nine years younger and might have been a more logical candidate, but the Queen and Prince wrote to him to express their hope that the Academicians would elect Eastlake 'as by far the best person to fill the office'; this was plain intervention, and Mrs Eastlake (her husband received the standard P.R.A. knighthood a few days later) wrote on 5 November 1850: '. . . how highly they thought of Landseer that they could address such praises of another to him'.

The Royal Academy liked its independence; it had saved up some money while at Trafalgar Square; and in any case it had great privileges, but these a man like Eastlake would not abuse, and he and Prince Albert had known each other for some years. They began to work towards a sort of *concordat*; largely in honour of the new President,

---

[1] Witness his long battle with Gilbert Scott at the end of the fifties over the style of the Foreign Office; Palmerston won.

[2] Steegman, *Consort of Taste*, p. 255.

the Prince made one of his best speeches at the R.A. annual dinner on 3 May 1851,[1] two days after his triumphal opening of the Crystal Palace. Burlington House, which has been mentioned above, was now offered for sale by one of the Cavendish heirs; the learned societies which could not be enticed to South Kensington were gradually persuaded that Piccadilly would be convenient; on 24 March 1854 the draft of a Treasury minute on the subject went from Gladstone to the Prince.[2] The appointment of Eastlake as Director of the National Gallery in 1855 helped smooth the way; it was not until after the Prince's death that the Academy, the Society of Antiquaries, the Royal Society, et al., moved to Burlington House, but the arrangement seems to have been completed by Disraeli (as Chancellor of the Exchequer) early in 1859. In the meantime, it had been possible to relieve some of the crowding of pictures in the National Gallery by providing new buildings in South Kensington.

The first of these was the famous 'Brompton Boilers', in corrugated sheet iron and glass, by Francis Fowke, a Captain of Engineers;[3] it was built in 1856 for storage, the display of patent models and of some of the 1851 purchases and gifts from exhibitors at the Crystal Palace, and perhaps in part for experiment; Cole called it 'that unlucky Iron Shed which will prove a most unfortunate Thorn'. It was later praised in the *Quarterly Review* by A. H. Layard, who as a critic was strong for suitability to purpose, and I think Semper must have liked it. Fowke came on to Prince Albert's team, and later designed the temporary buildings for the Art Treasures Exhibition at Manchester in 1857 and for London in 1862, as well as galleries which still form part of the Victoria and Albert Museum.

These galleries were built for the Vernon and Turner overflows from Trafalgar Square (nowadays divided between Trafalgar Square and the Tate Gallery), and for the Sheepshanks collection, a strong group of recent British painting much like Vernon's (Wilson, Stothard,

---

[1] Largely reprinted by Martin, ii, 372–4.

[2] *Archives*, F. 26/12.

[3] Thomas Arnold's Rugby had been considerably ahead of the universities in seeking to provide professional men and managers, but the supply was short. Cole began to depend on the Engineers, a trained group available to Government enterprises, during the construction of the Crystal Palace.

Constable, Turner, Etty, Leslie, Landseer, Maclise, and Eastlake were included). Cole began hinting to the Prince, though naming no names, as early as 18 September 1852[1] that such a collection was to be had under special conditions. Mr Sheepshanks, a Yorkshire industrialist, did not want his pictures to be under the control of a trustee, but in charge of a minister of the Crown; the Department of Science and Art being part of the Board of Trade whose President was in the Cabinet, all was well. Sheepshanks's other conditions – that some of the paintings be circulated to the provinces and that the gallery be open on Sunday evenings – were only too welcome to the Prince and Cole as popularizing devices; but there was so much public and press criticism of the donor's conditions that the Prince thought a visit by the Queen, although deserved by such munificence, would be unwise;[2] that was his opinion at the end of January 1857, but he relented as another triumph drew near, and the Queen celebrated the twentieth anniversary of her accession (20 June 1857) by opening the galleries.

In order to avoid reflections from skylights too close to the paintings, Fowke made the walls very high: thirty-four feet at the eaves, with the ridge of the roof fifty feet from the ground. Three more galleries were opened in April 1858;[3] and the present Victoria and Albert Museum was on its way.

The programme of the twentieth-century art-gallery or museum, with all its extension services, is so thoroughly taken for granted that it is hard to believe how crashing a novelty it was in the late 1850s. Mr W. Cowper, M.P., was quoted in *The Times* of 18 June 1858 as having said in the Commons that the Department had 'much improved the taste, elegance, and ornamental beauty of our manufactures', and that 'some parts of its system are about to be adopted in France'; he refers

---

[1] Cole to Grey (Cole papers, Victoria and Albert Museum, box 1).

[2] The Queen objected to Sunday's being made dreary by the prohibition of practically everything; but the people's representatives remained long in favour of strict Sunday observance; a resolution in 1856 to open the London museums for part of Sunday was lost in the House of Commons by 376 to 48.

[3] The *Fifth Report of the Department of Science and Art*, 1858 (by which time the Department was under the Committee of Council on Education rather than under the Board of Trade), pp. 56–64, has plans and elevations showing the attachment of these new permanent buildings to 'Brompton Boilers'.

to the activity which led to the Musée des Arts Décoratifs. A less friendly Member was Mr Danby Seymour, who said in the Commons (as *The Times* reported him on 3 March 1860), '. . . while no attempt was made to popularize the other national collections, large sums were being spent at [South] Kensington in giving lectures, in lighting with gas the buildings erected there, in establishing schools, opening the galleries at night, giving conversaziones, and sending out cards of invitation to all whose support might be valuable hereafter'. He was speaking in a debate on the motion to remove the Natural History department from the British Museum to South Kensington, which did not come about for some years, but which he was opposing – as a majority had opposed a Government bill of Palmerston's in 1856 to move the National Gallery on the ground of the 'dirtiness' of Trafalgar Square.[1] The Opposition liked to denounce moves away from the centre of Town to a 'luxurious' quarter.

The National Gallery, when Sir Charles Eastlake added the Director-ship to his P.R.A. in 1855, was innocent of extension services. Eastlake's great work for it (and he was a very great director) was to fill gaps in the collection, which, for example, contained at his appointment only four pictures earlier than Raphael. He and his wife, with their remarkable *expertise,* mobility, and knowledge of private sources, worked as one to build up what was already an important gallery. They hardly needed to consult Prince Albert, but knew he could be counted upon for help in a pinch and eventually for some paintings; the Queen, in fact, after his death gave the National Gallery a number of his best acquisitions. It is doubtful that the Prince's memorandum of 1853,[2] in which he laid out a plan for scientifically illustrating the history of art by choices for the national collection of paintings, was the sole reason for Eastlake's rehanging of the Italian pictures by schools; this sort of taxonomic

---

[1] The National Gallery Act of 1856, as finally passed, provided among other things for selling some unwanted pictures from the Krüger collection of Minden, early German paintings which had been bought *en bloc* at Prince Albert's suggestion; thirty-nine were sold at Christie's in February 1857 for £249.

[2] Martin, iv, 14. The lists of schools and masters included may have owed something not only to Lindsay but also to Hobbes's *Picture Collectors Manual* (2 volumes, 1849).

approach was in the air, and not only among Germans, for Lord Lindsay had published in 1847 his *Sketches of the History of Christian Art* (three volumes), and Ruskin had written a long and analytical review of them the same year in the *Quarterly Review*.

An odd side-effect of the arrangements which eased crowding in Trafalgar Square was the temporary presence of Ruskin in the tents of the ungodly, for the Turner Bequest was taken in part to Marlborough House, where he was given work-space in 1856-7 while he was arranging and cataloguing the thousands of drawings and watercolours. It seems inconceivable that he should not have had passing contact with Prince Albert in these years at least, but I find no record of it (see my chapter *1857 and 1862* for further speculations). Ruskin could not cure himself of the feeling that Cole was hopelessly and perhaps wickedly on the wrong track; when Cole persuaded him to give the lectures which were published (with additions) as *The Two Paths,* much of Ruskin's argument was directed against the flat oriental patterns that Cole and his team had been so pleased by in the Great Exhibition. Ruskin rather wrong-headedly insisted that eastern artists had not sufficiently consulted nature; his inaugural lecture, given in the Museum with Cockerell in the chair and Cole and Redgrave present, was titled *The Deteriorative Power of Conventional Art over Nations,* and he soon asked 'whether we are assembled here . . . to any good purpose'; then proceeded to lambaste Hindu art because 'it will not draw a man, but an eight-armed monster; it will not draw a flower, but only a spiral or zigzag . . . over the whole spectacle of creation they have thrown a veil'.[1] He continued unregenerate about ornamental art after his exposure to Cole and company: in a letter of 4 April 1859 he wrote, 'I would as soon decorate the warm end of a poker as a warehouse'.[2] He occasionally spoke courteously of Paxton's Crystal Palace, but always denied that a new style of architecture had been created or that the building was more than 'a single very admirable thought'.

Once it was clear that the Royal Academy could go to Burlington

---

[1] My quotations are from the New York edition (1859) of *The Two Paths,* pp. 19 ff.

[2] The letter was sold at Sotheby's, 4 April 1955, lot No. 237; the quotation is from the catalogue of the sale.

House and the National Gallery expand in Trafalgar Square, Prince Albert (though disappointed about the Gallery's not coming to South Kensington) was free to proceed with his plans for the large central portion of the Commissioners' eighty-seven acres. The land sloped down enough from north to south to allow terracing of excellent aspect; the Royal Horticultural Society (founded in 1804) was to develop the ground jointly with the Department of Science and Art. Horticulture nicely combined a science (botany) with an art (gardening); so a great pleasure-ground was to be formed, with parterres, bandstands, refreshment carts, shelters, a conservatory, and four thousand feet of arcades for sculpture and perhaps frescoes; a small fee could be collected at each of several entrances. Fowke was put in general charge under Cole, and Fowke designed the conservatory and the south arcade; Sydney Smirke (youngest of that family) designed the north and central arcades. Paxton seems to have been consulted, and the Hampton Court gardens had been carefully photographed in the interest of a partial return to geometrical formality;[1] in the end Nesfield, who had worked much with Barry (especially at Trentham for the Sutherlands) was given the garden design, which like every detail of the Arcades was closely over-seen by the Prince; a few quotations will show how closely.

The Prince's secretary Phipps wrote Cole on 23 July 1859 that the Prince did not much like a design for the Arcades that had been sub-mitted; he found 'the sort of Pilasters, the flat intervals that carry the columns, weak and poor, and particularly the narrow ones'; the capitals of the columns 'want more boldness'. Prince Albert had added in pencil to the drawings; he wanted the arches to have prominent keystones. By 31 July he had been shown a revision, but Phipps now reported that he found the keystones too tall. Again, on 1 May 1860 Grey writes Cole: 'The Prince says the bricks should be all of the lightest red you can manage, otherwise, as the whole effect of the Arcades depends on colour, you will have much more difficulty in preserving it'. It looks as if these red bricks were to be substituted for yellow brick used er-

---

[1] Cole, in a memorandum attached to his copy of a letter to Grey (22 October 1859, Victoria and Albert Museum, box 1), says, 'The thing wanted is simply [*simply* is crossed out] a beautiful geometrical garden to be in harmony with the architectural features already settled and those hereafter to be adopted.'

roneously at an earlier stage, for a letter of Grey to Cole on 27 March 1860 says that the Prince suggested 'black cement, or some other colour', to tone down 'the glaring effect of the yellow bricks'.

There was much terracotta ornament in the Arcades or Colonnades, all designed by Godfrey Sykes who had been an assistant to Alfred Stevens when Stevens was working for Hooles in Sheffield 1850-1, and of whom Cole thought well. Sykes probably designed the rich, dark terracotta ornament used on Fowke's later courtyard façades still visible in the Victoria and Albert Museum. The fragments of Smirke's central Arcade which until recently remained in exhibition galleries flanking the Imperial Institute, show that the scheme was one of groups of at least five arches, punctuated by slightly projecting pavilions of three arches, which latter were separated by broad piers each containing a niche. The arches were lightly moulded with specially shaped brick, the outer member of the moulding ornamented with small cockle-shell-like cast forms; the cornice, niches, and capitals in good terracotta of rather Stevens-Renaissance types, pleasantly varied; all the bases were stone, and the piers were of unmoulded stone. Photographs in the Victoria and Albert Museum library show many imaginative variations on column orders, some in twisted late-Gothic Italian style; some arches in brick and tile were without order and some were faintly Saracenic. Ingenious and decorative arrangements of steps led from terrace to terrace.

Not the least interesting fact about the Horticultural Society's gardens is that the Arcades were planned in part for a double purpose: some of them formed the ground floor for the temporary building of the Exhibition of 1862, and part of the gardens formed courtyards for the Exhibition. The Gardens and Arcades as such were opened by Prince Albert, with five of his children, on 5 June 1861 (the Queen was in mourning for her mother and would not appear). The financing of the whole layout must have been shared by the Department and the Society with the management of the 1862 Exhibition, and this will have lightened a burden which was on the Prince's mind from 1858 or earlier. A memorandum from him to Grey, dated Coburg, 1 June 1858,[1] proposes a possible solution to the problem of building funds for the Department

---

[1] *Archives*, F. 26/66.

of Science and Art: the Queen, who had some reinvesting to do, might take a mortgage at standard interest. The Horticultural Society was of course, like the Department, a tenant of the Commissioners; its gardens are now buried under the high-Victorian and Edwardian masonry of the quarter. There will be more to say about 1862.

I have already said that Cole's team held practically unanimous views about the exhibits of 1851 and the lessons to be learned from them. Not very many of the School of Design men from the School's pre-Cole days came to South Kensington. Dyce, whom Cole thought 'the first of artists' and the only effective previous head of the School, was busy with paintings for the Houses of Parliament, and so were Horsley and Herbert. Alfred Stevens, who had taught in the School 1845-7, was proposed by Cole as designer of a Royal waiting-room for Paddington in 1852-4, but nothing came of the suggestion; Stevens did enter the competition for the Memorial to the Exhibition of 1851 (his model is in the Victoria and Albert Museum) as well as that for replanning of the buildings of Church and State in Whitehall in 1856, in which Prince Albert was concerned; and he designed medals for the Department of Science and Art in the same year (wax models at the Victoria and Albert, drawings in the Tate Gallery). The aged Mulready, whom Cole also admired, continued to teach after the School of Design came into the Department, and his life class at Gore House produced drawings which were admired by the Queen even though someone else, who expected her to be prudish, tried during a Royal visit to hurry her past the door to Mulready's room.

Owen Jones and Digby Wyatt were asked by the new proprietors who re-erected the Crystal Palace at Sydenham – they may even have been nominated by Cole or the Prince – to design the various courts in historic styles which were a feature of that instructive resort. And Wornum, whom Cole had converted from critic to librarian, went on to become Keeper of the National Gallery and to do for the German schools of painting there what Eastlake had done for the Italian.

In distributing praise and blame for what became visible in 1851 and what happened afterwards, it is still difficult to be objective. The absolutists who took flight from ugly industry, such as Morris, came, in the end, close to industry through the manufacture (though with hand detailing) of wallpapers and light turned chairs, which became big business. It is easy to forget that Cole & Co. had to do their corrective work from a stance in a public place as civil servants, while Morris retreated to Merton Abbey and Ruskin scolded from Venice or the lecture platform, and the insensate industrialists ground out from the Midlands their gewgaws, gadgets, and grograms. In a generally useful and amusing recent book, for instance, a man who knows the field well goes thus far: 'Strange to say, the very causes of the decline in modern decorative art in the 1840s, namely the admiration and emulation of too many historic styles, were to be treated henceforward as the only possible remedy for the disease'.[1] This seems to me too pat; it ignores the derivation of principles of design from the study of museum material. The author does go on to say:

'The Great Exhibition taught the museums of the Continent that *every* school of the past was an example for the industrial arts. . . . Although the future Victoria and Albert Museum started fully a generation late [!] by Continental standards, French critics were obliged to admit, within ten years of the Great Exhibition, that the English were building up the best museum of applied arts in the world.'[2]

---

[1] Gerald Reitlinger, *The Economics of Taste*, 1963, vol. II, p. 96.
[2] *Ibid.*, p. 97.

11

Collecting

There have been some excellent studies of the habit, even the path-ology, of collecting: the Rigbys, Francis Taylor, Maurice Rheims. It is a delightful disease which often afflicts people who would have been interesting even without collecting. Prince Albert was too just and too deliberate in decision to be a brilliant collector but he was an acquisitive Coburg, and he could see through layers of neglect; his pioneering was abetted by a small purse. The Coburg acquisitiveness, which ran generally to thrones, sometimes ran only to clutter, as in the Duchess of Kent; in Queen Victoria it ran to lace and images and jewellery.

Almost from the moment of the Queen's accession there was a differ-ence with her uncle Cumberland, King of Hanover, and later with the representatives of her cousin, the blind King George, over the Hano-verian crown jewels which had been in the hands of George IV and William IV. When it was rumoured in June 1841 that the King would cede the jewels for money, the Queen asked, How to get the money? Peel put the Crown lawyers to work, but when they produced an opinion in December 1842 it was possible to read their despair between the lines; and when at last, in 1858, she had to surrender the jewels, the Hanoverian emissary Count Kielmansegge was surprised, for he was sure that the money would be forthcoming in order to keep the jewels in England (the valuations of course varied). For a good many years, the Queen's Privy Purse accounts show roughly equal expenditure for jewels, works of art, and Exchequer bills.

By 1858, however, the admirable financial management of the Prince Consort had long since produced adequate income. From 1843, when he put the Household on a budget and began to take a strong hand in the affairs of the Duchies of Lancaster and Cornwall, the income available to the Queen and eventually to the Prince of Wales augmented remarkably. Though Prince Albert never had more than £3,000 a year in or from Germany, and could not make lavish expenditure from the £30,000 a year which Parliament allowed him, he is said to have left his wife a capital of many times that sum.[1] His taste of course tended to guide even those choices of works of art which she made as presents for him, and the more expensive purchases were usually made nominally by the Queen; but their Christmas and birthday presents can seldom have included great surprises, for there are occasional evidences of previous discussion.

The Queen's attachment to persons often called for three dimensions in the image: Chantry and Francis, Francis's daughter, Mrs Thornycroft and Thomas Thornycroft, Gibson, the Theeds, the Wyons, and Marochetti provided those white marble busts which peopled the Corridor at Windsor, and the figures on porphyry pedestals for Osborne. The number of portrait sculptures commissioned is roughly equal to the number of copies of classic works made for Osborne and to the number of large and small subject-pieces. Some of the latter are of the 'parlour' description, as for instance *La Filatrice Addormentata*, *Paul et Virginie* (by the Belgian Geefs), or a silver and gold *Lady Godiva* which the Queen gave the Prince for his birthday in 1857.[2] The couple did patronize almost all the respectable sculptors of the day, except Baily and Calder Marshall (the latter was nevertheless represented by a Parian-ware reduction). The Prince liked J. H. Foley's *The Youth at the Stream* so much when it was entered in the Westminster competitions in 1844 that he ordered a small bronze version for himself and in the end set up the large one of that romantic but soundly sculptural work in the Royal Horticultural Society's gardens. E. G. Papworth, the lively John Bell, John Lawlor, and prolific John Thomas all worked at one time or another for him or the Queen; and many of them as well as Foley were employed after his death for various parts of the Albert Memorial.

In sculpture, then, the Royal choices were closer to the norms of

---

[1] *The Private Life of the Queen, by a Member of the Royal Household*, 1898, p. 202. This unauthorized work is certainly by someone who knew the Household intimately. Martin, on the other hand (iii, 22, note) says the Prince died 'leaving absolutely no fortune'. Happily, Royal wills are still a mystery. So is the authorship of *The Private Life*, but internal evidence suggests that the writer was a Scotsman and a Freemason.

[2] *The Private Life*, p. 63.

the time than in painting. The only startling acquisition was no purchase but a gift, three slabs from Assurbanipal's palace brought back by Layard; these eventually joined others of Layard's finds at the British Museum. An odd purchase by the Queen for a Christmas present in 1852 was a *Sappho and Cupid* in ivory by Baron de Triqueti, whom she afterwards employed to clothe the interior of Wolsey's chapel at Windsor as a second Albert Memorial. A very few antique marbles were bought: a restored bust of Marcellus and a similar *Flora*; a variant of the crouching Venus; the 'Egyptian' *Antinous* which had belonged to Jérôme Bonaparte and Lord Ward (long on loan to the British Museum); and the *Venus Anadyomene* which the Prince had admired on a visit to the Duke of Buckingham, and which the Queen was able to buy when the contents of Stowe were sold in 1848. The massive but graceful fountain group by Pietro Francavilla which is now in the Wadsworth Atheneum at Hartford, Connecticut, was offered by the Prince to the Royal Horticultural Society in 1861 and installed in one of the pavilions of the Arcades; but how it left the Society's hands is a mystery.[1]

Painting was a different matter: the Prince's taste was relatively advanced, extremely advanced in comparison to institutional taste before the National Gallery came under Eastlake's administration. In the first years of his marriage, acquisitions were not unconventional: the big Rubens-Snyders *Pythagoras* which was costly and therefore bought by the Queen, and a Jordaens head for ten pounds bought by the Prince in 1841; at the Nicholls sale in 1844 the Queen bought a Greuze head but her husband got a Cranach *Lucretia* and a Catena which was then called a Luini (Luini was fashionable, but not Cranach, and Catena was unheard of). In the next year began a period of fairly steady buying of early Italian paintings, mostly through Gruner from dealers in Italy; and the Royal couple began their lasting custom of giving each other presents of works of art more or less by agreement.[2]

[1] A. H. Scott-Elliot, 'Statues by Francavilla in the Royal Collection', in *Burlington Magazine*, 98, March 1956, pp. 76–84; and subsequent private communication.

[2] The Queen asked Landseer to finish a portrait of the Princess Royal with Prince Albert's greyhound Eros in time for his birthday, 26 August 1841. At eleven in the evening of the 25th she sent a footman from Windsor with orders to bring the painting, 'done or not done'. He woke Landseer at two in the morning and was back at six with the picture wrapped in a tablecloth.

Henceforth the Queen deferred almost entirely to her husband's taste; yet in 1845 she gave him one of the few pictures in George IV's taste that either bought, a van Schendel market scene with the artist's almost habitual night lighting; but she added a Bernardo Daddi *Sposalizio* (then attributed to Agnolo Gaddi) and a Perugino *St Jerome*. Prince Albert also in 1845 found one of his best buys, the small Duccio triptych, as well as a 'Memling' which turns out to be by the Master of the Lucy Legend.

Though a catalogue of all the acquisitions of 1840-61 might be of interest, this is not the place for it, and I shall continue therefore to name only some of the more successful purchases. In 1846, for example, came the Pesellino *Two Saints* which has long been on loan to the National Gallery as part of the Trinity altarpiece; a charming *Virgin and Child* by Gentile da Fabriano, and another distinguished catch, the tiny *Simon Magus* by Benozzo Gozzoli. The next year's best score was a Parentino *St Sebastian* which passed in that day as Mantegna.

In 1847 the Prince was at the expense of buying a number of old Coburg portraits which his brother Ernest II showed a 'want of feeling' in wishing to sell; Prince Albert bought and said no more. He also fell in with a sort of poor relation, Prince Ludwig-Kraft-Ernst von Oettingen-Wallerstein, who was in the Bavarian service and whom the Queen described on an earlier visit (6 November 1843) as 'gentleman-like and clever but slightly effeminate'. Oettingen-Wallerstein persuaded Prince Albert to be, in effect, co-signer of a note for three thousand pounds to Rothschild's, secured by a hundred paintings of early Northern and Italian schools. It is a wide-open guess whether Oettingen-Wallerstein ever intended to pay; not only did he not pay, he made difficulties; Prince Albert had to refuse to deal with him directly, and in 1848 he made an exhibition of the paintings at Kensington Palace, where he left most of them for years although he became absolute owner in 1851.[1] Admittedly 1848 and the following years were difficult ones for German princes.

The Oettingen-Wallerstein collection was a sort of modest version of the Boisserée collection on which the Alte Pinakothek in Munich was

---

[1] The whole story is recapitulated in a letter of Phipps to Oettingen-Wallerstein's legal representative; *Archives*, Add'l. MSS. T/26.

founded, and it contained a few misfortunes; but among its good things were the fine Bohemian fourteenth-century *Virgin and Child* attributed to Theodoric of Prague, a Jan van Hemessen, a Bernard van Orley, a Memling and a Gerard David (both now in the National Gallery by gift of the Queen), Herri met de Bles, Isenbrandt, and Giusto de' Menabuoi (also in the National Gallery).[1] As Prince Albert's earlier purchases show, his and the Oettingen-Wallerstein taste were much alike. In roughly the same period Peel was opposed to buying the early Italians, whom he called 'curiosities'; the National Gallery's purchase of the van Eyck *Arnolfini Marriage* was exceptional in 1842; Eastlake bought the Raphael *Vision of a Knight* in 1847, and Uwins (his successor as Keeper)[2] bought the first 'primitive', a Lorenzo Monaco, in 1848.

From 1848 until well after the Great Exhibition, most of the Queen's and Prince's acquisitions were commissioned from living English painters, including some additions to the ranks of portraits. But in 1853 there was a remarkable purchase, the large Justus van Ghent picture of Federigo da Montefeltro and his son Guidobaldo hearing a Humanist lecture; then attributed to Piero della Francesca and later (by Crowe and Cavalcaselle) to Melozzo da Forli, it was possibly known to Gruner and Eastlake as early as 1845, when it was in Florence in the collection of a Signor da Tivoli. It came into the hands of Samuel Woodburn, at whose sale the Queen had to give a good price for it. She cannot have found it very pleasing, and I suspect that it had to be 'sold' to her as an 'emanation of the giant Albion', for Federigo had the Garter – not truly a good reason for buying; but it was a grand purchase. Guidobaldo in his turn had the Garter: as thanks for which he sent Henry VII (by the hand of Baldassare Castiglione) the enchanting Raphael *St George* which left the Royal collection when Charles I's possessions were dispersed, and which, in 1853, could not possibly

---

[1] Kennedy North, the National Gallery's restorer, told a Trustee of the Gallery in the 1930s that he had found the haloes of many saintly personages in the paintings owned by the Prince were 'improved' with spiky pseudo-Gothic ornament. This may have been Oettingen-Wallerstein's doing or Gruner's or Prince Albert's.

[2] This was during the interval between Eastlake's Keepership and his return as Director.

have been bought out of the Hermitage (it is now in Washington). The Justus van Ghent had great meaning for Prince Albert because of its source in Urbino, birthplace of Raphael, where Federigo added the pleasures of learning and courtly entertainment to military glory. There is some possibility that the purchase was influenced not only by the beginning in that year of the systematic Raphael corpus at Windsor but also by the *Memoirs of the Dukes of Urbino* by James Dennistoun (3 volumes, 1851); Dennistoun was friendly with Gruner.[1]

1853 also saw much buying from the 'Spanish' gallery of Louis Philippe, who had died at Claremont, practically as Queen Victoria's pensioner, in 1850. Gruner did the bidding at the sale at Christie's: Carreño de Miranda, Sánchez Coello, Antonis Mor (a portrait of Philip II not then recognized as such), and Zurbarán (surprisingly, a 'portrait' of St Ignatius Loyola).

In 1854 the Queen made an odd purchase at the sale of Sir W. H. Lytton Bulwer: an Anton Raphael Mengs, *Charles III Abdicating the Throne of Naples in 1759*. Mengs had been the sleek international stylist of his day, yielding only to Battoni, but one doubts that the Queen saw in him a proto-Winterhalter; more likely she – and most likely Prince Albert – was interested in Charles III as the best of Spanish Bourbons (among whom even a good one was rare), Charles the promoter of good government and porcelain factories, and grandfather to Louis Philippe's Queen Amélie, whom Victoria liked. Scarcely anything else of the eighteenth century did she acquire: besides the little Greuze and a Hoppner portrait (an Eton 'leaving portrait') of Melbourne, she bought only a Reynolds of the marriage of George III; and the Gloucesters bequeathed to her and Prince Albert two Beecheys and a second Reynolds.

Another pleasant historical acquisition was Cornelis Janssen's portrait of William III as a young Prince of Orange, bought in 1858 (less dashing than the Honthorst of his father as a slightly older boy); a

---

[1] Dennistoun was considered in 1854 among candidates for the Directorship of the National Gallery, but Lord Aberdeen, writing to the Prince on 29 May (*Archives*, F. 26/14), said Dennistoun's knowledge of art was not 'sufficiently general' – 'confined to a particular school'; and his book 'a very laborious, but not very attractive work'. The illustrations were engravings and woodcuts done in Gruner's shop.

Dutch seascape by Adam Willaerts, acquired the same year, has had several historical titles and has come to rest as *James I Reviewing His Fleet at Spithead in 1623.*

In 1854 and 1856 Prince Albert bought two Cranachs of the *Virgin and Child,* the larger of which, a triptych with saints in the wings, was strangely attributed to Grünewald; he also found a Cranach portrait of Luther in disguise as 'Junker Jörg' during his concealment on the Wartburg; perhaps prices were driven up by these purchases, for in 1860 it was the Queen who paid for a Cranach, a stately travesty in which the *Judgement of Solomon* is enacted by Cardinal Albrecht of Brandenburg and his councillors, but a handsome picture. An exceptional act of 1860 was the Queen's purchase for the South Kensington Museum of an early Meissen *kakiemon*-design bowl and a fluted cup and saucer which are shown by incised letters and numbers underneath to have been in Augustus the Strong's ownership and use.

In acquiring paintings by his contemporaries, Prince Albert stuck to his rule of not over-favouring German artists. He commissioned an *Entombment* of Jäger in 1845, and in 1851 gave the Queen a Steinle *St Luke Painting the Virgin*; both of these are still in the Queen's rooms at Osborne; there too, in his dressing-room, is the large-scale *Hercules and Omphale,* a great chunk of fresco either cut out of a wall or deliberately made on a portable metal chassis; it is by Gegenbaur, and dated Rome 1830, but he bought it in England in 1844. He gave the Queen a Führich drawing, allowed room for a showing of Waldmüller at Buckingham Palace in 1856,[1] and asked Gruner to seek out for him the cartoon of Overbeck's mural *Religion Glorified by the Fine Arts.*[2] With the obvious exception of Winterhalter, everything else German was a duty purchase, this side of charity.

From 1842 onwards, when Winterhalter painted half-lengths of the

---

[1] Sir [George] Hamilton Seymour visited a Waldmüller show at Vienna, was impressed, but found it was on its way to Philadelphia; as a diplomat he was able not only to get the Prince's attention but also perhaps to manage the transport.

[2] It is sometimes called *The Triumph of Religion in the Arts;* the drawing is of cartoon size, and is probably a semi-final stage in the design, but the executed painting (Städel Institute, Frankfurt) of 1840 is still larger and varies in some details; see Keith Andrews, *The Nazarenes,* 1964, pl. 67, for comparison.

Queen and Prince (he in uniform and rather boyish), the artist from the Black Forest portrayed members of the Royal family in almost all possible combinations of persons at all ages from ten weeks to senility. Although the Queen seems to have thought of herself in profile as if on a coin or stamp, and although it is difficult for anyone to think away the image of that first admirable stamp, it was Winterhalter who created the iconology of the Prince, so to speak, and that of the Royal children; he made a cosy old lady of the Duchess of Kent, who in her photographs has a shrewd look; and his representations of the Queen and others were multiplied and filtered down in enamels, lithographs, and sometimes his own or Noël's watercolour reductions. In his late years, his brother Herman and other assistants painted rather awful draperies, jewellery, and other accessories, but such scamping was never done for the Queen. Winterhalter, too, was given a Palace showing, at St James's in June 1847; the ninety-eight thousand visitors were probably as curious about Royal images as about the art of portraiture.

Two or three Winterhalters deserve special mention. The full-length portrait of the three-year-old Prince Arthur (Duke of Connaught) in uniform inevitably puts one in mind of Manet's *Boy with a Sword* or *The Fifer*, which are bolder but later and possibly indebted: the Winterhalter portrait was lithographed in 1855 and published. *The First of May*, the group which records the triumphant day of the opening of the Crystal Palace, the first birthday of Prince Arthur, and the eighty-second birthday of the Duke of Wellington, was commissioned soon after that day, on the afternoon of which the old Duke came to Buckingham Palace with a present for his godchild. A pictorial record of this touching visit from the old national hero and true-blue Tory, was patently something to be desired. On 21 May the Queen wrote that a sketch already existed: 'It was originally my wish, but Winterhalter did not seem to know how to carry it out, so dear Albert with his wonderful knowledge and taste, gave W. the idea which is now to be carried out'. This idea was to make the picture substantially an 'Adoration of the Magi' with only one Magus. The Duke hated sitting for his portrait, and apparently he was not asked to sit; he is seen in lost profile, with just enough of his nose and chin showing to be unmistakable. In some ways it is rather an outrageous picture, and I cannot blame Winterhalter for having been a little embarrassed, or the present

Duke for having barely mentioned it in his *Iconography of the First Duke of Wellington*.[1]

Florinda, a large composition of nudes based on an episode in Southey's *Don Roderick* and hence in the anecdotal tradition of the Academy fifteen years earlier, was given by the Queen to her husband in 1852; but she must have noticed soon afterwards that Winterhalter had repeated the arrangement with some variations in his *Empress Eugénie among Her Ladies*, a watercolour copy of which the Queen gave to the Prince five years later; for a letter to Winterhalter from the Queen's dresser and amanuensis Mariana Skerrett early in 1857 asks whether *Florinda* had been engraved and whether there was going to be any multiplication of the picture of the Empress (whom the Queen admired for her beauty and unerring style); the watercolour copy is presumably the one mentioned in Winterhalter's answer as having been prepared for the use of Léon Noël, the printmaker who often worked on such multiplications.[2] On 13 October 1860 the Queen noted in her diary (she was at Coblenz and may have met the lady or have been hearing gossip) that the head on one of the *Florinda* figures was that of Princess Wittgenstein, 'still very handsome'. This was, of course, Princess Sayn-Wittgenstein, the companion of Liszt. It is hard not to imagine the very practical sense of humour of the Queen and Prince occupied privately with the resemblance between the two pictures.[3]

Among the draughtsmen and watercolourists employed for the souvenir albums was another German, Carl Haag, who like the Belgian Louis Haghe became a sort of fixture at Balmoral in season; some of Haag's torchlight scenes are fresh and sprightly. Besides the Belgian purchases already mentioned and a Cogniet (gift of King Leopold and rather a good one, an Arab head always hanging at Osborne), there were a few French: a couple of Dehodencqs, an Alfred de Dreux, a Meissonier bought by the Prince and another given him by Napoleon III, and an Ary Scheffer (Dutch by birth, French by practice) bought by the Queen

---

[1] Lord Gerald Wellesley and John Steegman, *The Iconography of the First Duke of Wellington*, 1935.

[2] Both letters in *Archives*, Victorian Add'l. MSS. C. 4/285.

[3] The gossip must have been general. The *Columbia Encyclopaedia* article on Winterhalter states the connexion as a fact. There is a replica of *Florinda* in the Metropolitan Museum of Art.

in 1844. She commissioned of Horace Vernet in 1856 a Crimean war subject (including the Zouaves whose costume she adored) as a present for her husband; and they bought a good deal of Delaroche (notably some of the artist's worshipful histories of Napoleon I). Delaroche was much favoured by the Lusso taste, and so was Eugène Lami whose lively elegance helped to give some air of *ancien régime* to Napoleon and Eugénie's doings. Without running down the great qualities of either Lami or Constantin Guys, it might be fair to say that in Guys's coloured drawings we have true reports on the appearance of personages who would have wished to appear as Lami made them look. Louis Philippe's gift of watercolours of the Royal visit to France in 1843 first brought Lami to the Queen's and Prince's eye; when he became a refugee in England after 1848, they employed him a number of times. His is one of the best reports on the opening of the Crystal Palace; and the Prince's asking him to design fancy-dress costumes for the Royal couple for a ball was one of the patron's real exercises of *flair*.

What Prince Albert may have thought of the works of Ingres and Delacroix at the Paris Exposition of 1855, and whether he even heard of Courbet's side-show, we shall never know. An interesting light is shed by F. S. Cary's report on the Exposition in the Society of Arts' *Journal* for 26 September 1855; he said that the English organizers in 1851 had 'shrunk from the greatness of the task' of including modern [or any] paintings; but now Napoleon had spoken and it was done. Ingres and Horace Vernet had each a room to himself in the Palais des Beaux-Arts; and Ingres, 'learnedly clever, hard, and repulsive', Cary simply passed over. Vernet, he said, was *real*, a man for the multitude. Delacroix he found 'gorgeous in colour, mild in composition, doubtful in drawing'.[1] The French liked Mulready, Millais (especially *The Order of Release* and *Ophelia*), Frith, and Leslie because they did not, like French painters, produce horror pictures of historic bloodshed. Cary liked among the French 'cabinet' pictures those of Decamps, Bellangé, Troyon, Meissonier, and Ziem.[2]

---

[1] Louis Philippe had known and employed Delacroix; Napoleon III preferred Ingres.

[2] There is a story of Claire Jerrold's (*The Married Life of Queen Victoria*, p. 370) about a sketch by Millet which she says the Prince bought in France and gave to the Princess Royal; it had been bought by the curé of Briquebec

In their purchase of British painting, the Queen and Prince followed common sense rather than the impulse based on experience and 'hunch' that the brilliant buyer obeys. If the Queen had had a better eye, her impulses might have been fruitful. She missed a good chance to buy an important Pre-Raphaelite painting which was sent to Windsor for her inspection,[1] and had ill luck once when she wanted to buy E. M. Ward's *Royal Family of France in the Prison of the Temple* (it was politic to let it go to the first enthusiast, an eminent Lancashire Maecenas, instead of asking him to cede it, as she did in a few cases of competition). Later she commissioned Ward to do two records of her meetings with Napoleon III, but neither picture was very successful.

Before her marriage, Queen Victoria had employed the fashionable portrait painters Grant and Hayter, but Hayter (though at first she does not seem to have minded his marital irregularities) became rather importunate about commissions and had to be cast off. In the early years of the marriage, Partridge and Ross painted a number of portraits before Winterhalter took over, and the Queen always felt Ross's profile of Prince Albert at twenty was the best early picture of him. Wilkie unhappily died too soon to do anything but the official panoramas of the Princess Victoria's confirmation and her first Council as Queen; the latter rather fine and fresh, for a composition of separate faces.[2] Something of Wilkie's strength turned up later in John Phillip, whose Spanish subjects of the fifties both the Queen and the Prince liked and bought; but their tenebrous free brushwork could not carry over into the portraits which Phillip was asked to do in the late years of the decade.

One of Prince Albert's earliest purchases was *The Eve of the Deluge*

---

near Cherbourg (Millet's country) in whose hands the Prince saw it. Claire Jerrold's details are sometimes unsupported.

[1] A. Paul Oppé, 'Art', in *Early Victorian England*, II, 113, reports that Millais's *Christ in the House of His Parents*, which made a sensation at the R.A. summer show of 1850, was sent to Windsor to satisfy the curiosity of the Queen, who was convalescent after the birth of Prince Arthur. Boase (*English Art 1800–1870*, 1959, p. 298) says that Holman Hunt's *Christ in the Temple* 'was sent to Windsor so that the Queen and Prince Consort might admire it at leisure'.

[2] The Queen later disliked it, perhaps only because it was inaccurate, for she had worn mourning for William IV, but Wilkie put her in virginal white.

56. *Entrance Hall, Balmoral Castle*; photograph by J. Reid, Ballater, before 1901

57. *Ball Room, Balmoral Castle*

58. G. M. Greig: *The West Drawing Room, Holyrood House*; watercolour, 1857 (?) 1859(?)

59. Sir Edwin Landseer: *Loch Laggan*; canvas, $13\frac{1}{4} \times 19\frac{3}{8}$ in.; 1847; gift of the Queen to the Prince, Christmas 1847

60. Carpet (detail), designed by Gruner and made by Blackmore Brothers of Burdensball near Wilton, 1850, for the Green Drawing Room, Windsor Castle

61. Anonymous: *The Prince Consort's Dressing Room at Altnagiuthasach*; watercolour, 1849 (?)

62. J. Roberts: *The Stairway, Balmoral*; watercolour

63. *Royal Dairy*, Frogmore, Windsor Greak Park, by John Thomas and Mintons for the Prince Consort, 1857–8

64. *Queen's Audience Chamber*, Windsor Castle. Photograph 1951 (courtesy
of *Country Life*)

65. *Duchess of Kent's Mausoleum*, Frogmore, Windsor Great Park; by Humbert from Gruner's designs, 1860–1

FORMERLY BELONGED TO H.R.H Pss CHRISTIAN

66. Leonard Charles Wyon: *Silver Medallions* of the first seven children of
Queen Victoria and Prince Albert; dated August and September 1850

by John Martin ('Mad Martin'), painted in 1840 and said by some writers to have been commissioned by the Prince, who paid for it in December 1841. Martin's impassioned and stormily-lighted Biblical or mythological compositions, a little repetitious in their combinations of architecture and crowds (with reminiscences of industrial ugliness), were so much and so badly reproduced in their own day that it is only now beginning to be possible to look at him again; he is not quite such a might-have-been case as Haydon. The Prince never acquired anything else so visionary, certainly never a Richard Dadd on the one hand nor a Turner on the other.[1] Of Biblical subjects there were a fair number: E. H. Corbould, Herbert, Dyce, and Eastlake (whose *Good Samaritan* Queen Victoria always kept at Osborne). Corbould was for some time drawing-master in the Royal family in succession to Leitch; and in the last year of the Prince's life the Queen commissioned Corbould to do two scenes from *Adam Bede* (which the Prince had admired) in water-colour, Corbould's usual medium which he treated like oils.

Of the freer water-colourists who are among the glories of the English nineteenth century, the Queen and Prince missed the earlier generation, but the Prince bought Callow, Varley, David Roberts, Copley Fielding, and of course Joseph Nash; G. H. Thomas, who became almost a specialist in military subjects for the souvenir albums, used water-colour and gouache in a gay Lami-like fashion that gives great pleasure today, and his *panache* was one of the things Prince Albert needed.

Occasionally a light subject came in, such as George Cruikshank's anecdotal *Disturbing the Congregation* (1850), but literary ones predominate: *L'Allegro* and *Il Penseroso* twice (once by Horsley of the School of Design); *Undine*, a rather queer picture by Maclise; and three

---

[1] Queen Victoria, visiting Petworth on 3 December 1846, said not a word in her diary about the famous Turners, mentioning only van Dyck and Titian by name; 'beautiful pictures, but they are badly arranged'. Turner at least once made a bid for Royal patronage. In Germany in the autumn of 1840, he sketched the comparatively new Walhalla and then travelled to Coburg. At the R.A. summer show of 1841 he exhibited (No. 541) 'Schloss Rosenau, the seat of Prince Albert of Coburg'. *The Times* review described this painting as 'eggs and spinach', and Royalty did not buy. A rather fine impressionistic view of the Festung, with water below it, was at Agnews in 1956.

Faerie Queene subjects by W. E. Frost, given by the Queen in 1847, 1848, and 1849. Frost, whose drawings are often delightful, was a pupil of Etty but more hard-edged and 'classical'.

Of those whom we might call the central but second-string Victorian painters there were fewer than one might expect: some fine horse portraits by Herring, some of the landscapes which Clarkson Stanfield painted all over the world when he was not designing for the stage, Augustus Egg's *l'Amante*, and a Pickersgill, *The Foscari*, which the Prince gave his wife in 1855 because of her fondness for the opera named for that family. But there was no Etty or Leslie after the time of the Buckingham Palace garden pavilion, not a single Pre-Raphaelite, not even a Watts (though he did some work in the Houses of Parliament and the Queen admired his big fresco in Lincoln's Inn Hall).

The Prince bought (perhaps commissioned) from Cope a large history in 1847 when Cope, too, was working at Westminster: *Cardinal Wolsey Dying at the Gate of Leicester Abbey*; and from the Academy show of 1855 the Queen bought with less enthusiasm Leighton's *Cimabue's Madonna Carried in Procession through Florence*, which in our day of criticism-of-criticism might be called a picture about a picture. 'Albert was enchanted with it, – so much so that he made me buy it'.[1] It is enormous and operatic. There can be no doubt that they were both delighted with a purchase from the R.A. show of 1854, Frith's *Life at the Seaside* (often called *Ramsgate Sands*). Lloyds the dealers had already bought it, but this time the Queen was in luck, for they ceded it to her, subject to the right to engrave it within three years.[2] It was rather a pioneer of contemporary genre without the 'corny' caricature of Cruikshank. Frith's report on Prince Albert's visits to his studio, bearing suggestions and a sharp instrument to point with, is well known. He was later commissioned to paint two Royal weddings, a task Landseer said he would not have undertaken 'for all the money in this world and the next'.[3]

Yet it is Landseer whose name, more than any other's but Winter-

---

[1] Diary, 3 May 1855.

[2] The engraving, almost as large as the painting, was distributed in thousands by the Art Union.

[3] W. P. Frith, *My Autobiography and Reminiscences*, 1888, p. 236.

halter's, is indelibly associated with Royal patronage in their time. It has had to bear a deal of opprobrium. Landseer, after all, did not invent the 'pathetic fallacy' (Ruskin named it); many a horse and many a dog with poached eye and self-conscious pose is to be seen in Parmigianino, Titian, and Rubens. Landseer's early works for the Queen, the macaws and dogs, monkeys and love-birds, cushions and curtains, were rather silly; but Melbourne encouraged *singeries*, and the Queen, for all her poise, was a girl entranced with her possessions. Landseer may have derived some amusement from the spaniel-like coiffure of the Coburg cousin Victoire duchess of Nemours, but when Prince Albert came on the scene, the artist began to paint, at least for royalty, in a somewhat altered fashion. The animals ceased their clowning. The well-known picture of the young couple at Windsor, with their first child and several dogs, introduces a sort of monumentality that turns up later in the idealized Highland subjects. The faults of Landseer were not all on the surface, but those on the surface were exaggerated by the engravings after his paintings by his brother Thomas, whose caressing manner increased the sentimentality. At best, Landseer now looks rather good, especially in those Highland pictures in which he seems to have shared the Prince's high opinion of the Scottish countryman, the stag, and the eagle. As early as 1842 the Queen gave her husband the *Stag Swimming* and *The Sanctuary* (a lone stag with birds); in the same year Landseer exceptionally painted a record of the couple in costume for a ball as Edward III and Queen Philippa – rather impressive, if not as gay as Lami.

After the Prince's death the Queen bought a strange, late Landseer, *The Baptismal Font*, in which sheep press around a watering-trough where doves flutter; it has the same queer unearthly quality as Thomas Cole's *Titan's Goblet*. She also added to the Noel Paton Crimean war subject bought in 1859 three religious ones for installation in the Prayer Room which she added at Osborne.

Prince Albert's most immediately influential collecting was his patronage of Landseer and Winterhalter; his early Italian and German pictures had their effect later. Perhaps his most useful collecting was his gathering of men who could extend his work. And in this, perhaps, he was a little like his grandfather, whose print-collecting could not match Liechtenstein's or Archduke Albert's, but could and did form a base for the *œuvre*-catalogues and the systematic curatorship and collecting of the nineteenth century.[1]

---

[1] A puzzling evidence of systematic attention to the Royal collection of drawings – but whether directly through Prince Albert's interest is not clear – is the addition by purchase at the Standly sale in 1845 of many Hogarth drawings to those already in hand from George IV's acquisitions. In the same year J. H. Glover, the Royal Librarian, had evidently been inquiring about certain prints and drawings of George IV's which had disappeared. See A. Paul Oppé, *English Drawings, Stuart and Georgian Periods, in the Collection of His Majesty the King at Windsor Castle*, 1950, introduction, p. 15, and catalogue, *passim*.

12

1857 and 1862

The Art Treasures Exhibition at Manchester and the second great International Exhibition in London might be seen, in different ways, as redemption of a pledge demanded by some critics of the Great Exhibition of 1851: attention must now be paid to Art.[1] It would be unfair to say that Ruskin's dislike of the 1851 Exhibition put any direct pressure upon Prince Albert, but Ruskin's star had risen very high, and he was expert at making a point and then emphasizing it.[2] When he wrote somewhat approvingly of the reopening of the Crystal Palace at Sydenham, he could not resist hitting 1851 by saying that while the 'petty arts of fashionable luxury' were being shown, 'the greatest pictures of the Venetian masters were rotting at Venice in the rain'.

When J. C. Deane, a member of the Manchester Royal Institution, put forward the idea of an encylopaedic art exhibition, it fell to Prince Albert to clear away some of the obstacles; both he and Ruskin were consulted about choices; Ruskin made an important speech during the show in Manchester; and several of the Prince's team were involved in the success of the affair, which had over a million visitors. It seems

---

[1] It was as a reaction to the absence of paintings from the Crystal Palace that a show of contemporary foreign painters, organized on French initiative, had been held during the 1851 season at Lichfield House in St James's Square. The Earl of Ellesmere had opened to 'respectable visitors' his gallery in Bridgewater House, even though the building was unfinished.

[2] It seems to me an error on the part of Roger Fulford to have said in his chapter on the Great Exhibition (in *The Prince Consort*, 1949, p. 216) that 'Under the influence of these [Ruskin's] fashionable doctrines, the Prince sought a moral justification for his own sensual enjoyment of painting and music by striving to spread the same enjoyment throughout all classes.' Sir Kenneth Clark has pointed out (in *Ruskin Today*, 1964, p. 11) that Ruskin's influence built up slowly, and that it was not until the mid-sixties that he had a really large public.

almost inconceivable that Ruskin and Prince Albert should have had no contact during the preparations, but there is no written evidence in all the Prince's papers, and in Ruskin's only a comment on his bride's presentation at Court in 1850. Although the elder Ruskin censored his son's public utterance so long as he lived, the younger managed to take an occasional pot-shot at '*Te-Deum*-singing Princes'. The closest thing to a comment on Ruskin in Martin's official biography of the Prince is his saying, apropos of the Prince's speech opening the Birmingham and Midland Institute on 22 November 1855, 'There were many austere critics present on the occasion, some of them themselves great speakers'.[1] This sounds like Martin's sort of circumlocution for a Ruskin, and Ruskin may have been there, but I cannot prove it. In the absence of written evidence, one can only assume that the Prince chose to have nothing to do with him;[2] perhaps letting Cole entice him was a bit of good staff work; see my chapter 7.

Elizabeth Rigby, who was married to Charles Eastlake in 1849, became the confidante of Effie Grey in the years of her unconsummated marriage with John Ruskin. If the Prince did not know something about this from Eastlake, he had other sources. Lady Eastlake later on wrote harshly about Ruskin: in reviewing the first three volumes of *Modern Painters* in the *Quarterly Review* in 1856 she spoke of his 'broad false principles'; again she said, 'Mr Ruskin's writings have all the qualities of premature old age – its coldness, callousness, and contractions'.[3] And she is said to have campaigned against him orally on many occasions; women sometimes hold their grievances overlong. The Queen, after the annulment and Effie Grey's marriage to Millais, would not receive her until Millais on his deathbed in 1896 asked her to.

---

[1] Martin, iii, 390.

[2] Sir Philip Magnus in *King Edward the Seventh*, 1964, says (p. 28) that the Prince consulted Ruskin in regard to the education of Albert Edward, but does not note his source. Often enough men of like interests and great eminence have failed to meet, or met only once. Newman and Dr Arnold, for example, met only twice, in 1828 and 1842, says G. Faber in *The Oxford Apostles* (1933, here quoted Penguin edition, 1954, p. 116); their second meeting was embarrassing, for by 1842 they were adversaries, and their host and interlocutor had a long and difficult day.

[3] *Quarterly Review*, XCVIII, p. 386; the article was of course, like all in that journal, anonymous.

There are always mysteries. I suppose there can seldom have been two men in one generation so thoroughly and deliberately prepared as Prince Albert and Ruskin were prepared by their elders for the careers which they in fact entered.

What about Manchester? 'It is singular', wrote Nathaniel Hawthorne, 'that the great Art Exhibition should have come to pass in the rudest great town in England'.[1] Manchester was one of the hives of the peace movement, and a capital of *laissez-faire* economics; but, unlike Birmingham which had many self-made men at the head of small enterprises, Manchester had a few great magnates. The Executive Committee for the Exhibition, which the Royal Institution asked to carry out the scheme, was headed by Lord Ellesmere and, after his death, by Lord Overstone; Milner Gibson and other M.P.s, the Mayor, and several of the Fairbairn family were members. A deputation from this committee waited upon the Prince in London on 2 July 1856 to ask his help; they were encountering great reluctance to lend among owners of works of art. He at once wrote Ellesmere a letter intended for publication, in which he said the plan had a 'great national object', and proposed 'a chronological and systematic arrangement' which might for the first time enable 'the most uneducated eye to gather the lessons which ages of thought and scientific research have attempted to abstract'.[2] He enclosed a copy of the list of schools and masters of painting which he, Eastlake, and others had made up for the National Gallery in 1853. The Queen's willingness to lend was also publicized, and *The Times,* which often sneered, spoke favourably, so all went well.

The Manchester Cricket Club used the large cricket ground of Sir Humphrey de Trafford at Old Trafford, next to the Botanical Gardens, and with a railway line alongside. For this site Fowke designed a tremendous set of temporary skylighted galleries covering more than three acres; C. D. Young, the contractor who was building at South

---

[1] *English Notes,* 1902 (Riverside edition), ii, 545; all Hawthorne's account of the Manchester show is excellent.

[2] Martin, iv. 35. See also page 126, note 2; a printed copy of the list is in the Commissioners' files, XI, 75. Another partial source, besides Lord Lindsay, might have been Hobbes's *Picture Collectors Manual* (2 volumes, 1849), which included lists of pupils and imitators of known masters, and a subject index.

Kensington, was the successful bidder. The great art-dealing firms of Agnews (who had originated in Manchester) and Colnaghi were asked to help in organizing and transport; the owners were insured against all risks.

Although the show was arranged chronologically and catalogued by classifications of material, there were a few special composite installations: Lord Hertford's large contributions were all shown together (was there already a hope that his collection might go to the nation?); the Soulages collection was shown as purchased by 'Members of the Executive Committee of the Exhibition'; and Marlborough House sent some of the Bernal collection; these last two groups were arranged by J. C. Robinson, who now had the title of 'curator of the Museum of Ornamental Art formed for the Department of Science and Art, London'. George Scharf, later to be first secretary of the National Portrait Gallery,[1] was in charge of paintings; water-colours and prints were got together by Edward Holmes, and J. M. Kemble chose the Celtic and Anglo-Saxon antiquities. Living painters and sculptors were invited to nominate their own works; in fact most of the sculpture was modern, but there were two Torrigianis and some Alessandro Vittoria bronzes, and examples of Roubiliac, Nollekens, Canova, and Thorwaldsen. A British Portrait Gallery (first sample of the future N.P.G., founded by Parliament in 1856 but long homeless) was put together by Peter Cunningham,[2] whose one-page preface to his section of the catalogue is graceful and amusing. P. H. Delamotte chose the photography. Besides the catalogue, there was a good semi-popular handbook by Tom Taylor.

The galleries were so well lighted that some darkly-varnished pictures lost their reputations, but on the whole it was a superb exhibition,

---

[1] Scharf, knighted just before his death, was (before Manchester) a stage designer for Charles Kean. In 1856 Kean, having to produce *A Winter's Tale*, was troubled by the famous implausibility of its setting on 'the seacoast of Bohemia'. Scharf, who had travelled in the East, was able to provide suitable scenery, complete with the correct flora, from his own drawings of Bithynia: a nice bit of Science and Art. Buckley, *The Victorian Temper*, 1951, p. 135.

[2] Cunningham had a good eye. A painting sent to the Exhibition as a Turner was recognized by him as being from the hand of James Stark, *A View on the Yare with Fishermen and Their Nets*. When it was sold at Christie's on 24 July 1959, the story was told in the catalogue entry (No. 66).

and the first really great general exhibition of works of art. Among the paintings were three Rubenses from Windsor, several great Poussins, the Wilton Diptych, Prince Albert's Duccio, his best Cranach and his Kulmbach and van Orley, the Queen's Mulready *The Wolf and the Lamb* (bought by George IV), many of Stirling's Spanish pictures and some from Louis Philippe's posthumous sale, as well as the Velásquez *Admiral Pulido Pareja* from the Duke of Bedford and the *Olivares on Horseback* from the Earl of Elgin; Mr Drury-Lowe's 'Pollaiuolo' *David* on a shield (the Castagno later in the Widener collection and now at Washington); many ducal Canalettos, the Panshanger Raphaels; Mr Dingwall's Bellini *St Francis* (now in the Frick Collection); the Hampton Court Tintorettos and the Earl of Yarborough's great Veronese; a Fra Filippo Lippi lent by John Brett the painter whom Ruskin lectured until he was 'completely wretched';[1] fifty Reynoldses; and a fine lot of Hogarths. Hawthorne, in his long account of the Exhibition, called Hogarth 'the only English painter, except in the landscape department . . . unless it be some of the modern Pre-Raphaelites'. Ruskin doubtless frowned on Hogarth, for he could never get it out of his head that the English taste for the burlesque would always prevent English art from being 'successful in the highest fields of ideal or theological art'.[2] But Reynolds – like Velásquez – was one of his latest enthusiasms; and having been recently converted to the visual delights of the late Venetians, he stoutly defended (in this same year 1857) the National Gallery purchase of the great Veronese *Family of Darius before Alexander*, which had been meanly criticized. The Manchester galleries of watercolours and drawings included Jordaens, Rembrandt (the well-known *Woman Leaning over a Half-Door* so well reproduced by Ploos van Amstel and now no longer attributed to Rembrandt himself); Cipriani, Cozens, and all the great latter-day English, dominated of course by Turner (Ruskin again).

Prince Albert, having opened the Exhibition in early May, came back in late June with the Queen, who was entranced by a large composite photograph by O. G. Rejlander, *The Two Ways of Life,* rather in

---

[1] The rather shocking story is told in Robin Ironside's *Pre-Raphaelite Painters*, 1948, p. 46.

[2] *Lectures on Art*, 1870.

the style of Couture; she bought it for her husband.[1] Then, with the *Te-Deum*-singing Prince out of the way, Ruskin came on to deliver on 10 and 13 July at the Manchester Athenaeum the pair of lectures which he called *The Political Economy of Art*; this title was pointed straight at Manchester – a member of the Manchester Statistical Society once said it would better have been called the Political Economy Club. Ruskin had written the speeches[2] earlier in the summer, largely at Cowley, with Charles Eliot Norton visiting daily from Oxford and hearing most of the matter read aloud. The proceeds of the actual presentation before a 'very large and exceedingly fashionable audience' went to Ruskin's Working Men's College; his recent biographer Rosenberg calls the lectures 'a prelude to *Unto This Last*'.[3] His subject is basically the finding of artistic genius, its nurture, and its turning to good account: his sub-titles are Discovery, Application, Accumulation, and Distribution. He was denouncing competition in Manchester, and inviting government to pay attention to the social and economic lives of the governed, and to the commonwealth's patrimony of art. He poured upon his hearers some of his most eloquent wheedling, but then scolded them with his pearliest paternalistic scorn for permitting art to decay in Italy and elsewhere; and whacked South Kensington (of course not by name) for struggling to produce new wallpapers and teapots while 'we let the walls fall that Giotto patterned, and the canvasses rot that Tintoret painted, and the architecture be dashed to pieces that St Louis built'.[4] It was superb; if he had been a Gospel revivalist (which he was almost) the sinners would have come in droves to the mourners' bench. And oh, how Ruskin detested the pollution of land and water that surrounded Manchester (not of course by name)! Prince Albert, with his restraint, perhaps rubbed the same sensation into himself by looking at the water-colour view of Manchester that he had commissioned of William Wyld

---

[1] This composition had been prepared by many outline drawings with trial photographs cut and pasted in. The Queen's finished example has disappeared, but the Gernsheims tell me two others have been preserved.

[2] In the collected works of Ruskin the two lectures are called *A Joy Forever*.

[3] John D. Rosenberg, *The Darkening Glass*, 1961, p. 103. Clark, in *Ruskin Today* (1964, pp. 263–4), says, 'No doubt his sponsors expected a speech of congratulation on the prosperity and enlightenment of their city. Instead they got an attack on false values in Ruskin's best Socratic style. . . .

[4] *The Political Economy of Art*, 1857, p. 120.

in 1851 or 1852, in which chimneys smoke in the distance beyond a threatened lake.[1] If only the two men could have worked together.

Late in 1858 there was a move to hold in the Crystal Palace at Sydenham in 1861 an international fair which would have been the first in a series of decennial renewals of 1851. But South Kensington was preferred, and several considerations (probably among them the general financial crisis of 1857) combined to postpone the show to 1862. Cole, ever since the Manchester plans were realized, had wanted a great London show to stress the fine arts, including music; but by the middle of 1859 the emphasis (partly in memory of 1851 and partly because of the industrial sources of guarantee funds) came around to Arts and Industry jointly. There was quite as much of machinery, industrial products, and 'art manufactures' as in 1851, but there were also galleries of painting and sculpture (here Manchester had its effect, for the English school was heavy with Hogarth, Reynolds, and Lawrence). But Cole had, in the meantime, become rather controversial because of his bold methods,[2] and he kept as much out of sight as he could in the planning of the 1862 show.

No competition was held for the design of the building – a fact which caused some published complaint; but it was still a day of violent newspaper partisanship and great freedom to editorialize. As Fowke had been working on the site for some time, and his South Arcade was to be incorporated in the Exhibition building, there was logic in employing him. Paxton, now a Member of Parliament, was perhaps too busy with other interests (such as the design of the château of Ferrières for James de Rothschild) to be thought of for the new Exhibition; but he approved Fowke's design though he did not like the financing or contracting methods. Some lessons had been learned from the Crystal Palace, notably the lesson about trapped sun-heat combined with glare from above; this time the large glass areas were almost all in the form of a

---

[1] Reproduced in Randall Davies, *Victorian Watercolours at Windsor Castle*, 1937, pl. XV. Queen Victoria, describing the industrial landscape of the region in her diary on 14 October 1852, said, 'In the midst of so much wealth, there seems to be nothing but ruin. As far as the eye can reach, one sees nothing but chimneys, flaming furnaces, many deserted but not pulled down, with wretched cottages around them . . . a thick & black atmosphere. . . .'

[2] See page 84, note 1.

clerestory with opaque roofs. The chief display of glass as a sort of trade-mark was in two vast domes; these were at the east and west ends of a long central hall or nave where it met other elements of the building lying on north-south axes; these formed two large covered courts, the more southern of which was closed on its south side by brick pavilions intended as exhibition galleries for use by the Society of Arts after the end of the Exhibition itself.

All the rest, like the Crystal Palace, was prefabricated (to a twenty-five-foot module, one foot larger than the 1851 module); and it too was relocated much later, on the Alexandra Palace site. The whole rectangle with its contained courts took up the southern one-third of the Commissioners' central land, from the north side of Cromwell Road to a little north of the north side of Imperial Institute Road, with almost a million square feet under cover. The glazed buildings had a decent arcuated rhythm, and the 'permanent' brick ones were rather Dutch-eighteenth-century-looking, with mansard roofs punctuated by small shaped dormer-gables with bull's-eye windows; and there was also some resemblance to the side elevations of Duban's contemporary École des Beaux-Arts in Paris. Inside, the scale was, of course, colossal, but the colour was not the consistent 'functional' colour of Owen Jones and Semper; now it was the browns, blues, dark reds, light greens, and gold of the decorating house of Crace, following rather Renaissance patterns.[1]

It is impossible to say how different the Exhibition might have been if Prince Albert had not died on 14 December 1861. The man who received praise and blame was Cole, but while the Prince was alive he followed the preparations as closely as his endless and increasing labours allowed. Just after the opening, Lord Torrington wrote General Grey (who continued as secretary to the Queen) that mistakes had been made which the Prince would have foreseen and avoided: planks and brick-layers were still about here and there; the food was bad and expensive; Lord Granville was too amiable to be demanding; Cole had not been given quite enough authority, and the Prince was sorely missed;

---

[1] Betty Bradford 'The Brick Palace of 1862', in *Architectural Review*, vol. 132, July 1952, pp. 15–21; and *The International Exhibition of 1862*, catalogue of a memorial show at the Victoria and Albert Museum, 1962.

nevertheless, the opening was a success and the Exhibition was a better one than that of eleven years earlier.[1] *Punch* later complained that crinolines took up what floor space under the dome was left by the great ornamental trophies, and that what should have been a nice view of the Horticultural Society's gardens from the refreshment rooms was spoiled by a lot of tents put up for a flower show and never removed. The worst mistake, however, was the handbook; Francis Palgrave, compiler of the *Golden Treasury*, had written such a nice preface to the art section of the catalogue that the Commissioners asked him to prepare a handbook on the order of Tom Taylor's for Manchester; they failed to edit his manuscript which, when it appeared in print, contained inaccuracies and some very tactless criticism of Baron Marochetti and other sculptors. The star turn in sculpture at the Exhibition, by the way, and the 1862 equivalent to Powers' *Greek Slave,* was Gibson's *Tinted Venus*; and a milking machine was perhaps the equivalent to the reapers at the Crystal Palace.

The categories under which objects were catalogued were even more fussily hair-splitting than in 1851; they may reflect the Germanic taxonomy of Minutoli (see my appendix on his work); and *Punch* ridiculed them. From hindsight, two of the more important exhibits for the history of taste were a large group of Japanese prints (which are often said to have been shown first at Paris in 1867) and the entries of Morris, Marshall, Faulkner, and Co., William Morris's answer to the machine-made imitations of carved complexities which had dismayed him in 1851. It would be fair to say that some of the preachments of the South Kensington team had had an effect elsewhere: there was a certain amount of frankly archaeological imitation of approved examples out of the past, especially in ceramics, but there was also an improvement in over-all shapes, with fewer lumps and very little of those crashing contrasts of scale between pictures painted on porcelain and their ornamental surrounds, which had marked the show-pieces of 1851. The French thought the British had made great progress in ten years. The 'naturalistic' school of furniture design (carved, for instance, with twining ivy)[2] was coming to the fore in special or hand-made work,

---

[1] 4 May 1862; *Archives*, F. 27/149.

[2] Peter Floud, 'Furniture', in *Connoisseur Period Guide No. 6, The Early Victorian Period 1830–1860*, 1958, pp. 35-50.

and in serial production the shapeless completely-upholstered chair or sofa was being replaced by thinner upholstery on visible frames. There was plenty of both good and bad to come. Another interesting feature, repeatedly noticeable from about 1860 and especially in the catalogue of the 1862 Exhibition, may be in part a result of School of Design indoctrination: the outermost points of rather elaborately detailed things such as mirror frames lie in the line of a simple enclosing shape, not expressed but implied; however rich the curlicues, they will fall just within an invisible boundary, oval or lozenge-shaped or of some other simple silhouette, instead of straying anywhere. The Exhibition was followed by as many reports and lectures on its results as the Crystal Palace had been; best of all, probably, both Owen Jones and William Morris began to design wallpapers and send them to market.

Again there is an epilogue. Alfred Stevens was commissioned (by whose initiative I do not know) to design the certificate of award; his first drawing included at the base two cherubs carrying escutcheons, one with a V, the other with an A, the latter in shadow; and the cherub hiding his head on the other's shoulder. Someone thought this would be too shattering to the Queen (it is said by some that she herself saw the drawing, but I tend to doubt this); and Stevens modified his design for the final wood-engraving, which has a single cherub with VR on a shield.[1] It is one of his best and most original compositions, with something of Holbein as well as something of Raphael about it, but all Stevens's; and I like to think that the Queen would have accepted the original form, and that the Prince would have approved the quality as superior to that of the 1851 certificate.

---

[1] Both are reproduced by Hugh Stannus in *Drawings of Alfred Stevens*, n.d. but *c.* 1900, plates XXXIV and frontispiece.

13

Design, Intervention and Management

Prince Albert influenced a number of buildings besides those Crown or private royal dwellings with which he was directly concerned, and he designed or influenced a good many objects and events, among which might be especially mentioned some of the Queen's jewellery and the Duke of Wellington's funeral, as well as many concerts.

His minor buildings began with the mausoleum at Coburg for his father, who died early in 1844. The Prince and his brother Ernest II put Streib to work on the problem; there are Byzantine and Gothic designs signed W. Streib and dated from Paris 1844-6, still at Coburg; but even the octagonal shape was not settled until 1846, and the building on the Eckardtsberg was designed in the end from the brothers' suggestions by Eberhardt: a rather Italianate octagon with wings, which Queen Victoria described on 27 September 1860 as 'not at all gloomy'. There was also a project for an Ernst-Albert-Museum in Coburg; a plan and section, signed by Streib and dated 10 September 1845, also in the local archive, indicate that Prince Albert had something to do with the programme, which called for an *Antikensaal*, a *Münzencabinet*, and a *Bildergalerie*, all of a rather classic, even Pompeian, style, suggesting the Glyptothek in Munich, but with deep-toned wall surfaces. Nothing came of this plan, and the autographs, Coburg earthenware, and other gatherings of the brothers were merged in the Veste Coburg collections. The Mausoleum, however, undoubtedly influenced the style and shape of the one which Queen Victoria had Humbert build from Gruner's design for her husband and herself at Frogmore. The octagon and the fine marble floor particularly made themselves felt. The Coburg costs were shared by the widespread Coburg family.

As nice a contrast as one could find to these splendours are the model houses for working-class families which Prince Albert asked Henry Roberts (a pupil of the elder Smirke) to design as a contribution to the work of Lord Ashley's Society for Improving the Condition of the Labouring Classes. Ashley, who succeeded his father as Earl of Shaftesbury in the year of the Great Exhibition, had had the ear of the Prince for some time; and the latter had not only built many cottages at Windsor, Osborne, and Balmoral, but had interested himself in other groups with the same aims as Shaftesbury's. He had insisted, for instance, against Lord John Russell's advice, on presiding at the Labourers' Friends Society in May 1848, when it was supposed that any such meeting might end in revolutionary doings. The model houses, a pair of semi-detached ones, were built near the Crystal Palace in Knightsbridge, and another model building by Henry Roberts, smaller, was inside the Exhibition. The pair from Knightsbridge may still be seen at Kennington.[1] Hitchcock, with sound reason, remarks that 'it is probably just to attribute to Albert's own taste the unhappy combination of straw-coloured and red bricks, the unstructural flat-pointed arch that covers the entrance way, and the silly Jacobethan scallops that mask the flat roof. As always, Albert was a sounder patron of technical innovation than of advanced architectural design'.[2] The building was fire-proof, and had running water and a water-closet for each family. The flat roofs drained to the soil-line, and their hollow-brick shallow arches, tied by wrought-iron rods to cast-iron springers, were levelled with concrete and covered with 'patent metallic lava' such as had been used for the waterproofing of fountain basins at Osborne. The hollow bricks, patented by Roberts, were also used for the walls and everything but the foundations, which were solid brick; the hollow ones had one diagonally-cut end, and they could be used without special bedding as window-sills or water-tables. Heat could have been passed through them in the hypocaust way that had kept the Romans comfortable in Britain; but this was perhaps too much to expect.

The Prince was consulted about the design of St John's Church, Eton, in 1852, and about the remodelling of Edinburgh Castle in 1857; he also tried hard to persuade Eton College not to cover up with modern

---

[1] The Duchy of Lancaster owned much of Kennington and still does.

[2] *Early Victorian Architecture in Britain*, I, 42; illustrated in II, XIV, 14. The Prince had certainly read Edwin Chadwick's *Report on the Sanitary Conditions of the Labouring Population*, 1841; can he have read Engels's *Conditions of the Working Class in England*, 1845?

oak stalls the considerable remnants of medieval wall-painting in its chapel, which were not again revealed until this century. In the mid-fifties, possibly as part of his campaign to bring the National Gallery to South Kensington,[1] he took some part in a city-planning scheme for Westminster with the Sub-Dean; Westminster School was to be removed to the country, the Abbey was to be surrounded by a park, and a new street was to be cut from Buckingham Palace to the Abbey.[2] Earlier he had discussed with Peel the possibility of adding to the New Palace of Westminster a sort of Hall of Fame; 'in which to place monuments, etc., to distinguished men', says the Queen's diary on 15 March 1844; this would have kept further memorial encroachments out of the Abbey. Many of these ideas came to naught; one that took thirty years to reach fruition was the proposal to set up 'Cleopatra's Needle' in London, broached in a letter from the Prince to Lord John Russell on 20 January 1847.[3]

In 1855, the many concerns of the Prince with the new concentration of military strength at Aldershot, south and west of Windsor Great Park, resulted in the construction of a Royal Pavilion for use on reviews. This was not much more than a specialized barrack; a few years later he asked Fowke to design a building, which stands in use today close to the highway A.325, for the library of military history which the Prince gave to the Aldershot establishment. Fowke, whose skill in inexpensive building Paxton admired, and who was to build the 1862 Exhibition for as little as twopence a cubic foot, here looks rather underdone and dreary; but perhaps Aldershot was already as grim as it is now, and if so it may have affected him; his Prince Consort's Library was finished late in 1860. (Even drearier, perhaps, is the fate of the rather bad equestrian statue of Wellington by M. C. Wyatt which had been proposed for the top of the arch at Hyde Park Corner; it came to rest at Aldershot on a little mound in a ratty garden.)

---

[1] Rumours began to circulate in the middle of 1851 when a commission (including Eastlake, Westmacott, and Ewart) was appointed to consider possible sites for a new Gallery. In the autumn of 1853 Pennethorne drew plans for a Gallery in South Kensington or Kensington Gardens.

[2] Martin, ii, 304.

[3] Roger Fulford prints the letter in full in *The Prince Consort*, 1949, pp. 214–15. The clearing-out of supernumerary monuments from the Abbey has taken four times thirty years to reach fruition.

In his overworked late years the Prince spent a tremendous lot of time on another of the Duke's memorials, Wellington College, for which he chose Dr Benson (a future Archbishop of Canterbury) as first headmaster in 1859. Five years earlier he had begun looking for a site at Sandhurst and even at Epsom, and still earlier he had apparently fomented some architectural thinking, for the young Norman Shaw, then a pupil of Cockerell, took a prize at the Royal Academy school in 1853 for a plan which Hitchcock reproduces.[1] It was very monumental and Vanbrughian and, though not built, it may have influenced the eventual choice of the executed design by John Shaw II. When the site was marked out in December 1854, the Prince was anxious to have the chapel copied from Eton College Chapel, but he did not persist. The main group of the College, built 1856-9, was meant to look like the work of Wren, but with its separate tall pavilion roofs it looks suprisingly French, even a little like the Château d'Eu where the Queen and Prince had visited Louis Philippe years before.[2] The Queen's diary records whole days in 1857-9 spent by her husband on Wellington College business.

The rebuilding of Whippingham Church in Norman style I have mentioned in my chapter on Osborne. On balance, the Prince as a patron of architecture seems a thorough eclectic. It may not be surprising that when he died, *The Builder* (of which he had been a regular reader) came out with its front page in mourning leads; it did such honour to only one other man, Professor Cockerell.[3] But it is possible to trace in his building (with Balmoral III as an exception called for by a notion of what was suitable to Scotland) a diminution of romantic flavour and an increasing fineness of ornament.

In naval architecture, the Prince's interest in engineering and all problems of design must have led (in spite of his tendency to sea-sickness) to his involvement in the design of the successive royal yachts, but I find no real information about them, and only a few representations in the souvenir albums, which show them to have been suitably

---

[1] *Op. cit.,* II, X, 33.

[2] Hitchcock, *op. cit.,* I, 331–2; II, X, 34; Hitchcock remarks that Sandhurst, built soon after, has 'guts (*Victorianicè*, "go")'.

[3] Of course all the newspapers wore black, but *The Builder* was not a daily paper.

dashing in silhouette but rather uninteresting and retardataire as to their interiors.[1] The royal railway carriages, on the other hand, though they never in the Prince's lifetime achieved the convenience of a continuous side corridor, were the pinnacle of cushioned comfort, padded throughout for safety and quiet, and even rather chic.

The Queen loved jewellery; her husband designed some of the new settings into which she liked to put good stones old or new, and he often gave her jewellery in which we can find both his own taste and the general nineteenth-century taste for associations of precious and semi-precious stones, which lasted through the *art nouveau* style but now seems – what shall I say? – insufficiently rich. Dark blue enamel with pearls, a white enamel bracelet with emeralds in the centre, appear among the Prince's gifts; but he also gave his wife as a wedding present a large sapphire; later he designed her ornaments of turquoise with diamonds. His own favourite was the opal. He certainly designed the marvellous wreath with a matching brooch and earrings which he and the Duchess of Kent gave her at Christmas 1845 and for the wedding anniversary on 10 February 1846. The wreath has orange leaves of frosted gold, with white porcelain orange blossoms and tiny green enamel oranges: a highly special and luxurious example of the sort of thing commonly seen in the odd brooch with 'bloomed' or granulated gold. Not unlike this wreath in spirit is the porcelain frame by Mintons to the dressing-glass of the toilet service which the Prince gave the Queen in 1853 and which is still in her dressing-room at Osborne: angel figures support the glass, and the frame grows more complex and colourful as it rises to a crown at the top; but there is a restraint which spares one the feeling of fragility that china flowers often give.

The Prince, who intervened in the cutting of the Koh-i-noor, also designed the collar and star of the Order of the Star of India,[2] the Life Guards' helmets, a silver centrepiece for the Society of Arts, 1842

---

[1] The Prince, however, was inquisitive enough about anything excellent to make a thorough inspection of the *America*, which was sailed round from Cowes to Osborne for the purpose on 23 August 1851, the day after the Cup was won.

[2] The lotus, as a Buddhist symbol, was not welcome to Brahmins, and had to be changed; just as the Shah had to be provided with a Garter star without a cross.

(shown at the Society of Arts in 1849 and later at the Great Exhibition), and some other silver which I have mentioned as having too many ideas and not enough silverness. He composed two less successful headpieces, a military one which was laughed out of existence and a Wellington College one which was only abolished after many years when the Prince of Wales found it was mistaken for a railway cap; Albert Edward was always exacting about uniform.

The Prince Consort was always being consulted about such things as Morison's *Views of the Ducal Palaces and Hunting Seats of Saxe Coburg and Gotha*, a colour-plate book (also issued plain) of 1846 which was inspired by the royal visit to Coburg in 1845. He also suggested such designs as that of the certificate of award for the Exhibition of 1851, designed a gilt-latticed sleigh for the Queen, and perhaps designed the cradle which was made for the Princess Royal (carved in boxwood) and used by all his children.[1]

The fancy-dress balls which the Queen occasionally gave were sometimes arranged with charitable intent: at least one was meant to encourage the textile industry in hard times; not only the one that Lami designed and the one that Landseer recorded so far as the Royal couple's costumes were concerned, but others too, are recorded in the souvenir albums at Windsor. Many of these festivities have been shown to us in Helmut and Alison Gernsheim's excellent picture-book *Victoria R.* (1959). The appendix to the first volume of Martin's official biography of the Prince gives such full particulars of the concert programmes chosen by him that I need not rehearse them, except to say that he frequently introduced either to the Ancient Concerts or to the Philharmonic Society compositions old and new which had not been heard before in England, including works of Schubert, Mendelssohn, and Schumann.

The numerous comments on music in Queen Victoria's diary represent her own taste probably far more than her comments on visual

---

[1] There was also a less stately cradle, a seventeenth-century gilt one with the arms of Saxony, bought by the Prince in 1843 and believed to have belonged to Augustus the Strong; it appears in a Landseer portrait of Princess Alice, and is now at Kensington Palace. The boxwood cradle carved by Rogers is reproduced in both the official 1851 catalogue and the *Art Journal* one-volume catalogue.

art; so there is perhaps more to learn about the Prince from his choices than from any of the Queen's comments on performances. His programmes were almost always well-balanced; the most 'Victorian' one I have noticed is that of a band concert at Windsor on 2 October 1853: the overture to Auber's *Gustave*, Meyerbeer's 'Romance' from *Le Prophète*, a selection from Méhul's *Joseph*, an 'air de ballet' from Flotow's *Stradella*, and the Mendelssohn wedding march. In his last years the Prince encouraged a company which performed opera in English and English operas (it languished after his death).[1] We do find an occasional judgement of his: he wrote to his daughter, the Princess Royal, in 1860 that Glück's *Orfeo* was the 'poetry of drama' in contrast to the episodic Italian opera with its show-pieces and the modern *Geräusch* ('noise' – he may have meant Berlioz). He was fond of *Nun Danket*, 'O Isis and Osiris' from *The Magic Flute*, and his mother-in-law's dance and march tunes from the réveilles which were such a feature of birthdays and other anniversaries. His own *Te Deum*, the hymn tune *Gotha*, a setting of Morning Prayer, several anthems, and other compositions were of course much used, especially at christenings and weddings, for which he also designed special decorations (he liked to use a large *labarum* in flowers in the Buckingham Palace chapel). He and the Queen certainly heard as much good music as anyone but a fanatical concert-goer could have heard in their day. For private concerts they occasionally had oddities and prodigies; but such a prodigy as the young Joachim returned many times as he grew up. The royal children may have profited from some of these exposures; they were all taught to play instruments, but Prince Arthur was allowed his heart's desire, which was to have lessons in drumming (unconventional though military).

By far the most interesting of the productions in which the Prince took a leading part was the funeral of the Duke of Wellington, a *Gesamtkunstwerk* in the great tradition, though not without the follies and ridiculousnesses that such pomps beget. That great man must obviously have a funeral as fine as Nelson's; in the coloured aquatints published soon after the event there was plenty of information about Nelson's neo-Grec hearse and the procession. More recent state funerals must

---

[1] William Harrison and Louisa Pyne's English Opera Company; see G. M. Young, editor, *Early Victorian England*, 1934, II, p. 257.

also have been known to the Prince and his team from representations: for example, the ceremony in 1841 of the return of Napoleon's ashes from St Helena included a vast float with a dozen sculptured female figures upholding a coffin (this was even made into a wallpaper).[1] Jacques-Louis David's tall car for the *Triomphe du Peuple Français*,[2] however republican, may have offered a precedent; and Dr Ettlinger has demonstrated that Semper, who designed the Wellington funeral car, had an archaeologist's knowledge of the descriptions of Alexander the Great's funeral.[3]

The Duke died on 14 September 1852, and his burial in St Paul's took place on 18 November; everything except the funeral car was apparently settled by late October, Prince Albert having returned from Balmoral on the 14th.[4] He talked with Cole and Redgrave on the 22nd, and committed the design of the car to their Department; but Semper and his students worked until the last minute available, and their construction was assembled in an imperfect state, so that it threatened to collapse during the long procession from Chelsea Hospital to the Horse Guards, then past Buckingham Palace and St James's to the Strand and the City. The Duke's lying-in-state at Chelsea Hospital had been committed by the Prince to Professor Cockerell, who designed a handsome setting of black-hung walls, a silver canopy over the coffin which had a red velvet pall, and gigantic candelabra alternating with Yeomen of the Guard. The Duke's orders and field-marshals' bâtons were disposed on black velvet cushions; but his son Lord Charles Wellesley did not like these doings, and wrote to Angela Burdett-Coutts on 11 November, '. . . you will not be pleased with the arrangements there, the effect tawdry, and the decorations (foreign orders I mean) are made quite subordinate to the gewgaws of the Heralds and Ld. Chamberlain's department'.

---

[1] Reproduced in *Antiques*, September 1960, p. 260.

[2] David L. Dowd, 'Art and the Theatre during the French Revolution: the Rôle of J. -L. David', in *Art Quarterly*, XXIII, No. 1, spring 1960, pp. 3–22.

[3] Leopold D. Ettlinger, 'The Duke of Wellington's Funeral Car', in *Journal of the Warburg and Courtauld Institutes*, III, 1939/40, pp. 254–9.

[4] He would have had time, meanwhile, to recall the dramatic funeral of Marie of Württemberg, which he attended in Pisa Cathedral (letter to Florschütz, 7 January 1839; *Archives*, Add'l. MSS. A/6; translation in Add'l. MSS. 7.

For St Paul's, Redgrave designed six great candelabra of a plausible high-Renaissance sort, over seven feet tall, in fibrous plaster on a wooden core, and with some wooden details, all painted as bronze. That they were better designed and made than the funeral car is demonstrated by the fact that it was possible to use some of them at the funeral of Sir Winston Churchill in 1965.[1]

As to the car, it was twenty-seven feet long, ten broad, and seventeen tall: quite a machine for twelve horses to draw, with its Empire-style podium topped by a bier with projecting poles and then a coffin with cocked hat and sword. Redgrave made a preliminary design and Semper a final one from which the undertakers and Semper's students (who did the ornaments and lettering) worked. The ubiquitous John Thomas did the coats-of-arms. Dickens, who liked the military part of the funeral, thought that 'for forms of ugliness, horrible combinations of colour, hideous motion, and general failure, there was never such a work achieved as the Car'.[2] Dickens hated undertakers and was not fond of Prince Albert, who rode alone in a modest carriage in the procession.

Yet to the Queen, who adored the old Duke, the Car looked as Redgrave and Semper and the Prince would have wished it to look. Having seen it pass, she later drew in her diary a memory image of it, all clouds of glory. Let us leave it at that except for a word about the music. It included Spohr's funeral march from *Weihe der Thöne*, the familiar 'Dead March' by Handel from *Saul*, and some of the burial-service music by William Croft. For the actual committal,[3] the Prince passed over Purcell's music written for the funeral of Mary II (1694) and Croft's and Parsons', choosing the oldest music to the burial service in English, Thomas Morley's setting of the 1559 Prayer Book. This music of about

---

[1] They were overhauled in 1960, a steel core inserted, and the arms replaced by a single candle-socket.

[2] Edgar Johnson, *Charles Dickens*, 1952, II, p. 756.

[3] To light the ceremony, gas jets were introduced into St Paul's: 'One line of diamonds', wrote Lady Eastlake the next day, 'round the Whispering Gallery and outlining the whole cornice of the building, was very successful.' She though the lying-in-state 'somewhat insincere', but liked all the rest. It may be worth adding that the Churchill funeral showed not only a careful study of the Nelson and Wellington funerals but also Sir Winston's own witty use of his remembrance of the old French song about the burial of his forebear the first Duke of Marlborough.

1620 had perhaps last been used complete at the funeral of George II.[1] What moved the Prince most in St Paul's, however, was the anthem *And the King Said* by John Goss, organist of the cathedral, whom the Queen later knighted. It is worth mention here that Prince Albert also loved Haydn's *Seven Last Words*, the Mozart *Requiem*, and *Elijah*.

What the Queen called 'his greatest amusement and delight' was the print-room of the Royal Library, and the work which took him there most often was the compilation of a corpus of the works of Raphael, based upon Passavant's book of 1839. Ludwig Gruner had done much engraving of Raphael and his school, especially in his work on the decorations of the Vatican. Woodburn's facsimiles of Raphael drawings from Sir Thomas Lawrence's collection had appeared in 1841, and there were older 'imitations of drawings', such as Rogers' and Chamberlayne's and Young Ottley's. With these and any and all engravings after Raphael's paintings, the Prince and Dr Carl Ruland began a systematic illustration of the *œuvre*, ordering photographs of the originals whenever it was possible to have them made. From 1853 they worked steadily whenever the Prince was at Windsor; and after his death the Queen asked Ruland to continue. The resulting book, privately published in 1876, was the best thing in its field until Fischel's appeared. The great value of the Windsor Raphael corpus – in addition to its pioneer status as art-history illustrated by photography – is its inclusion of all compositions *connected* with Raphael's name, however loosely. In time, of course, photography replaced engraving completely. An interesting part of the Prince's campaign was undertaken in 1859: while the Oxford University Galleries were under repair, the Raphael drawings (the largest group in the world) were lent to the Department of Science and Art, and at South Kensington they were all photographed for the use of the Prince and Ruland and of J. C. Robinson, whose *Critical Account of the Drawings by Michel Angelo and Raffaelo in the University Galleries* (1870) was another of the accomplishments of that sound member of the Cole team. The almost solitary work of the Raphael corpus, though it was again an example of that visual order which

---

[1] Morley's music was published complete in the same year (1760) in *Cathedral Music I*, edited by William Boyce. John E. Uhler, 'Thomas Morley and the First Music for the English Burial Service', in *Renaissance News*, IX, No. 3, autumn 1956, pp. 144–6.

Prince Albert always sought, must have come close to his solitary organ-playing as an escape from politics.

Though I can offer no emendation in matters of music or mere sound, I want to try to interpret a little the look of certain Victorian objects as we now think they looked. Certainly Berlioz does not sound to us as he sounded to Queen Victoria, just as much of Ruskin's social programme, which seemed revolutionary to his time, is now taken for granted. We know that the mid-nineteenth century saw the eighteenth century not at all as we see it; and it is a wonder that Ingres's or Delaroche's views of the costume of Paolo and Francesca or of Henri IV do not seem to us almost as ludicrous as the 'troubadour' get-ups of French romantic music-covers or the misunderstood seventeenth-century costumes in which the staffage figures of *Mansions of England in the Olden Time* wandered about. In such cases and in many others where we believe that we understand historic costume better than they did in the 1850s, we almost unconsciously apply charitable correctives (which we may need ourselves in future). Cats looked very different to eighteenth-century and to nineteenth-century printmakers; a rose in a French woodcut *cul-de-lampe* of 1775 is not the rose that early nineteenth-century aquatinters or mid-century chintz-designers saw.

One reason why we have tended to think ill of some decent average exhibits of 1851 (not only of the horrendous show-pieces) is that we have to see most of them through the not very good woodcuts hastily prepared for the official catalogue of the Great Exhibition. The wood-engravers employed for those three volumes and for the one-volume *Art Journal Illustrated Catalogue* were not the very fine craftsmen of Gruner's shop, still less those who were to be the glory of the establishments of the Dalziel in the sixties, the great era of British illustration. The 1851 cuts were, in many cases, frankly ungainly. By 1862 the technique available for such reproduction woodcuts had, to judge by the catalogue of that year's Exhibition, greatly improved; but they were still subject to the engraver's own misunderstanding or misinterpretation of a drawing or photograph. And although the *Art Journal* cuts were often better than the official catalogue's, if we compare its cuts (p. 206) of Osler's glass candelabrum for Osborne with a good photographic halftone (see my pl. 15), we find that the wood-engraver gave almost no notion of the brilliance of that *tour de force*.

The steel-faced engravings, prepared more slowly and carefully than the usually journalistic woodcut, in such a periodical as the *Art Journal,* often gave fuller information. Prince Albert (as we shall see) came to depend upon them as a way of spreading information about works of art in his own or his wife's collection.

14

Prince Albert's Taste

In the early years of her marriage, Queen Victoria's diary often portrayed her husband as battling against bad contemporary British taste. That she was not a detached observer we already know; aside from the question, 'Whence did she get this idea?' there is the problem of what taste he was combatting and what taste he recommended as a replacement.

The Queen also described the Prince's taste more than once as inherited from his father. Ernest I's taste is clear from the watercolours of his interiors: it was based in the classic elegancies of Goethe, but brought up to date by Empire styles in furniture, and slightly romanticized by the buildings which the Duke inherited; – a simple, rather severe taste that makes one feel a little better about him, a taste with a few whims of colour or scale but without the coarseness, even the suggestion of cruelty, that one might expect. His son's taste is not so easy to wrap up in a package.

Much of this book will, I hope, have allowed answers to the above questions to be read between the lines. Much remains unspecifiable because Prince Albert did not devote himself to leading fashion as the Duchess of Sutherland did; nor did he choose the nation's great works of art, for this task was in the good hands of Eastlake during much of the Prince's most active period as a mediator and popularizer. His great creations were his wife as an admirable monarch; the modern sort of art museum; and the notion that art and science could and should both be applied to products of industry.

It may be significant that, despite his efforts to correct his wife's hot temper, one of his own favourite portraits of her was the oval Winterhalter one with loose hair and half-opened lips, in which she is lovely and a little willful, not the Queen as he made her, but the natural Victoria. Because he understood her so well, the correctives which he applied probably made her too dependent upon him; for this, with his death, there was no remedy and, sad to say, the Government waited five or six years before it provided her with so much as additional secretarial help to take the place of the Prince who had drafted her letters.

'This most kind, eccentric, infallible, and unfathomable German', as Henry Dunckley called him,[1] was a man whose great capacities (all used to the full) included tremendous powers of absorption or reception. He had a corresponding need to put out what he took in. This putting-out he did largely in the form of work; he was intolerant of unproductive activity and, though he was willing to amuse himself with whist, shooting, complex pencil-and-paper games, deer-stalking, play with his children, and other recreations, his attention span was short except when he was truly on holiday at Balmoral. He was a good shot, but he thought shooting was an amusement for a few hours, not all day. He probably needed to be able to shift from one activity to another; because of his classifying mind, he fortunately could shift easily. In small matters he often became impatient, as did his son Edward VII; and he was certainly a 'worrier', but he did not soak himself in a mood as his wife did. By the same token, he had not her English and 'Victorian' capacity to enjoy his sensations frankly, but he was enough a man of his time to like what was obviously well made, and to feel that work, and evidence of work in a work of art, were desirable. Just as an art to conceal art was too sophisticated an idea for an increasingly materialist society in a period of optimistic outreach, so an art for art's sake was too irresponsible an idea for a man of Prince Albert's purpose and control. He would not have believed with Ruskin that 'Taste is the only morality'.[2]

He always liked *belle facture*. If we look at some of his choices – say the Gozzoli, the Wyatt *Penelope*, the Osler candelabra, the Darnley Jewel, the orange-blossom wreath, the Parentino, the Audience Chamber

---

[1] 'Verax', *The Crown and the Cabinet*, 1878, p. 14. Dunckley was a Manchester Liberal who was reviewing the first three volumes of Martin's *The Life of His Royal Highness the Prince Consort;* he argued that the publication was a political act, provocatively meant in foreign affairs; and that the Prince had been a meddler.

[2] Quoted without source by J. H. Buckley in *The Victorian Temper*, 1951, p. vii, but see page 31, note 1.

at Windsor, the Maclises at Westminster, the seventeenth-century Saxon cradle – we see well-made things. He liked to see that an artist had taken trouble and presumably pride in his work. If we look at his own most intimate rooms, his dressing and sitting rooms, we see furniture severely arranged, pictures symmetrically hung, the portable chairs very light, the work-table encumbered only by reference books, the ornaments few and usually concentrated on the chimneypiece or on the flat top of a cylinder desk. At Buckingham Palace the Prince used for years a fine ormolu-mounted and galleried table in George IV's palace style, and a modest Empire bookcase with blue silk stretched in the doors. His Windsor dressing room had a superb early eighteenth-century silver kettle for hot water on a matching silver tripod. He almost always used slip-covers in small blue and white patterns; the furniture he bought for private rooms at Osborne was rosewood and chintz.

He was not a dandy, nor yet consistently odd and personal in his clothes like the Duke of Wellington; he was a careful man who liked an occasional lively touch. He wore with evident pleasure the fancy waist-coats his mother-in-law gave him; but he always wore straps to keep his trousers stretched (it is on record that Abraham Lincoln often left his trouser-straps undone). There are some colourful glimpses in the Queen's diary: Prince Albert at Osborne in 1846 using a red silk handkerchief; at Balmoral in 1847 in a kilt of the Royal Stuart tartan and a green doublet, with the Garter used as a real garter; shooting at Windsor in 1848 in a black velvet jacket and high red leather boots. He wore uniform well, even when he had begun to grow heavy. He was graceful in motion as the Queen was; in his later years, when he probably did not exercise as much as in his youth, he ran rather than walked when going about the house – and although he ran because of haste and pressure of work, the running shows a sort of balance as well as a sort of desperation. In many ways he makes one think of the modern executive who is a good organizer of staff but who keeps long hours, works and plays hard, and dies of a heart attack in his prime because his company pushes him as much as he pushes himself.

In the end, the Queen concluded that he had not the will to live. Three years earlier (5 November 1858) she described him as 'so terribly busy and troubled, he really fags himself too much'. Yet at Balmoral on 10 October 1859 she said he was 'never cross or disappointed' though he sometimes came in 'dead beat'. At least when he was deer-stalking he did not run into criticism, which was what really disappointed and dismayed him. In his speech to the Royal Academy annual dinner on 3 May 1851[1] he remarked on the need for criticism in the arts, but added that an unkind word and injudicious praise of the undeserving were equally bad. Even after many years in Great Britain he remained sensitive; on 23 January 1854 the Queen noted that 'attacks on Albert (which are fast disappearing) have the result of making him afraid to do what I should think to be right'; and on 23 October 1855 her diary mentions a discussion of 'the lack of talent & genius of our age, which Albert attributed to the baneful & depressing spirit of criticism, which is the misfortune of this country, – & which people should *not* yield to'.

He would utter criticism privately, as when on 6 May 1852, having gone 'to hear the Choirs from the different Cathedrals, sing at Westminster Abbey, he said nothing could have been worse'. But most of his criticism – and this again in a small circle – was expressed in mimicry, for which he had a great gift. Along with this went his fondness for caricature; he sometimes drew comic portraits, and he made a great collection. 'If you want to know what public men are like', Martin quotes him as saying, 'you must study the caricatures of their day'.[2] Unhappily, the Prince's sense of humour never was visible in the outer world. Dunckley[3] says,

'All the gaiety of heart which the Prince could spare from his domestic circle broke out in his letter to the Baron [Stockmar]. . . If he had treated the English gentlemen whom he met on business or in society with one-half of the gushing amiability which he lavished on the German recluse he would have been the most popular man in the realm, instead of being, as he was, intensely disliked'.

Without having that passion for privacy which marked the Queen, Prince Albert nevertheless was at his best in a small group and among

---

[1] Martin, ii, 372–3. Steegman, in *Consort of Taste*, 1950, pp. 321–2, gives an excellent analysis of the speech.

[2] Martin, ii, 298, note.

[3] 'Verax', *op. cit.*, p. 26.

people whom he could respect for their accomplishments. As I have said earlier, his secretaries, his friends in government, his South Kensington team, and all with whom he worked closely, were shattered by his death, two days after which Granville wrote to Canning, 'The most valuable life in this country has been taken.' Lady Eastlake's long memoir says, 'No artist employed in the works of the Commission, ever approached the Prince without recognizing a clearness of perception, regarding the purposes and principles of art, which contrasted curiously and refreshingly with the vague, and often false conventionalities to which the votary of art is generally doomed to be a listener'.[1]

With all this understanding, what was the Prince's taste? He liked not only the well-made and the meaningful, but also rather hard finishes and what we should now call easily-maintained surfaces. The works of art which he bought for the Queen or himself were primarily for their pleasure, as works of art bought by individuals should be; they must be differentiated both from the objects bought under his influence for the nation, and from his own great work in South Kensington; that was for the public pleasure but also for public improvement. The concept and direction of that work, never forgetting Cole's part, and not omitting possible contact with Minutoli, were as unprecedented and as successful as those of any other nineteenth-century *Gesamtkunstwerk* of distinction: they might be compared to the composition and direction of a symphony, with Cole as *Konzertmeister*. What is especially remarkable about the Museum is that the acquisitions made during the Prince's lifetime were so good, though they were in a sense chosen by a committee – and it is never wise to send a committee to choose works of art. The leading spirit really led.

Oddly, he was following, not leading, in his patronage of Landseer; but the real leadership in patronage of living British artists had passed at about the time of Thomas Lawrence's death (1830) to 'unheard-of' provincial collectors such as Vernon and Sheepshanks – and this in the end was good for the nation. The success of Winterhalter was certainly promoted by Royal employment. A few exceptions such as the Frith, almost a pioneer example of *contemporary* (not literary) genre-made-monumental, or the Dyce fresco and Dyce *Madonna* at Osborne, or the

---

[1] *Quarterly Review*, January 1862, p. 171.

unusually good and uncluttered John Martin, show that Prince Albert was not bogged down in what we tend still to think of as the drears of Victorian painting. It was in the active and persistent buying – and hanging for personal enjoyment at Osborne and elsewhere – of Gentile da Fabriano and Cranach and those early Florentines who were then lumped under the name of Orcagna, that the Prince was ahead of his time. In actual buying he was well ahead of Eastlake, although Eastlake travelled repeatedly in Italy and had opportunities on the spot which were denied the Prince. For many Italian acquisitions, as for his institutional doings, he had to depend on staff; as an expert chooser of personnel he could and did depend on Gruner and others; we do not need to know what he rejected from among Gruner's or Metzger's or Warner Ottley's offerings to see how good his acceptances were.

His persistence – even though it has been called meddling and officiousness – supported Eastlake and the National Gallery, which in its first thirty years was often in precarious standing;[1] and of course substantially created the South Kensington institution, whose stature increased so rapidly that Members of Parliament were alarmed and Frenchmen could speak of the three museums of London (the Gallery and the British Museum being the others).[2] It was probably due to the Prince's classifying mind, which was nimble enough to skip across categories, that many fine ceramic objects which belonged to the Geological Museum in Jermyn Street (as *Verarbeitungen mineralischer Stoffe?*) wound up as works of art in South Kensington.

In forwarding great enterprises, he was skillful at finding the opportunity to make the points that seemed to him of first importance, but most of the occasions were private; the public ones were carefully chosen, for as a promoter of institutions he liked to use institutions

---

[1] It was not until 27 March 1855 that a Treasury Minute defined the relationship of the Director to the Trustees, set up a regular purchasing fund, and provided for a responsible and resident Keeper. The old upper-class attitude to such undertakings may be represented by Lord Althorp, Chancellor of the Exchequer in the early thirties, who despite his help in driving the Reform Bill through the House of Commons, said that if he had his way he would sell the National Gallery and have nothing of the kind.

[2] H. de Triqueti, *Les Trois Musées de Londres*, Paris, 1861. Mulready once said that in his youth a student could see old masters only at the exhibits in the British Institution and in the auction room.

67. Franz Xaver Winterhalter: *The Prince Consort*, 1859; canvas, 7 ft 11 in. ×
5 ft 2 in.; commissioned by the Queen

68. Daniel Maclise: *The Meeting of Wellington and Blücher* (detail)

69. Daniel Maclise: *The Death of Nelson* (detail)

70. F. W. Sperling: *Imaum*; watercolour, about 1846; commissioned by Prince Albert

71. John F. Herring, senior: *Said*; canvas, 1 ft 10 in. × 2 ft 6 in., signed and dated 1856; gift of the Queen to Prince Albert, Christmas 1856

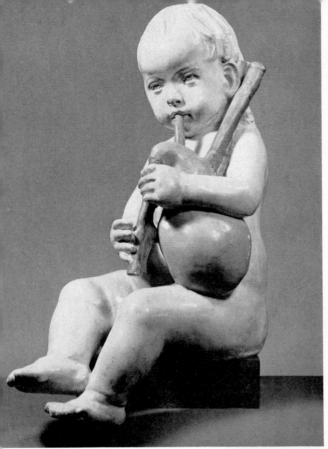

72. Andrea della Robbia: *Cherub with a Bagpipe*; glazed terracota; gift of Prince Albert to the South Kensington Museum, 1858

73. *Venus Anadyomene*; marble, 4 ft 5¾ in., found in the baths of Caracalla; bought by Queen Victoria from the Duke of Buckingham's collection, 1848, and given to the Prince on 28 August

74. Alfred Stevens: *Model for prize medal* for the Department of Science and Art; wax, 1856

75. John Thomas: *St Eustace* or *St Hubert*; stone relief, 1856

76. A. W. N. Pugin: *Chalice*; silver-gilt, with enamel and cabochon stones, executed by Hardmans of Manchester, 1850–1

77. Billiard table, designed by Prince Albert and made by Thurstons, 1846–7

78. *Refreshment Rooms* (part of the Arcades) *from the east dome of the Exhibition of 1862*, photograph taken 16 December 1861

79. *View across the Royal Horticultural Society's Gardens to the east dome of the Exhibition of 1862*, photograph taken probably in October 1861

80. *South-east corner of buildings for the Exhibition of 1862*, photograph taken 19 December 1861

that were rising; thus, for instance, he chose the laying of the first stone of the Midland Institute in Birmingham for an important speech on the application of science and art to productive industry. A promising organization was most pleasing when it occupied a fine building, such as St George's Hall in Liverpool; Queen Victoria's diary for 9 October 1851 says, 'Albert was delighted. He never really admires what is small in purpose and design, and frittered away in detail'. Birmingham, Manchester, Liverpool, or the National Gallery of Scotland – these were as important places for outreach as London, in some ways more important because they were not so subject to the heavy hand of the old upper class. 'Truth to say, the "Swells", as a class, did not much like the P[rince] and still less, do they like Lectures and Concerts', wrote Lord Henry Lennox to Cole.[1] Nor did they like his understanding of machines, which they on the whole did not want to understand, so long as they produced income. And they did not observe that the understanding of machines and the feeling for institutions of complex structure came from the same instinctive perceptions of balance and space and kinetic relationships that make a man a good dancer or fencer or swimmer.

One of the Prince's most ingenious tastemaking devices was the use of the *Art Journal* after 1854 as a place for publishing objects from the Royal collection. The *Art Journal* under S. C. Hall's proprietorship had become well disposed toward him even when it was battling Cole in the days of Cole's *Journal of Design;* and during the last seven years of the Prince's life a systematic publication of the Queen's pictures ancient and modern was carried on – about two dozen per year, engraved and provided with comment in letterpress. A few pieces of sculpture from the Queen's and Prince's acquisitions were also reproduced. The large circulation of the *Art Journal* guaranteed what nowadays we should describe as a large exposure, and produced a considerably effect.

The *Illustrated London News* regularly carried a good deal of intelligence about the current art world, but its woodcuts were not nearly as good as the *Art Journal*'s engravings, and there is no feeling of a working relationship such as one gets from the steady publication in the *Journal*

---

[1] 14 October 1862; Cole papers, Victoria and Albert Museum, box 5.

even though the *News* occasionally carried cuts of Royal acquisitions.

In spite of Prince Albert's apparent stiffness and sobriety, his lack of interest in beauty-for-its-own-sake, his moral endeavour, he was yet entirely capable of delight, especially when temporary freedom from routine burdens gave him time. This of course was the case when he and the Queen travelled. St George's Hall, the picture galleries at Antwerp (where he pointed out early and late Rubenses but was just as pleased with modern Belgian artists as the Queen was with the varieties of nuns' habits in Bruges), the treasures of Castle Howard and Chatsworth, all 'enchanted' him. In 1860 he delayed the Queen and their schedule by taking his Prussian son-in-law Fritz to see the beauties of the Bishop's Palace at Würzburg (including no doubt the Tiepolo rooms).

The great came to realize that the Prince knew and enjoyed works of art, and others besides Peel began to take trouble about him. It was natural to refurbish if the Queen came to visit; a very fine eighteenth-century pier-glass was regilded and sent from another Atholl house,[1] for instance, when the Queen and Prince visited Blair Castle in September 1844; and the Duke of Bedford was careful to hang a Hayter, a Landseer, and an Eastlake in their rooms at Woburn Abbey in July 1841. But it was not until after the Duchess of Sutherland (who had means, motive, and opportunity) added a whole modern wing to Dunrobin Castle above the Moray Firth to receive them in 1846 that the Prince's taste seems to have been observed in this way. Thereafter there are many examples, which the Queen well understood as testimonies. I shall name only a few of the latest.

In June 1858 she and the Prince were at Birmingham and lunched at Aston Hall, a noble house of 1618-35 which had been threatened with destruction in 1857 and 'to obtain which, the working classes have worked very hard & subscribed very largely'; the rescue, an early case of that kind of good effort by a large public acting almost spontaneously, was deserving of Royal approval. 'Many fine old pictures had been lent',

---

[1] George Cole had made it in Golden Square in London in white and gold in Chippendale's *Director* style; it left Dunkeld for Blair Castle, and is still there; Anthony Coleridge, 'Chippendale, the Director, and some Cabinet-Makers at Blair Castle', in *The Connoisseur*, January 1961, pp. 252–6.

wrote the Queen, and Elkingtons' plate was used on the lunch table: a good mixture.[1] When the Prince went alone to open the Manchester Exhibition in May 1857 he stayed at Abney Hall, Cheshire, which he described to his wife as 'magnificent'; it was a neo-Gothic house decorated by Crace. The Prince's bedroom[2] was dressed with a damask-like wallpaper, a neo-Gothic half-tester bed, and an ingrain carpet; the white marble chimneypiece had a Gothic cast-iron grate, and there was the usual stuffed sofa with armchairs to match; but there were also two very good late Sheraton chairs. A day or two before the Birmingham visit, the couple had spent a night at Stoneleigh Abbey near Kenilworth. Lord Leigh, whose house by Francis Smith of Warwick had wonderful Georgian stucco interiors, redecorated a series of rooms for them which delighted both. Fine Chippendale furniture in their bed- and dressing-rooms was painted white and gold for the occasion; the Prince's dressing-room contained an Austrian baroque bed, said to have belonged to Napoleon's Marie Louise, and the 'Christopher Columbus' table from the Crystal Palace. The charming breakfast room had and still has a wallpaper of jays and other birds among passion-flower vines, and the Minton ceramic jambs to the fire-place echo this motive. 'Very handsome and well done', wrote the Queen on 14 June 1858; and so the Prince must have thought. The next day at Kenilworth, when the weather was hot, the Queen who had seen Kenilworth before did not get out of their carriage; the Prince did, and that was the difference between them.

The Prince's broad effort to persuade industry to take art as well as science into partnership was sometimes hampered by that independence of spirit and character in the factory-owner which expressed itself by brooking no interference from London, and also hampered by a general misreading of some of the functions of machinery. It was a marvel that the machine could reproduce easily the work of hands; this marvel blinded all but a few to the fact that mechanical reproduction of both the perfections and the imperfections of handwork became unbearable. Further, admiration for what the often beautiful unadorned

[1] Diary, 14 June 1858.
[2] Reproduced by Elizabeth Aslin in *19th Century English Furniture*, 1962, pl. 73.

early machines could do was not followed until years later by admiration for the new beauties of the machines themselves;[1] and in the meantime those machines began to be smothered in ornamental costumes cribbed from anywhere – costume from which they were not freed until well into the twentieth century in most cases. The whole South Kensington complex and its spiritual descendants helped in that freeing. Who shall say that the best modern industrial design is not in its way another memorial of Prince Albert?

The Prince who, when he was not in uniform or full dress, always wore the riband of the Garter inconspicuously under his waistcoat, was a man who would rather have been missed than noticed. Let that be a new epitaph for him.

---

[1] Washington Allston was one of the exceptions.

15

British Tastes after 1861

Although it would be improper to suggest that *post hoc, ergo propter hoc*, it would be wise to try to assess the share which the Prince Consort and his team and apparatus had in the trend of British taste after his death. It might be still wiser to make no overt claim, but to give some material from which inferences may be drawn. In offering such material, I am aware that it is as much a question of opinion as the formulations in my chapter on *British Tastes in 1840*.

The effect of the Prince's 'tastemaking' was felt at different levels in different areas. The general shape and style of an Osborne or a Balmoral could be disseminated by publication of all sorts; and although those houses were private and were not meant by either Queen or Prince as trial balloons or demonstrations, in fact they were influential beyond any of the works intended as examples, such as the workmen's housing. The knowledge of Royal patronage of particular artists was less widely spread, but it affected many collectors and all who read newspapers, as well as the community of artists. Acquaintance with actual Royal choices (at a time when the best illustrated papers gave but a thin notion of what was reproduced by wood-engraving)[1] was limited. Beyond the court circle and the South Kensington group, any influence of these choices was delayed or indirect. South Kensington's influence was the direct and powerful one (a manufacturer of cast-iron stoves advertised

---

[1] The decade of the fifties saw great improvement both in the quality of the drawings made for *Punch*, the *Illustrated London News*, and other weeklies, and in the technique of wood-engraving. Gleeson White, *English Illustration/ The Sixties: 1855–1870*, 1906. Not that Tenniel and Leech were not already fine by 1850; but of their like and the rising firm of Dalziell much finer was built. See also my comments in chapter 14 on the *Art Journal* for relative quality. Compare the reproductions in *I.L.N.* (wood-engraving) and *Art Journal* (engraving) of the *Letterwriter of Seville* by John Phillip.

in the late fifties that his heating apparatus was used in two cathedrals and the Museum).

The influence of the Raphael corpus was of course not felt until after Ruland published in 1876. But, if the court taste at the beginning of the Queen's reign was ten years or more behind the times, it was by the end of 1861 sufficiently caught up with the general taste in most respects to provoke reactions not only from *Punch* but from such conscious tastemaking quarters as Ruskin's; and in other respects, as we have seen, it was in the lead. It was, then, a positive taste, perhaps most in the lead where least consciously so. It should always be borne in mind, however, that Prince Albert's taste was generally that of the just popularizer, not that of the man of flair or the uninhibited inventor. It was necessary to make reasonably sure in advance that Royalty should not be associated with a failure.

Several historians, notably Nikolaus Pevsner, have tended to shorten (without further specification) the early Victorian period, and to consider the high Victorian to have been perfectly defined by the time of the Exhibition of 1851. It may be too late to modify their classification, but a more nearly even division into early, high, and late Victorian might better recognize the sixty-three years of the Queen's reign if not the existence of her husband. The slow change of style from about 1815 to about 1840 has already been remarked; Hitchcock makes a clear case for a distinct change about 1860; 1830-60 or 1840-60 might well be called 'early Victorian'.

The Great Exhibition did a great deal of harm by causing complex mechanically carved work and woven pictures to be admired by a large public;[1] it also did a deal of good in facilitating the creation of the bureau of standards which South Kensington became (*pace* Quentin Bell, who sees Henry Cole as essentially a bureaucrat if not a dictator)[2] But it does not seem to me that 1851 is a point of maturity, any more than Butterfield's All Saints' Church, Margaret Street, is the crest of

---

[1] Mrs Gaskell in *North and South* (1855) described post-Crystal-Palace furnishing as of an 'icy, snowy discomfort', having a 'painfully spotted, spangled, speckled look'; quoted by Francis D. Klingender in *Art and the Industrial Revolution*, 1947, p. 121. As she was writing for Dickens, she may have allowed Dickensian prejudices full sway; but she had a point.

[2] *The Schools of Design*, 1963.

the high Victorian (there is a difference between becoming and being).

As my chapter *1857 and 1862* suggests, the Exhibition of 1862 represents better than that of 1851 the end of the 'battle of styles' and the consolidation, in almost all areas of design, of an unmistakable Victorianness and Englishness. By that time, Hitchcock's 'High Victorian', the developed and comparatively homogeneous style of Butterfield, G. G. Scott, Street, and E. M. Barry, was in full view and was being emulated widely. In the Exhibition of 1862 there appeared not only the showing of Morris & Co. (Morris himself as a younger man having been dismayed by the industrial horrors of 1851) but also a bookcase-aedicule by R. Norman Shaw in the style soon to be called 'Eastlake' from the illustrations in the younger C. L. Eastlake's *Hints on Household Taste* (1869, first American edition 1872); Norman Shaw seldom again designed in the Eastlake style, his own later styles were plural and 'prettier', and they appealed to more than one of the tastes I am about to classify. It could be argued, I think, that from the early sixties to the time of obvious *fin-de-siècle* manifestations there were three sorts of taste, which I shall call Donnish, Parvenu, and Sincere. They represent regroupings of the sorts of people whose taste in about 1840 I called Grec, Lusso, and Olden Time; the boundaries of a taste did not coincide with those of a particular style.

The taste which I call Donnish was a taste for correctness in an historical or archaeological sense, to some extent a taste for the correct in terms of function or sanction (the Ecclesiologists began after all at Cambridge, that scientifically-oriented university, not at Oxford); but not for correctness on arbitrary grounds à la Lord Melbourne; there was always a reason given. The Donnish taste contained obviously an intellectual (or as Mr Lynes would call it, a highbrow) element from the Grec taste of (dare I say?) 1808-48.[1] There was also an element of a

---

[1] 1808 for the date of Hope's and the London Chair Makers' publications of 'Grecian' furniture; 1848 for a débâcle that changed many things. One of the last pieces of full-dress Grec was the exhibit of the King of Sardinia (Victor Emmanuel) at the Crystal Palace: a very handsome and luxurious *klismos* and a table inlaid in ebony and ivory are reproduced in the *Art-Union Illustrated Catalogue*, p. 323; but Victor Emmanuel survived 1848 with credit and might be allowed to be old-style in taste even when he was beginning to be advised by Cavour.

merely romantic sort from the Olden-Time taste; but by 1860 or there-abouts the Olden Time's sentimental and ungrammatical view of the past had been purged by empirical trials and by the study of facts which the South Kensington party had almost forced upon it. So the cheerfully vague, or vulgar but animated, performances of the forties were now followed by more academically plausible varieties of Gothic, Tudor, and François Premier. The Gothic of Norman Shaw's early Holy Trinity church (1866-7) in Bingley, Yorkshire, or of G. F. Bodley's St Augustine's Pendelbury (Lancashire) of 1870-4, was pleasing to the Donnish; François Premier was a bit rich for this taste, however, and (especially in E. M. Barry's hands) it appealed more to the Parvenu. Norman Shaw came closest to being the favourite Donnish architect; personally and geographically he was often so close to the South Kensington group that one might almost call this taste Museum rather than Donnish. Shaw's first client was the painter Horsley, long attached to the Schools of Design; and Shaw worked for many other painters of the prospering sort, almost all of whom built in Kensington. His fine Albert Hall Mansions of 1879 stand on the Commissioners' land, and so does Lowther Lodge of 1873-4 next door, which was the first appearance in London of his country-house style which Hitchcock calls 'Shavian Manorial' though it has detail as of about 1700. It is now the Royal Geographical Society; it may have influenced, more immediately than the seventeenth-century buildings that both emulated, the Friedrichs-hof which the Princess Royal built at Kronberg near Frankfurt[1] in the early nineties. For J. P. Heseltine, the broker who was a great collector of drawings, Norman Shaw designed a house in Queen's Gate of a museumish late-Stuart persuasion; and at the corner of the same street and Imperial Institute Road (again on the Commissioners' land) he designed in 1887 for the American diplomat Fred White the most Donnish of all his houses, a careful sleek brick one with stylistic detail only at the doorway and a prominent dormer. The discreet sort of American twentieth-century 'Georgian' learned much from it. Dons and diplomats tended to be international.

The Donnish taste was of course informed and to some extent led by the collecting and exhibiting of the South Kensington Museum. The

---

[1] Both buildings also have German sixteenth-century characteristics.

rather broad renaissance of interest thus promoted helped to save much that might have been destroyed. The modern well-instructed trade in antique furniture is based more in the Donnish taste than in the Wardour street shams of the Olden Time; the Donnish was a 'decently-and-in-order' more than a romantically aroused taste. It helped to clear away (or at least to segregate in vitrines) some of the clutter which the nineteenth century dearly loved; but it did not go so far as the Sincere taste, which was all for true simplicity, for sweeping away trumperies and gauds. Yet like the Sincere, the Donnish liked blue-and-white porcelain, thin black frames and white mats for the watercolours hung on its Morris-papered walls, and photographs of classical antiquities. The description of a certain shade of reddish brown as being 'the colour of a very good photograph' is thoroughly Donnish. But it also pleased this taste to see antiquity through the eyes of Alma Tadema, and the eighteenth century in the tidy anecdotes of W. Q. Orchardson, correctly costumed. In its latest manifestations it went into those yearnings over Marie Antoinette and the lost Dauphin which occupied the time of some Jamesian or Whartonian ladies. It also tended to encourage very careful and, in their time, dangerous reproductions of older furniture. To our eyes now the gold leaf on the otherwise excellent Louis XVI carved detail looks a little too green, but the reproduction Chippendale of the eighties is almost convincing until one realizes that the carving is a little dry, the knees of cabriole legs too sharp. In the end, the Donnish taste led to so original an historian among practising architects as Lutyens; it had opened many eyes on the way, but it did tend to look backwards.

Containing elements from both the Lusso and the Olden Time tastes, the Parvenu was obviously devoted to creature comfort more than its fellows; it may be well to say here that I try not to use any of these tags in a pejorative sense, such faint mockery as may be perceived in them being the result of habitual cynicism mixed with affection. The Parvenu taste was the one which demanded 'character' in suburban architecture; the 'realism' which it also tended to demand was realism in the political-economy sense rather than in the sense in which the Pre-Raphaelites and the Sincere taste used the word. The Parvenu was not interested in antiquarianism as such or in moral or historic 'rightness'. It liked well-buttoned upholstery but it also liked more visible structure in its furniture than the Lusso had cared for; indeed, all the post-Albertine tastes wanted furniture to show its structure fairly honestly, for the structure-concealing curves of the Louis XV, whether real or 'second rococo', had become tiresome even when they were not mishandled by designers and manufacturers. Hence the Louis XVI favoured by the late Donnish taste; hence the rugged structure of Eastlake; hence the slender stick-furniture of Godwin, of some of Morris & Company's less expensive lines, and later of the Glasgow school. The Parvenu did not care much for these, but rather for the 'Eaton Hall' sort of chair which, although the design went back perhaps before Waterhouse's remodelling of that Gothick house, was the movable chair most seen in plutocratic *Punch* interiors from Keene to late DuMaurier. It had rather light legs, the back legs well splayed, and a number of uprights rising from the seat-rails to support a low and level back, horseshoe-shaped in plan, which was upholstered on its broad top so that it could be leaned against or even sat on by the long-legged, while the short-legged were comfortable on the upholstered seat. It other words, the 'arms' were also the back: it was a sort of special development of the low-backed Windsor chair, and its mixture of comfortable padding with clearly visible structure (the legs and posts were only lightly turned) is the Parvenu equivalent to the 'Morris' chair with its wooden frame everywhere exposed, its upholstered seat and movable back and back-cushion. The Morris chair was for the study, the Eaton Hall chair for the drawing-room; obviously there were many other sorts of chairs, among which post-Victorians and anti-Victorians have had most fun with the 'conversation' chair for two people seated side by side but facing in opposite directions, the two seats having an S-plan back in common.

We must also perhaps pin upon the Parvenu taste (and its American equivalent the General Grant) some less attractive furniture, notably those illogically interrupted pieces in which the apparent material is suddenly changed by the application of a contrasting veneer, usually with no transition but a gouged line painted black. The same thing occurred in women's clothes, where bows or bits of ruching would be stitched to a ground of a different material or colour, often with the same sort of transition in the form of a dark satin or velvet edging. When the hoopskirt went out (with a bang not a whimper) in 1868, the sculptured-and-frozen thing which replaced it below the waist, and the rigidly corseted and buttoned shape above, were peculiarly Parvenu, even more in embellishment than form. The Donnish taste reacted by a move towards softer pseudo-eighteenth-century forms, and the Sincere revolted towards simple sacks. The Sincere never liked the bustle.

The Parvenu taste was fond of such hard and brilliant and well-machined surfaces as those of the Albert Memorial; the tile, brick, or marble polychromy of Butterfield *et al.* spoke to its condition; and it liked sharp (not flat) combinations of colours, as for instance cocoa, electric blue, and olive, or sulphur, crimson, and grey. Not for it the muted 'arrangements' of Whistler, which were more for the Donnish, still more for the Sincere. The aniline dyes, of which purple was first discovered in 1856 by William Henry Perkin, helped the Parvenu wealth of colour. When this taste took the trouble to 'understand' Rossetti, it liked his work for its lush colour and languor, whereas the Sincere liked it for its 'intenseness'. The Parvenu might be said to have swallowed much of Ruskin without bothering to try to understand, still less believe, him. It preferred Albert Moore to Alma Tadema, liked Holman Hunt whose high prices were almost in themselves convincing as to his good value for thorough work; thought Frith perhaps old-fashioned, and loved the circumstantial Egyptian delights of J. F. Lewis's productive old age. Its water-colours had gilt mats, not white.

The Parvenu taste even liked and bought Tissot, who made its chic look *more* chic and more French that it really was; but it may have suspected Tissot of teasing it (and Tissot's way of designing a picture was Sincere or Degas-like rather than Parvenu). The historical pageants of Sir E. J. Poynter were more dependable; Poynter, the son of an early Victorian architect, might be said to have switched from the Donnish world to the Parvenu when, having begun as one of the staff of the South Kensington art school, he wound up as President of the Royal Academy. When the South Kensington team in 1857 confirmed the 'Englishness of English art' (Dr Pevsner's good phrase) by so handsomely displaying the Sheepshanks collection, the Parvenu taste took Haydon, Mulready, Webster and other temporarily eclipsed old-timers to its young bosom. In its latest phase it led to such splendours as Collcutt's Imperial Institute of 1887-93, to Bentley's Westminster Cathedral of 1894 ff., and to Norman Shaw's late Piccadilly Hotel; this last even hints of Lutyens.

The Sincere taste looked forward, not backward like the Donnish; it called for revolution more than reform. This does not mean that it had an inflammatory programme, simply that a *tabula rasa* would have suited it better than academic revisions. It included elements from the Grec and the Lusso tastes, both of which had been discriminating, as the Olden Time had not been. It might be said that, whereas the Donnish taste tended to believe in Ruskin and sometimes followed him, the Sincere believed him but did not much need to follow him, because its practice was closer to the best of Ruskin than anything that was built to his party line. Many of the Sincere adherents were 'advanced' in political thought as in their approach to form, but few were overt Socialists like Morris. Morris & Co., founded in 1860, was both a place for the capable devotee to work and a source for 'sincere' craftsman-like furniture and eventually printing and wallpapers. Yet Morris & Co., being craftsmen rather than simplists, were glad to use their skills in other interests; and it is to the credit of High Victorian architects, especially the church-builders, and of clients both Donnish and Parvenu, that there were so many commissions for the admirable stained glass which Morris produced, often from Burne-Jones's designs.

The architects most to the Sincere taste were of course Philip Webb and E. W. Godwin; the former was above all a craftsman in brick and slate and timber; the latter, emulating the Japanese interiors which he saw in the prints shown at the 1862 Exhibition, purged his own dwelling of all that he considered extraneous, but seldom had a full opportunity to work for a kindred spirit. The house he designed for Whistler fell prey to the costs of Whistler's suit against Ruskin. Webb and Morris received one Royal commission which they executed in a fashion which I believe the Prince Consort would have liked: in 1867 they were asked to redecorate the Armoury at St James's Palace, which remains an effective performance with just the right odour of *Macbeth*; there are panoplies of arms on the walls, and the walls themselves are stencilled over gilt leather or canvas with brocatelle-like designs of a high-Renaissance character. The command was probably inspired by the South Kensington officials, who earlier in the year had had the refreshment room of the Museum decorated by the same pair.

Besides the special 'Arthurian' decorated furniture of which several specimens survive, with paintings by Rossetti, Burne-Jones, and others generally of the wider Pre-Raphaelite fellowship, Morris & Co. of course produced stock items, partly or largely hand-made but certainly in quantity. Such excellent light furniture as the inexpensive rush-bottomed and bamboo-turned chairs seen in many *Punch* interiors of the seventies and eighties, and often taken for earlier 'fancy Sheraton', came in fact from Morris. The company advertised them, and it is amusing that in some of the same periodicals one sees also advertisements for the Indian copies or emulations of second rococo furniture of the forties and fifties; one suspects from the shapes and the prominent piercing that many of these Indian chairs were imitated from the American work of Belter. The inexpensive light furniture and the less opulent of Morris's wallpapers had by intention a 'cottage' spirit, yet a high degree of sophistication actually underlay their design; and here there is a kinship with Whistler. Though the most Sincere might reprove Whistler's wordly wit and worldliness, yet his cultivated but spare harmonies and his luxury-with-economy-of-means fell in precisely with the Sincere mood; and he certainly did not look backward. Like Webb, he influenced later generations (including above all our own) far more than Norman Shaw or Alma Tadema.[1] Whistler's Peacock Room, incidentally, represents an interesting 'correction' of another taste, for its lush but calculated splendour overlies a not very distinguished High Victorian interior with grooved-board wainscot and a chimneypiece of spool-turned étagères, originally ebonized in a rather Parvenu way.

We must also allow under the Sincere heading the taste of the younger Eastlake, whose *Hints on Household Taste* reads almost like Bauhaus doctrine and hence looks to the future. If his illustrations do not seem always to suit his words very well, this is not the only such case. Despite occasional vagaries (decorative tiles set cornerwise, for example, in large expanses of oak), Eastlake furniture in its insistence upon structure and its fondness for natural finishes was as forthright as the Sincere taste could have wished, even if a trifle heavy-handed. As we have seen,

---

[1] Alma Tadema was later to head a committee which redecorated the Athenaeum's dining room in a fine Donnish version of Greek revival design. He also created some remarkable furniture in ebony inlaid with ivory and coral: the choice of materials and their colour almost Sincere, but the budget Parvenu. This furniture, which adorned Henry Marquand's house in New York in the nineties, was rediscovered by A. Hyatt Mayor in the Martin Beck Theatre in the 1950s.

an early design of Norman Shaw's a cabinet shown in 1862, was East-lake *avant la lettre*. The culmination, of course, of the Sincere taste's structure and simplicity was in Voysey and Mackintosh; as the culmination of the Whistler strain of subdued-colour elegance was the black-and-white of Aubrey Beardsley.[1]

Along the black-and-white way, which was so superbly paved by the British illustrations of the middle third of the century, were many artists of the Sincere party or taste, many of whom were also of the wider Pre-Raphaelite connexion. Arthur Hughes was one of the finest, and so was Boyd Houghton (William Morris owned Hughes's painting *April Love*); their limpid unpretentious directness, with Hughes's occasional charming original symbolism or eerie suggestion of the supernatural, and Boyd Houghton's clear reports on interiors more fully detailed than *Punch*'s made *Good Words for the Young, London Society, The Graphic*, and other illustrated papers a gold mine still mineable. Frederick Sandys, almost as highly gifted, falls with his rather loaded costume pieces more into Donnish territory; but Boyd Houghton and the excellent Pinwell and Ford Madox Brown also served the demand for costume pieces which was part of the general Victorian appetite for novelty; and Madox Brown approached the Parvenu lushness of Albert Moore's painting in his Oriental black-and-whites.

I am afraid I should have to put Edward Lear, who might have been Sincere if he had let his beautiful landscape drawings alone, into the Donnish camp, because he dried up and spoiled his drawings made on the spot during the day in pencil by retracing them with a pen in the evening. Caricaturists it is hard to place: they tend eventually to fall into the taste they caricature, in which case Keene was Donnish[2] and DuMaurier was Parvenu. An odd and little-known black-and-white artist is the admirable poet Gerard Manley Hopkins (who had a low opinion of Burne-Jones).[3]

---

[1] Superb though the accomplishment of the Kelmscott Press was, the vein of deliberate antiquarianism, amounting often to quaintness, tends to Donnishness.

[2] In a self-portrait (reproduced in Derek Hudson's *Charles Keene*, 1947, frontispiece) he sits in a good Dutch Queen Anne chair such as the Museum approved. Keene represented many a swell, but his friends included Rossetti, Edward Fitzgerald, and Millais.

[3] Geoffrey Grigson reproduces some of Hopkins's drawings in *English Drawing from Samuel Cooper to Gwen John*, 1955, pp. 132–3; and p. ix.

The painters to the Sincere taste were of course in the first rank the Pre-Raphaelites; but few of them remained true to those principles of Truth which the original Brotherhood announced. The young Millais, if he had not already changed by 1861, would have qualified as Sincere, but as painters he and Hughes went bad about the same time in the mid-fifties before the tastes I am now speaking of had 'jelled'. The young Madox Brown was too didactic to be anything but Donnish, and as an illustrator in later years he was Parvenu. Only John Brett and Rossetti remained more or less true; Dyce and Augustus Egg would have qualified if they had not died in 1864 and 1863 respectively. Burne-Jones, who in his romantic and yearning way continued some of the Pre-Raphaelite search up to his own death in 1898, was Sincere in his wish for a better world, for better design, but so backward-looking that one is inclined to call him a subscriber to the Donnish taste.[1] Like Holman Hunt, he sold well to people of Parvenu taste and even to people of the *fin-de-siècle* variant of the Sincere, because of his mixture of luxury with other-worldliness. Ruskin's piercingly honest but somehow pearly drawings and water-colours from nature are thoroughly Sincere, but in his day they were hardly in the public domain. As is suggested above, Whistler's subtleties, harmonies, and 'arrangements' were certainly also Sincere, if not always sincere with a small *s*.

It might be possible to split hairs over the portrait-painters who, though they worked across class lines, might be expected to show some leanings toward one or another of my three tastes; but I think it better to say no more than that the tastes themselves crossed conventional class boundaries. Millais and Watts and Leighton all had both aristocratic and merely plutocratic sitters; Herkomer perhaps was more of the Donnish taste than anything else.

It is an open guess whether the Morris-Webb-Whistler-Mackintosh-Voysey reaction would have appeared without the Crystal Palace, without the High Victorian consolidation, without the South Kensington Museum's academicism. We are now as willing to be at peace with a sound bit of second-rococo *papier mâché* or a decent ingrain carpet or

---

[1] He designed armour 'on purpose to lift it out of association with any historical period', but based it on fine Venetian and Milanese armourers' work of about 1460.

a lady's Davenport desk as we are with the Kelmscott Chaucer, a Morris or Dresser or Mackmurdo wallpaper, a piece of Tiffany or Lalique glass, or some of C. R. Ashbee's arts-and-crafts furniture. But we have to admit that the first three examples were *typical* of the Albertine period, while the later ones were rather exceptional in theirs. If we admit this, we have to ask whether in fact the whole 1851 experience (however we react to it), the Schools of Design, and the South Kensington programme, improved taste generally. We may be willing to believe that it was necessary to pass through all those stages to arrive at the enlightenments of twentieth-century architecture and industrial design, without being willing to think that all those steps were *good*. I for one am very glad that the Prince Consort's efforts produced in London so great a bureau of standards as the Victoria and Albert Museum. Haydon and Cole and Ruskin and van Gogh and Gropius and Albers were, all of them, right in their several ways, and we still have not got an all-purpose art school or a perfect school of industrial art.

Appendix: Minutoli

The failure of the librarians who succeeded Glover and Becker to keep the Windsor archives in the order devised by the Prince Consort, is reported amusingly (or one might say bittersweetly) by Lord Sysonby;[1] as the dispersal of much of the Prince's library is reported by Sir Lionel Cust.[2] Various sins, negligences, and ignorances have deprived us of much that we should like to know. One of the things we shall never, probably, find out is whether the Prince knew before 1854 of the work of Alexander Freiherr von Minutoli in Liegnitz, Silesia, where from 1845 there existed a South Kensington Museum *avant la lettre*. The Prince may have known about it as early as 1851, when Minutoli was one of the Silesian committee to choose exhibits for the Great Exhibition in London (Minutoli himself was an exhibitor). But the only evidence now visible is the Prince's book-stamp on the title-page (1855)[3] of Minutoli's serial publication, begun in 1854, the *Vorbilder* which I shall mention farther on. The fascicules of this publication, given by the Prince to the Department of Science and Art, are still in the library of the Victoria and Albert Museum.

Alexander von Minutoli (1807-87) was a Prussian civil servant, the third son of a general in the Prussian service who was also an Egyptologist and a globe-trotting collector; both older brothers were

---

[1] Sir Frederick Ponsonby (Lord Sysonby), *Recollections of Three Reigns*, 1952, pp. 105–10.

[2] *King Edward VII and His Court*, 1930, pp. 12–13.

[3] This book-stamp, which also appears on some copies of the *Almanach de Gotha* and other books at Windsor, has the arms of Saxony surrounded by the words *Vertrag vom 13. Mai 1846*, which must refer to some sort of agreement between the Prince and his brother Ernest II about the use of funds deriving from their father, who had died in 1844; but there is no record of such a contract at Windsor or Coburg. The date of the Prince's gift was 16 May 1855.

collectors, and one of them, Baron Adolf, court chamberlain in Meiningen, founded a drawing-school in the toy-making town of Sonneberg, only fifteen or twenty miles from Coburg. Baron Alexander, having served in the *Technische Deputation für Gewerbe* in Berlin (a sort of high-thinking factory-inspection bureau), was sent to Liegnitz in 1839 as *Regierungs-Assessor*, with instructions to try to improve the condition of the Silesian wool-textile, glass, and cast-iron industries which had suffered in the general depression of 1837.

Minutoli saw that the Silesian product was old-fashioned and so poorly designed that it could hardly compete in the European market in hard times. Setting out to improve the designs, he soon discovered that many workers could not read a designer's drawing. So he began again, late in 1840, with drawing classes for foremen, factory hands, and apprentices; for models he used objects from his own and his family's collections: small sculpture, arms and armour, illuminated manuscripts, cast-iron stove-plates, medals, pottery and porcelain, Renaissance embroideries, near Eastern glass. He was able to raise a little money from factory owners (he knew that sharing the cost increased interest), but mostly he used his own funds, which seem to have been comfortable.

By April 1844 he had 3,700 objects in hand; having apparently found the experience of three years useful to all, he announced in the *Amts-Blatt* of the Prussian provincial government that the 'owner of the Institut Minutoli' would open it to foremen, workmen, apprentices, school teachers, and their pupils from 1 January 1845. His intent then and always was to improve industry with the aid of works of industrial art of the best sorts, dating mostly from handicraft times; he never called his undertaking a museum during its active life – it was 'for study and improvement, not merely for general amusement' – but a museum it was.

Shortly before or after this opening, Minutoli was able to beg from Friedrich Wilhelm IV the use of a double range of rooms in the south wing of the Piastenburg, the old castle of the dukes of Liegnitz. It had been damaged by fire in 1835, and rebuilt as a palace for the occasional visits of Prussian royalty.[1] Minutoli remodelled the vaulted rooms in

---

[1] Liegnitz (now Legnica, Poland) evidently impressed Friedrich Wilhelm III, for when he made a morganatic marriage after the death of Queen Luise,

the upper floor during the years 1845-9 while carrying on his Institut. By 1851, when his colleague Dr Sammter published the first formal account of the work,[1] the collection was shown in two parallel ways, by categories of raw material and by region and time. Certain wall treatments with reassembled old panelling, or Spanish stamped and gilded leather, provided period backgrounds. There was a sort of lunch counter and a proto-laboratory for restoration, as well as a lodging for Minutoli himself. As soon as daguerreotypy was practised in the region, he caused many of his best objects to be recorded by that means, and he was willing to circulate the daguerreotypes to *Gewerbevereine*[2] whose members were too far from Liegnitz to travel. There were even a few paintings and sculptures: in a later catalogue,[3] Altdorfer, Baroccio, Clouet, Rubens, Velásquez, and Giambattista Tiepolo are listed. In other words, the whole apparatus of a small general museum specializing in the decorative arts, with drawing classes, reference library, photographic records of objects, travelling exhibitions, and the whole 'uplift' of museum extension as we now know it, was in operation in a provincial town. There was nothing like an art school or a public collection of objects of art in Silesia, except in very small ways at the University of Breslau. No one seems to have complained that Minutoli was 'spoiling' the working classes, perhaps because he was using his own money rather than public revenues (cf. Mr Danby Seymour's strictures on South Kensington quoted in my chapter *Second Royal Commission*).

Minutoli had been under the influence in Potsdam of Peter C. W.

---

he created his wife (who was a Harrach of Vienna) Princess of Liegnitz; Prince Albert knew her, as letters about her from the Princess Royal to her father in June 1858 indicate.

[1] *Das Minutolische Institut der Vorbilder-Sammlung zur Beförderung der Gewerbe und Künste*, Liegnitz, 1851; same 'zweiter Teil', Liegnitz, 1866; this was advertised in the Liegnitz *Stadtblatt* newspaper by a bookseller on 12 December 1851, p. 771.

[2] This word probably means something more like a club than an industrial union, which hardly existed then and there; the *Vereine* must have found the daguerreotypes disappointing, for they showed large groups of objects none of which can have been very legible.

[3] *Catalog der Sammlungen von Musterwerken der Industrie und Kunst des Instituts Minutoli zu Liegnitz*, Berlin, 1872; in the foreword as in several other places, priority is claimed for Liegnitz.

Beuth (1781-1853),[1] founder of the *Gewerbe-Institut* in Berlin (1820) and of provincial industrial schools. The Parliamentary Select Committee of 1835 on Arts and Manufactures heard considerable evidence about the Gewerbe-Institut, which Prince Albert may have read later; Dyce visited it and reported on its methods when he travelled on the Continent in 1838 to prepare for the Schools of Design. Between 1821 and 1837 Beuth (with the help of Schinkel as draughtsman and the applause of the aged Goethe) published his series called *Vorbilder für Fabrikanten und Handwerker*, pattern books which attempted to bring art, handicraft, and industry together, and whose purpose and even title were echoed (with due acknowledgements) in Minutoli's own *Vorbilder für Handwerker und Fabrikanten aus den Sammlungen des Minutolischen Instituts zur Veredlung der Gewerbe und Beförderung der Künste*. This work appeared in fascicules from 1854 through 1863; in 1855 a general title-page was issued, on which Minutoli described himself as, among other things, an honorary vice-president of the 'Universal-Society for the Encouragement of Arts and Industry in London'; he had said the same thing on the title to his book on Trondhejm Cathedral (1853).[2] In other words, he was claiming honorary office in an imaginary but deceptively-named organization like the Society of Arts; there is no record of his having been elected to the Society of Arts, nor can we tell whether his invention was disingenuous. But it is possible that this pretentious bit of work queered him with the Prince and Cole, who unquestionably knew of him by 1854. To the *Vorbilder* I shall return.

In the summer of 1853 Alexander Redgrave, of the British factory-inspection service, visited several Continental industrial centres,

---

[1] Beuth was a picturesque 'character', an old cavalryman who collected prints after Raphael compositions and gathered an *œuvre* of Dürer; he held Sunday evening art pow-wows. Waagen said he had 'remarkably fine and right taste'. P. O. Rave, *Das Schinkel-Museum und die Kunst-Sammlungen Beuths*, Berlin, 1931, pp. 107–15. Beuth's *Vorbilder* (see below) are mentioned by Eastlake and F. S. Cary in the *Journal* of the Society of Arts for 13 October 1854; which suggests that this sort of thing was 'in the air' but that Eastlake and Cary had not yet seen Minutoli's first fascicule dated 1854. Prince Albert early in his married life drew a caricature of a Count Beuth of Bonn who was a guest at the Queen's table, but this must have been another Beuth, I think.

[2] *Der Dom zu Drontheim*, Berlin, 1853; the comparative material among the lithographed illustrations already included the puzzling stone tower at Newport, Rhode Island, as a work of Norse colonial outreach.

including Liegnitz, where he met Minutoli and saw the Institute. Redgrave was a younger brother of Samuel and Richard Redgrave, authors of *A Century of British Painters* (1866); Richard we know from the South Kensington team. Alexander Redgrave's visit must have been known to Cole, who was in daily contact with his brother, and it may be that Cole or the Prince suggested the visit. At any rate, Redgrave's report to his Service was quoted in part in the *Journal* of the Society of Arts for 20 March 1854, and in a letter to the *Journal* printed a few days later (7 April) he expanded his account of the work in Liegnitz, saying that Minutoli's Institut was 'a memorable instance of the devotion of private energy and of private generosity in the discharge of the public duties of his office'. Prince Albert and Cole, both active in the Society of Arts, must have read the *Journal* if they had no previous knowledge of Minutoli; and the first fascicule of the *Vorbilder*, which incidentally is the first German publication illustrated with paper-positive photographs, will have come to the Prince's eye before long.[1]

The Prince and Alexander von Minutoli were both well-brought-up Germans (old General Heinrich von Minutoli had been 'governor' to a Prussian prince); they were thoroughly exposed to Goethe and Froebel and Pestalozzi's ideas about popular education as a duty. The time and the cultural background doubtless explain much of the extraordinary resemblance between Minutoli's taste as we see it in the *Vorbilder* and the Prince's taste as we see it in the choices of objects bought for the Department of Science and Art in the early years when he was close to it. Even if these choices represented the team's taste without any influence from him, the resemblance would be suggestive; but there is almost sure visual evidence of Prince Albert's choices in a volume of photographs in the Royal Library. It is titled *Works of Art Exhibited at Marlborough House 1854*; the photographs, all mounted within ruled borders and many signed *F. Bedford 1854*, include representations of objects lent by the Queen, objects from the Gherardini collection, and other recent purchases for the Department. Not only the style of the photographs but the choices of objects remind one powerfully of Minutoli: the Marlborough House volume shows, for instance, Isnik and

---

1 Prince Albert had proposed early in the summer of 1851 to photograph the best exhibits in the Crystal Palace and to make a hundred sets of talbotypes for sending to regional committees.

Wedgwood ceramics, Chinese, Indian, and Italian Renaissance textiles, a relief by Clodion as well as some of the Michelangelo or near-Michelangelo wax models, fine seventeenth-century locksmiths' work, pewter, and swords. Minutoli's sharp wet-plate photographs include in many cases a black-and-white scale labelled *Institut Minutoli*; the subjects include bronze and iron age metalwork, mosaics, enamels, rock crystal, lace, stained glass, ivories, Campanian, 'Habaner', Leeds, and Savona earthenware, and Meissen porcelain.

One would not want to take away a particle of credit from either undertaking, but one has survived, the other not. Prince Albert's genius in organization and in choice of personnel, together with royal prestige and central location, made the London work viable. The Liegnitz work, far from being unappreciated, was so successful that the central Prussian administration could not leave it in the provinces. In 1858 the new royal museum in Berlin reached out and bought the majority of Minutoli's ceramics for 48,000 marks. Minutoli, who as a civil servant could hardly refuse a quasi-royal command, sold; and set to work at once to replace the missing pots. He added to the money in hand by selling at auction in Leipzig in May 1858, and in March 1859 at Brussels,[1] what he did not want from his father's large collections. In ten years he had rebuilt his ceramics section so well that in 1869 the Prussian Ministry of Trade bought it and all the glass and metalwork for 150,000 marks.

The immediate reason for this was that the Crown Princess of Prussia, who was Prince Albert's eldest daughter, had been propagandizing for better industrial design; she had noticed that German representation at the London Exhibition of 1862 was poor, with correspondingly few awards, whereas in 1851 German work had taken many prizes. An official investigation had as one of its results[2] the founding in 1867 of the Deutsches Gewerbemuseum in Berlin; it was to this that the two large purchases from Minutoli eventually went. His superb material was the real backbone of that museum, but I suspect that his taxonomic fussiness came in with the objects; for the labels, when I first saw the

---

[1] Weigel's catalogue of the sale of 31 May is in German but has an *Avantpropos* in French, in which the 'goût rococo' is mentioned. The Brussels sale was held on 7 March by LeRoy.

[2] Part of the campaign was Dr Herman Schwabe's *Die Förderung der Kunstindustrie in England und der Stand dieser Frage in Deutschland*, 1866.

Kunstgewerbemuseum in 1930, were absurdly stuffy.[1] As I have suggested, his arbitrary classifications may have affected other men, including the cataloguers at Manchester in 1857. Minutoli listed furniture, tapestries, and even moulded Chinese ink-sticks, as *Verarbeitungen vegetabilischer Stoffe.*

When it was all over he was willing to say that the Institute had been a *Gewerbe-und-Kunst-Museum;*[2] but his original intention, like Cole's, had been the improvement of industrial products:

The collection is neither a museum of art nor of antiquities. It is rather a collection of works of industry and was originated in the desire of aiding in the improvement of the fabric,[3] by the examination of examples of attested excellence, adapted, not only to those branches of industry already developed in Silesia, but to others, which from local advantages might be introduced. The subjects therefore, bear upon the artistic products of industry, partly works of classical antiquity, partly of the quatro-, cinque-, and sei-cento period, when the regeneration[4] of art flourished, and art, in connexion with industry, created works which will remain examples for all time.[5]

This sounds very much like Cole as I have quoted him in my chapter 10 from his budget message for the year 1852-3.

In his old age, Baron Alexander grew rather testy and jealous about the priority of his work at Liegnitz: in the foreword to the (we might almost say posthumous) 1872 catalogue and in the notes to the auction

---

[1] For example: 'Teller, K'ang Hsi, mit der Darstellung, einer mit ihrer Dienerin in einem Garten wandelnden, blumeneinsammelnden, vornehmen Chinesin.'

[2] 1872 catalogue; see note 3, page 193. Sammter's foreword in 1855, issued with the *Vorbilder* title-page, said as much.

[3] This was probably *Fabrik* (factory) in the original, which I have not found.

[4] This may have been *Wiedergeburt* or some such word in the original, which we would now translate by 'renaissance'; but Renaissance was rather a new word, apparently first used in English to describe a style of art by T. A. Trollope in *Summer in Brittany*, 1840; Palgrave in 1842 spoke of 'the period of the Renaissance' in his Murray *Guide to North Italy*; Eduard Kolloff spoke of the *Epoche der Renaissance* in German in 1840. But J. C. Robinson of the South Kensington Museum was still titling a Museum publication in 1862 *Italian Sculpture of the Middle Ages and the Period of the Revival of Art.*

[5] Thus Alexander Redgrave, quoting Minutoli himself; *Journal* of the Society of Arts, 20 March and 7 April 1854.

catalogues he claimed, very properly though repetitiously, that his Institute underlay South Kensington, the Paris *Union centrale des Beaux-Arts appliqués à l'Industrie,* and the *Oesterreichisches Museum für Kunst und Industrie* in Vienna. And it does seem likely that he made himself annoying to such an extent that no one wanted to remember his good work during the active years of the forties and fifties; the *Festschrift* for the opening of the new building of the Berlin Kunstgewerbemuseum, while speaking of the Minutoli collection as the base, said not a word about the activity in Liegnitz; and Minutoli's disciple Justus Brinckmann, when he produced a similar *Festschrift* for the opening of his Kunstgewerbemuseum in Hamburg, likewise ignored the Silesian prototype. Yet, for about ten years (1849-58), Liegnitz was the seat of an extraordinary concentration of museum objects of quality made available to the public; for after the death in 1846 of General Heinrich his father, and the murder during the revolutions in 1848 of his brother the Hofmarschall Adolf, Alexander brought most of their collections to Liegnitz, and apparently he had the use of the Spanish material of his brother Julius, who died in 1860 as envoy in Persia. Baron Alexander also bought *en bloc* the collections of Graf Ross and Stadtrath Friedmann of Berlin, and traded away a good deal of secondary material. He had a sale of *Resten* (leftovers) in Cologne in 1875; from this and the two sales of his father's things, arms and armour, illuminated manuscripts, ceramics, and enamels have passed to latter-day collections.

Whatever may be the facts of contact between London and Liegnitz before 1854, it seems clear to me that Minutoli's collection and his educational outreach helped to swing the South Kensington undertaking towards its eventual character. The Victoria and Albert Museum now uses the same method of parallel displays that Minutoli devised in the Piastenburg's double range of rooms in 1894 (composite installations by period and culture of some of the finest pieces; the bulk of the collection classified in type-series, e.g., wrought iron, cast iron, steel).

Finally, there are faint hints in Dr Decker's *Amtlicher Bericht über die Londoner Industrieausstellung 1862* (Berlin, 1863) that Prince Albert may have meant to give Minutoli a hand in the 1862 Exhibition. One can never solve all the mysteries.

ACKNOWLEDGEMENTS

Extracts from the works listed below are reprinted here by kind permission of the publishers.

Albert: Prince Consort by Hector Bolitho: Bobbs Merrill, U.S.A.

The Connoisseur Period Guide:Early Victorian Period:1830-1860, 'Furniture' by Peter Floud: *The Connoisseur.* 1958.

Consort of Taste by John Steegman: Sidgwick & Jackson Ltd.

The Creevey Papers by Sir Herbert Maxwell, ed.: John Murray.

The Darkening Glass by John D. Rosenberg: Columbia University Press, U.S.A.

Early Victorian Architecture in Britain by H. R. Hitchcock: Yale University Press, U.S.A.

The Economics of Taste by Gerald Reitlinger: Barrie & Rockliff.

English Art 1800-1870 by T. S. R. Boase: The Clarendon Press.

English Drawings . . . at Windsor Castle by A. P. Oppé: Phaidon Press.

English Furniture at a Glance by Barbara Jones: The Architectural Press.

Georgian London by Sir John Summerson: The Cresset Press.

Here Lies the Heart by Mercedes de Acosta: Reynal & Company, Inc., U.S.A.

Letters from the Earth by Bernard de Voto: Harper & Row, Publishers, Inc., U.S.A.

Louis XVI Furniture by F. J. B. Watson: Alec Tiranti.

The Nazarenes by K. Andrews: The Clarendon Press.

The Order of Release by O. James: John Murray.

Paxton and the Bachelor Duke by V. R. Markham: Hodder and Stoughton.

Pre-Raphaelite Painters by Robin Ironside: Phaidon Press.

The Prince Consort by Roger Fulford: Macmillan & Co.

Queen Victoria by Lytton Strachey: Chatto and Windus.

Queen Victoria, Born to Succeed by Lady Longford: Weidenfeld & Nicolson.

The Schools of Design by Quentin Bell: Routledge & Kegan Paul.

Three Howard Sisters by Lady Leconfield and John Gore: John Murray.

The Victorian Home by Ralph Dutton: B. T. Batsford.

Windsor Castle by Sir Owen Morshead: Phaidon Press.

NOTES TO THE ILLUSTRATIONS*

1. Theodore Rothbarth: *Ernest I's Bedroom at the Ehrenburg in Coburg*
The Gothic and Classic panoplies in moulded plaster in the spandrels,
the generally severe arrangement of furniture, and the alabaster vases
and clock are very much of the period; the frank stopping of the wallpaper frieze at the corner against the plaster arch, and the bare floor,
are very Ernestine. What seems to be a Renaissance *Virgin and Child*
over the fire-place has been given a new Empire or Restoration frame;
the fire-place itself is exceptional in the German stove region. This is
one of the more ambitious of the interiors in which the young Prince
Albert grew up.

2. *The Riesensaal in the Ehrenburg*, Coburg; about 1693
In this robust late seventeenth-century room Prince Albert was ca-
techized and confirmed. It seems to have left no trace in his later
enterprises, but may have been too barbaric for his taste. Its smaller
accompanying rooms, set off at each end by a screen of columns, may
have combined with the similar subdivision of large rooms in Adam's
work (which the Prince saw at Sion House on his first visit to England) to
influence the design of the drawing room and billiard room at Osborne.

3. Caleb Robert Stanley: *Aviary, Frogmore*
Some of Prince Albert's earliest building, for housing the exotic birds
which he collected, was a romantic prolongation of what he found
already in hand among minor buildings at Windsor. Adelaide Cottage,
for instance, a neat stone Tudorish vicarage-style house which greeted
him when he began managing the Windsor farms, had wooden 'lace'
at the eaves. The range of aviaries shown here, with chimneys to warm

* All works of art, pictures and palaces, the ownership and location of
which is not specified, are reproduced by gracious permission of Her Majesty
Queen Elizabeth II.

tropical birds, and dovecotes and cages for hardier ones, is the Prince's most 'English' performance.

4. Douglas Morison: *The Picture Gallery, Buckingham Palace*

John Nash, or more likely his successor Blore, must have been alarmed by the idea of an entire ceiling of glass in one plane, such as Continental architects were beginning to use over the courtyards of palaces turned into museums; the pendant ornaments and the faceted glass of the domelets may have helped to diffuse the light. This ceiling has now become a glass segmental vault, but the four fire-places and some of the pictures are still present. One of George IV's Wilkies is recognizable; the lower tiers including some of his small Dutch paintings.

5. Joseph Nash: *The Queen's Birthday Table*

The Christmas and birthday tables were almost unfailingly recorded by camera or by hand. Here we see, in a room at Osborne, the typical garlands and, among them, several bronze busts (probably Elkingtons' electrolytic copies of the antique) for the Osborne terraces or corridors Winterhalter's portrait of the Queen's mother, another of Prince Alfred and Princess Helena, one of the porcelain garnitures which the Queen loved, and Troschel's *Filatrice Addormentata* (see pl. 6). The Queen made a water-colour copy in her diary of the portrait of the Duchess of Kent.

6. Julius Troschel: *La Filatrice Addormentata*

Troschel worked, like half the high-toned sculptors of Europe after Thorwaldensen had set the pattern, in Rome where professional stone-cutters abounded; it took a really tough and original inventor to make his design shine through the sleek professional mannerisms of those operatives. The *Filatrice* is just old-fashioned enough to have a re-miniscence of the Grec; she even sleeps on a *klismos* chair. But she is also obviously parlour sculpture in her unheroic proportions, the anecdotal title and subject, and the tidy treatment of the nude. Yet the figure looked more 'Victorian' to the water-colourist Nash than to us.

7. Sir Edwin Landseer: *The Queen and Prince with the Princess Royal*

Wearing shooting costume and sitting on a piece of the Green Drawing Room suite made by Seddons for George IV, Prince Albert pets his greyhound Eos. Through the window we see the East Terrace with some of the great Windsor oaks beyond. Landseer had difficulties with the picture and did not complete it until 1843; his heirs gave the Queen an unfinished sketch for it after his death.

8. Franz Xaver Winterhalter: *Queen Victoria*

This, the least pretentious of Winterhalter's portraits, is not without artifice. The Queen at twenty-four was growing plump; by echoing the shape of the face in the oval canvas, and by showing the shoulders as broad as possible, the painter minimized the weight of the head. The hair and eyes are marvellously rendered. The Queen recorded five sittings in early July 1843 for this 'surprise for Albert' – but he seems to have liked even better the profile of his wife in her wedding veil.

9. Sir Edwin Landseer: *Prince Albert with the Princess Royal*

When he did not apply too much 'finish', Landseer could be charmingly direct; here he is at his least laboured. The intelligent eldest child, as she grew up, was better able than the Queen to share the Prince's searchings in the arts and his confidences in questions of taste.

10. *Wreath, Earrings, and Pair of Brooches*

The wreath, mounted on green velvet, represents orange flowers and leaves, with four tiny green oranges in enamel for the four children the Royal couple then had. Prince Albert designed the set, perhaps wishing to provide fade-proof flowers for his wife, who liked to put flowers (and diamonds) in her hair. The gold leaves are so finely engraved with close lines as to have a very *matte* or 'frosted' effect. The whole is one of the Prince's nicest inventions.

11. *Cradle*

The ornament is in the *Ohr- und Muschel-Stil* widespread in the early seventeenth century through Flemish and German engravings; and the arms are in the even earlier sixteenth-century style in which German heraldry rather froze at the time of Holbein. The cradle, variously represented as having belonged to Augustus the Strong and to Marshal Saxe, was used in the Queen's private sitting room at Windsor; one of the younger princesses had her portrait painted by Landseer while she sat in it.

[202]

12. W. L. Leitch: *Osborne House under Construction*

Leitch, drawing-master to the Queen from September 1846, records an earth-moving operation by Cubitts' navvies in which the terraces are being prepared. The previous day some of the scaffolding of the House-hold wing (left) had fallen, and three men were hurt (one of them died). Leitch's sketch made on the spot shows uprights of scaffolding pro-jecting above the unfinished wall. In the larger and more generalized water-colour made from this sketch for one of the Windsor albums, the building is shown complete (it was roofed in by the seventh of May). The alcove in the terrace wall, where the Queen and Prince often break-fasted, is ready, but the soil of the terraces takes time to settle, and they will not be finished until the summer of 1849. The corridor and its open upper storey to connect the Pavilion to the rest of the House do not appear here, but were built in 1848-9. Cubitts often had as many as 250 men at work; in the summer of 1846 the Queen had an outdoor party for them.

13. *Osborne House*

The adjustments of building to land, which Prince Albert studied and laboured over for years, whether standing on the tower or walking over the terrain, are visible in a modern air view. The elaborate and subtle modifications of symmetry away from the obvious are also clear.

14. *Hall Chair*

In the tradition of the wooden-seated hall chair which kept footmen and unwelcome visitors humble, this is nevertheless an original per-formance of real style. The curule form of the legs may be intended as a reminiscence of the so-called Dante or Savonarola chair for an Italianate house, but it looks more like Hope or even Duncan Phyfe.

15. *Candelabrum*

Though these candelabra were not quite such a *tour de force* as the glass fountain by the same manufacturers which spouted in the tran-sept of the Crystal Palace, they were and are spectacular in their con-sistent use of material. Prince Albert was involved in the design, having a model sent to Osborne in December 1847 and asking for revision. The candelabra may have been thought of as a sober but splendid artistic and technical counterblast to the frivolous standing lamps in ormolu with lotus-like tops in coloured glass, which went up to Windsor from the Brighton Pavilion when the Queen sold the Pavilion to the Brighton Corporation.

16. Sir Edwin Landseer: *Queen Victoria and Prince Albert in Costume*

The Queen made a drawing of the same costumes in her diary for 12 May 1842. Landseer was already a favourite with her before her marriage; he was still painting the informal double portrait when called upon to do this rather untypical picture.

17. *Silver-gilt table centrepiece*

The composition of the piece, which was shown at the Society of Arts in 1849, is not unlike that used later for the memorial to the Exhibition of 1851; without the rather inept dogs it would be imposing. The Renaissance ornament, though not very grammatical, is handled generously and with 'snap'.

H.M. the Queen (on loan to the Victoria and Albert Museum)

18. *Silver Statuette of Prince Albert*

Garrards' modeller, Cottrell, visited the Windsor stables in January 1841 to see 'several of our horses which we wish to have modelled for a piece of plate'. He was successful with the Prince's 'Mercury', a fine beast precisely in the taste of Géricault; but it is to be observed that a practically identical horse supports the Duke of Wellington in a statuette by Robert Garrard made in 1838 (sold at Christie's 17 November 1965). Prince Albert here wears the uniform of the Eleventh Hussars. In 1848, we learn from Joseph Nash's water-colour and lithograph, this statuette stood under a glass bell on one of George IV's *guéridons* in the Queen's private sitting room at Windsor, with the Saxon cradle (pl. 7) facing it from the fireside.

19. *Silver-gilt Baptismal Font*

The routine scrolls and cherubs are part of the Regency repertory, but the water-lily and lily-pads are early Victorian naturalism; the arms in a ozenge are the Royal arms with Saxony in pretense and a label for difference. All the Royal children were baptized from this font

20. Gegenbaur: *Hercules and Omphale*

In some ways this work forecasts the *Age d'Or* of Ingres; it is startling to see it through the door of a wardrobe as one looks into the Prince's dressing room at Osborne. There is in fact little suggestion in the picture that Hercules was in bondage to Omphale. Gegenbaur made other versions of this subject, one for Thorwaldsen.

21. Friedrich Overbeck: *Triumph of Religion in the Arts*

The huge drawing (on several pieces of paper) is a finished but still preliminary design for a painting now in the Städel Institute in Frankfurt; the final cartoon is in Karlsruhe, and varies in size and in many details from this drawing. The title is sometimes given as *Religion Glorified by the Fine Arts*. Along with strong influences from Raphael, there are traces of Dürer's *Allerheiligenbild* and of Holbein's physical types. If Prince Albert met any other Nazarenes than Schnorr von Carolsfeld, he will have met Overbeck, who was in Rome in the year of the Prince's visit.

22. Emil Wolff: *Prince Albert*

Wolff's first (1844) version of this sculpture, barefooted, is on the main stair at Osborne; the formalized waves and dolphins surrounding the George on the shield refer to the nautical theme of the Dyce fresco on the facing wall. Wolff knew a good iconological programme when he met it: the breastplate is ornamented by a Victory with wreath and palm, while the lappets of the tunic are carved with rose, thistle, shamrock, and the arms of Saxony. The present sculpture was made for Buckingham Palace.

23. Richard James Wyatt: *Penelope*

The tradition of Flaxman and Chantrey is here made more 'statuesque' and luxurious by the Italian surroundings in which the *Marble Faun* generation of sculptors worked; it is parlour sculpture at its most finished, saved from being purely anecdotal by a degree of simplicity in the detail and by a decently sculptural compactness. This figure was at Windsor by October 1844, and in November the grand old man of the British group in Rome, Gibson, walked through the Castle with Victoria and Albert to find a place for it. Wyatt later did a series of figures for Osborne, but he almost never came home; it is said that the *Penelope* was ordered on one of his few London appearances.

24. Joseph von Führich: *Saints Peter and John Confirming the Churches*
The Prague-born Austrian Nazarene here works rather in the figure style of Schnorr von Carolsfeld. The scene (Acts viii. 17), however complex the composition, is given a sort of Lutheran decorum by the bishop's chaplain, complete with pastoral staff, who accompanies each apostle. Like many Nazarenes, Führich moved into the academic world, and was professor in the Vienna Academy from 1840; he made drawings for one of the albums originally included in the Gothic bookcase given by Kaiser Franz Josef to the Queen in 1851 (pl. 55).

25. William Dyce: *Neptune Resigning the Empire of the Sea to Britannia*
The Sketch for Dyce's decoration of the Pavilion stair at Osborne is rather pleasanter in colour than the fresco, which however has remained in remarkably good condition. There are obvious references to Raphael and even Poussin, which have modified the often chill fervors of Nazarene painting as Dyce practised it in the House of Lords. Truth to tell, he was really more at home as a teacher and easel-painter than in fresco. Only Maclise and sometimes Etty, and in other ways David and William Bell Scott, could manage the scope and swing of big figure compositions in the 'forties. Dyce made a laudable try.

The Lady Patricia Ramsay, Windlesham, Surrey

26. Lucas Cranach: *Apollo and Diana*
A sound standard performance of which there are variants elsewhere. Cranach was so thoroughly a Saxon painter that the Prince bought more of his work than of any other artist's except Landseer's and Winterhalter's. This one at a hundred guineas was a wise single purchase in the period when the Oettingen-Wallerstein collection was not yet in hand.

27. William Wyld: *Manchester*
Wyld, a friend of Bonington and an exhibitor at the famous Salon of 1824, lived much of his life in France, but worked at Balmoral and

Brussels on some occasions for the Queen and Prince. The present water-colour, commissioned in memory of a visit to Manchester on 10 October 1851, seems to suggest that even the Claudian goats in the foreground, the picnic on the greensward, or the curving stream cannot fend off the dark satanic mills; yet the mills are rather romantically presented. This was one of the modern works from the royal collection chosen for engraving in the *Art Journal*, 1857 (opposite page 204).

28. George Cruikshank: *Disturbing the Congregation*

A rather histrionic performance which might have been more amusing as a black-and-white, this painting is one of the few of the early-Victorian anecdotal sort acquired by the Queen or the Prince. The Queen, who saw painting as theatre, may have liked it as a *tableau vivant*; the Prince may have seen it as a sort of echo of Spitzweg, the Munich humorist whose work he had liked as a boy; and he will have appreciated the artist's treatment of the parish church as a minor museum of sculpture.

29. John Gibson: *Queen Victoria*

The Welsh doyen of the British sculptors working in Rome, Gibson had worked for Canova and with Thorwaldsen. Unlike many of his contemporaries and juniors, he had been apprenticed to a mason, and he cut his own stone instead of leaving that work to Italian technicians. Besides this highly official portrait, he produced a slightly more informal statue of the Queen for Buckingham Palace and a public monument (with some colour in the costume) for Liverpool. This Westminster portrait now stands alone after the removal of the flanking figures of *Justice* and *Mercy*. Gibson skilfully accommodated his classicism to Pugin's Gothic detail by setting Grec bas-reliefs in Gothic panels, and putting the Queen in almost the attitude of Mrs Siddons on the Coronation chair.
Prince's Chamber, Houses of Parliament

30. Louis Gallait: *Le Sentiment de la Maternité*

Contemporary Belgian painters and sculptors were well organized, and were rather carefully promoted by King Leopold. Both Queen and Prince liked what they saw on several visits to Antwerp and Brussels, and they bought at good prices (two hundred pounds for this Gallait, more than the Prince had to give for some of his pioneer acquisitions of *quattrocento* painting).

31. William Dyce: *Virgin and Child*

Exhibited at the Royal Academy in 1846, this painting is an only slightly altered repetition of one of 1838 which is now in the Nottingham Art Gallery. When Prince Albert received it on 9 August 1845 his wife described it in her diary as 'so chaste, & exquisitely painted . . . in the style of Raphael'. The Aberdonian Dyce made at least two stays in Rome in the second half of the twenties, when the Nazarenes whom he met were being called 'pre-Raphaelites'. From them he learned fresco technique, which certainly influenced the smooth flat tones and big scale of this painting.

32. C. W. Cope: *Embarkation of the Pilgrim Fathers*

Interesting chiefly for its subject and technique, Cope's picture is one of those painted in various trial materials after the failure of the first great fresco experiment in the Houses of Parliament; the series of which it is part is well preserved. Cope's earlier and much larger oil painting, *Cardinal Wolsey Dying at the Gate of Leicester Abbey*, was commissioned by Prince Albert in 1847, and is still in the billiard room at Osborne House.

New Palace of Westminster (House of Lords Corridor)

33. Franz Xaver Winterhalter: *Florinda*

Echoing high-Renaissance compositions of *Parnassus* or *Apollo and the Muses*, this vast picture also has connexions with such eighteenth-century subjects as *La Comparaison* or *La Toilette de Vénus*. The title, however, has the literary sanction of Robert Southey, for the scene is an episode in his *Roderick, the Last of the Goths*, a Spanish romance of 1814. There seems to be little doubt that Winterhalter here made an anthology of beauties, not compressed into one *à la* Raphael, but treated as a bouquet (see text, chapter 11, for the Queen's comment on one of the faces). There is also little doubt that the composition became the base for the slightly later painting of the Empress Eugénie with her ladies-in-waiting. Finally, it is odd that the Queen gave this picture to her husband who, by her own statement, was practically immune to 'female beauty'. A replica is in the Metropolitan Museum, New York.

34. Pietro Tenerani: *Flora*

The statue was created, or at least used, as a pendant to R. J. Wyatt's *Glycera* at Osborne. Tenerani, though spirited, has not quite the *chic* of Wyatt; in most of the mid-century work influenced by professional Italian marble-cutters, one feels that the fleshings worn by dancers, acrobats, and opera choruses in that day have crept over the marble nudes, blunting and smoothing and averaging-out the forms. Tenerani in 1840 had designed the tomb of the Saxon princess who married the younger Marchese Massimo, second patron of the Nazarenes in Rome.

35. *Antinous*

Hadrian caused his favourite, who drowned in the Nile in 130, to be apotheosized in the guise of various gods; this *Antinous* is oddly pathetic in its mixture of idealized portrait, *kouros*, and Pharaonic effigy. Other portraits show that Antinous had a huge chest, but the weak square shoulders and the small head on its short neck look like Egyptian conservatism invading the image. A similar statue from Hadrian's villa is in the Capitoline Museum. This one, captured in 1806 by a naval vessel from a ship carrying antiquities belonging to Napoleon and Jerôme Bonaparte, was given by Gibraltar merchants to George Ward, father of Lord Ward, the collector whose taste seems to have changed about 1850; for after his sale he showed to the public in Piccadilly during the Great Exhibition summer a 'collection of pictures recently formed' which included many choices reminiscent of Prince Albert's, Eastlake's, and Oettingen-Wallerstein's taste.

H.M. the Queen (on loan to the British Museum)

36. Pesellino (Francesco di Stefano Ginochi): *The Trinity with Four Saints*; lower left, *St James the Great and St Mammas*

Gruner bought the trapezoidal panel from Warner Ottley for the Queen, and again it is a fair guess that the gift was not exactly a surprise. The altarpiece, painted in the last year of Pesellino's life (1456-7), is now reassembled from three ownerships after a long separation. The Florentines before Botticelli had a great attraction for Prince Albert, and during his most active collecting in the mid-forties he made some consistent acquisitions: Daddi, Fra Angelico, Benozzo Gozzoli, Lorenzo di Credi; that some of them came under other names does not affect their character.

H.M. the Queen (on loan to the National Gallery)

37. Bohemian or Moravian: *The Virgin and Child*

Scenes from the Life of the Virgin in colour alternate, around the frame, with figures of apostles stippled or punched on the gold leaf. Sir Lionel Cust, Surveyor of Pictures in the time of Edward VII and George V, suggested that the frame might be a generation or two later than the panel, which is, with the frame, one of the stars of the Oettingen-Wallerstein purchase. Recently an attribution to Theodoric of Prague (active 1348-67) has been suggested.

38. Benozzo Gozzoli: *Fall and Judgement of Simon Magus*

One of the Prince's most distinguished small acquisitions (twenty-five pounds), this panel was part of the predella to an altarpiece contracted for by Gozzoli in 1461, and now in the National Gallery; it is in excellent condition. The compact bodies of Benozzo's personages are of a physical type later favoured by Raphael; this is the sort of thing Prince Albert would have noticed.

H.M. the Queen (on loan to the National Gallery)

39. Giovanni Bellini: *Saint Dominic*

It would not be accurate to call this picture one of Prince Albert's choices, but it helps to illustrate his methods; for it is an example of some of the good things acquired during the series of purchases by which in less than ten years the South Kensington collections were given basis, form, and direction. Whether the Prince noticed this painting or not, he was an initial subscriber to the purchase of the Soulages collection, because he trusted his team to find what was needed. Soulages may have bought the picture because the first important house of St Dominic's Order of Preachers was in Toulouse where Soulages lived; but as a collector of Gothic and Renaissance decorative arts he will

have enjoyed the book-binding and the textile background. Such a museum document underlay William Morris's wallpapers and Owen Jones's, Walter Crane's Christopher Dresser's.
Victoria and Albert Museum (on loan to the National Gallery)

40. Justus van Ghent (?): *Federico da Montefeltro and his Son Guidobaldo Hearing a Humanist Lecture*

Federico's mantle is embroidered with the cross of St George surrounded by the Garter, which he received in 1474; the painting is perhaps five years later. The decorum of little Guidobaldo is such as Queen Victoria would have wished for the Prince of Wales. Duke Federico liked learned men and musicians, as Prince Albert did. For some identifications of other personages in the picture, which probably hung for years in the library at Urbino, see the catalogue of an exhibition, *Juste de Gand, Berruguete, et la Cour d'Urbino*, Ghent, 1957, No. 20.

41. Duccio di Buoninsegna (?): *Triptych*

When Kennedy North cleaned this Franciscan portable altarpiece at the National Gallery in 1930, he found it in good condition except for regilding of the ground. In Prince Albert's time it had a rather good recent Gothic frame with grapevines in the spandrels; the present modest framing emphasizes the separate elements of the triptych, which is no longer universally given to Duccio himself. It is none the less a pioneer acquisition of the Prince's, made at a time when he still had some leisure for collecting, and when Gruner was very active on his behalf.
H.M. the Queen, (on loan to the National Gallery)

42. Franz Xaver Winterhalter: *The First of May*

The Crystal Palace in the background, the branch of may at upper left, the lilies-of-the-valley for May Day, all help to load with reference the programme of this picture for which Winterhalter was paid five hundred pounds. A copy was later sent to Walmer Castle, where the Duke of Wellington, as Lord Warden of the Cinque Ports, regularly spent part of every year. See the text, chapter 11, for more detail. At almost the same time as this painting, Winterhalter was doing a small sketch of the Queen and Prince as Charles II and Catherine of Braganza, costumed for a ball held at the Palace on 13 June 1851.

43. Eugène Lami: *Baptism of Prince Arthur*

The future Duke of Connaught, born 1 May 1850, was christened in the private chapel of Buckingham Palace. Lami could not manage portraits, but he caught precisely the mixture of familial atmosphere with festive costume; the stock figures of elegance at the left are nevertheless very different from the real actors in the ceremony. But Lami has given to Prince Frederick of Prussia an attitude borrowed (though in reverse) directly from that of young Lorenzo de' Medici in the Botticelli painting in which the Medici enact the *Adoration of the Magi*; if Lami had not seen that picture in the Uffizi, Prince Albert certainly had done so. Prince Fritz's turning out and away from his father and the other sponsors makes this pose the more obvious; the others were the Duke of Wellington and the Grand Duchess of Sachsen-Weimar, for whom the Duchess of Kent stood proxy.

44. Benjamin Edward Spence: *Highland Mary*

The Roman stone-cutters managed to make a sort of wool taffeta out of the plaid of Burns' heroine, but at least there is some animation in the fringe, and a faint tartan-like criss-cross incised in the sugar-like marble. The sculpture is saved by a certain sense of envelope, as of the original shape of the quarried stone, in that same plaid. The figure was at Osborne for years, but in 1859 it was moved to Balmoral, and its owners discussed with the sculptor a possible pendant to it, *The Lady of the Lake*. It is interesting that Prince Albert was far more active in buying sculpture than the Queen, who was less timid about painting.

45. Franz Xaver Winterhalter: *Prince Arthur* (detail)

Few of Victoria and Albert's gifts to one another were surprises. Internal evidence suggests that the little boy's father knew what was being done; for the Queen's birthday in May 1853 he had given her a Marochetti marble figure of the child with a Roman sword – not a success. It looks as if a new try had been made, this time with a Perugino drawing in mind. The drawing, itself based upon the well-known Donatello *St George* in Florence, was in the Royal collection, and well known to the Prince who was beginning his Raphael research this year. The child's pose is borrowed directly from Perugino, and the painting was an instant success; like all images that pleased the Queen, it was promptly multiplied. It may have been an influence on Bénédict Masson's portrait of the Prince Imperial (aged five, in military costume on a pony) which the Empress Eugénie commissioned in 1861; and one of the reproductions may have come to the eye of Edouard Manet, whose *Fifer* of 1866 uses a boy in uniform against a blank background.

46. Eugène Lami: *State Ball at Buckingham Palace*; water-colour 5 July 1848

Lami, recommended by Louis Philippe and Queen Amélie, received several commissions from Queen Victoria when he came to England as a refugee at the same time as the French royal family (Alfred de Dreux also came over, and was employed at least once for a horse-portrait, now destroyed). Obviously there was no revolution in England such as shook the Continent in 1848. The palace stair, one of Nash's best efforts, lent itself as well to a Lami performance as to the funneling of guests from Grand Hall to Throne Room (then still serving as a ball-room). The portraits on the landing are Dawe's of William IV and Queen Adelaide.

47. Louis Haghe: *Ball Room, Buckingham Palace*

Pennethorne and Gruner's ballroom, at its first showing in the Season to the court and guests, is here recorded for the souvenir albums by a Belgian who worked much at Balmoral. The red, blue, gold, and white of the Raphaelesque decoration have now vanished, and all that remains of what we see is the throne-niche and the cornice, now whitened. In this water-colour the scale is not falsified, as is sometimes the case with such pictures.

48. *Buckingham Palace*, east front by Edward Blore, 1846–7; (*Radio Times* Hulton Picture Library)

Nash, whose Palace courtyard is concealed by this wing, had built around Regent's Park those terraces in which individual dwellings were combined into one great-scaled building. Here Blore managed to suggest seven or nine houses linked. The best part of the composition was the animated skyline. Whether or not Queen Mary disliked the Victorian, the refacing [by Sir Aston Webb] in 1913 was already over-due, for the Caen stone used by Blore had suffered.

49. Eugène Lami: *Opening of the Great Exhibition*, 1851

Lami made the best of a good show with all the *chic* of epaulettes and orders, heralds and bishops in antiquated costume, the Queen and her ladies up to date; but he also took the trouble to draw the structure and glazing of the Crystal Palace accurately with a ruler. Not only the building but the installation had a style: the colossal statues and trees punctuated the great spaces while a variety of draperies in the exhibitors' bays enlivened the cellular and modular scheme.

50. Edward Matthew Ward, R.A.: *Queen Victoria at the Tomb of Napoleon*

The Queen had been hugely impressed by this visit to the ashes of her grandfather's old enemy, as well as bewitched by Napoleon III's rather gallant attention. Her usual interest in recording events was so intensified in this case that no mere water-colour for the souvenir albums would do. There were sittings (one actually by candlelight) for this painting and its companion in 1858, and the Queen described them as 'greatly improved' after further sittings in 1860. The other, which shows Napoleon III being invested with the Garter, betrays the influence of photography.

51. George Housman Thomas: *Prince Albert and Napoleon III at Boulogne*

The Prince's September visit to the new Emperor was a trial, initiated by the need for discussion of the Crimean situation, of intended visits between the two royal couples. It was amply recorded for the souvenir albums by Thomas, who had learned much from Lami. Napoleon kept considerable state, and Prince Albert's German stable-master, who enjoyed all the parade, was annoyed not to be allowed to use a particularly splendid saddle-cloth. The Emperor later spoke of the Prince's 'desire to leave nothing obscure or vague', and the Prince's memorandum of the visit noted: 'his [the Emperor's] French is not without a little German accent'.

52. William Powell Frith: *Life at the Seaside*, or *Ramsgate Sands*

So charmed was the Queen by this popular favourite at the R.A. summer exhibition in May 1854 that, in order to acquire it, she was willing to surrender to the dealers who had already bought it the right to engrave it. The painting takes a rather detached, not unhumorous view of events; and it has itself survived several generations of criticism.

53. Augustus Egg: *L'Amante*

Though Egg could paint devastatingly 'real' social-problem pictures if he pleased, he usually preferred literary or romantic subjects. The studio light and smooth surfaces of the costumed group contrast oddly with the backdrop. It would not be altogether objective to omit from an account of Prince Albert's collecting a few of the choices which now seem unsuccessful.

54. *Dressing-glass and toilet service*

Herbert Minton, whose great Staffordshire works produced every sort of ceramic, was the model of the intelligent industrialist after the Prince's own heart; friend of Henry Cole, active in the Society of Arts, a promoter of the Exhibition of 1851. The small pieces of this service made in his factory reflect, in their bands of *rose Dubarry* and their bouquets, the Sèvres ware of which George IV had bought so much, which Cole admired, and which Mintons learned to reproduce rather deceptively; but the stand and frame of the glass, with cherubs in bisque, the rest in creamy white, rose, and gold, is a Victorian *tour de force*, well designed and modelled, superbly fired.

55. *Oak Cabinet*

Shown at the Great Exhibition and later installed in one of Prince Albert's workrooms at Buckingham Palace, the cabinet seems to have contained, as part of the Kaiser's gift, albums of Austrian views, which have vanished. It is interesting to see so rich and fanciful a piece of Gothic coming so early from Austria; the Gothic revival dawned there with a revolt in 1848 against the Renaissance design of a suburban church by one of the court architects, and by 1855 all the designs submitted in competition for the mid-city *Votivkirche* were Gothic. Either Leistler had absorbed a lot of Pugin, or he was near the heart of the revolt (suprising in a *Hoflieferant*). The cabinet was given to its present owners by King George V.

The University of Edinburgh, Department of Forestry

56. *Entrance Hall, Balmoral Castle*

The statue of Malcolm Caenmore is signed, 'W. Theed Sc. 1861. Electrocast by Elkington & Co'. The fender and the hanging lantern both have thistle finials. Above the stags' heads on the right we see part of the great apparatus of articulated bell-wires which, before electricity, activated the jangling clappers that summoned Victorian servants. The echo in the ceiling-pattern of the design of the floor is typical of Prince Albert's architectonic inclination; but the chimney-piece, its Boulle clock, and the ewers in 1851 style, are vagaries.

57. *Ball Room, Balmoral Castle*

The generous chandeliers, the star-studded ceiling, the tartan cutains, and the upper wall, marbleized like that of the entrance hall and stair-case, somehow do not agree well with the woodwork, which Queen Victoria varnished a marmalade colour long after her husband's death; originally it was much blonder. In the orchestra-niche the royal arms of Scotland are above the central glass, with Prince Albert's arms to the right. The room has been decorated for a party, with the Queen's initials on the stair; the date is presumably before 1876, after which V.R.I. would have been used.
Photograph by J. Reid, Ballater, Aberdeenshire

58. G. M. Greig: *The West Drawing Room, Holyrood House*

Prince Albert is dictating to a secretary. Even though he and the Queen seldom used Holyrood, the atmosphere of serious business, without clutter, is characteristic of him. Into the Charles II room with its Georgian furniture, only some typical Victorian mantel ornaments, the necessary clock under a glass bell, and some light portable chairs have crept.

59. Sir Edwin Landseer: *Loch Laggan*

The Queen's sketching equipment, the Prince of Wales's kilt and doublet, the stag shot by his father, and the Princess Royal's tartan costume, are all well set in the Life-in-the-Highlands mould the year before Balmoral I was acquired. The Queen and Prince were spending three weeks at Ardverikie, the Marquess of Abercorn's house, in rainy weather but in that privacy which the Queen so loved; there was not another house within four miles. The walls of Ardverikie were hung with Landseer drawings of stags.

60. *Carpet*

An industrial product but hand-knotted, this was one of the most admired Royal exhibits at the Crystal Palace in 1851, partly of course because of its great size and special T shape. Although the flowers are in most places naturalistic, the general plan is formal, and the main lines reflect precisely (as did some carpets designed by Robert Adam) the divisions of the ceiling of the room.

61. Anonymous

The tent-like wallpaper was presumably chosen to emphasize the 'roughing-it' nature of life in one of the shiels on the Balmoral estate. Actually Altnagiuthasach was a solid enough house, built in wood as an addition to two huts which Queen Victoria called 'our little "bothie" ' (*Leaves from a Journal of Our Life in the Highlands*, American edition, 1868, p. 114). It must have been the first of Prince Albert's Balmoral constructions: 'a charming little dining-room, sitting-room, bed-room, and dressing-room, all *en suite*; 'we . . . were amazed at the transformation'. Here we see the Prince's shirt and shoes laid out on the *chaise longue*, his stockings and doublet on the armchair, and his kilt and sporran on the tabouret.

62. J. Roberts: *The Stairway, Balmoral*

The uncompromising and unmistakable 'Victorian' and domestic character of Balmoral is clear in spite of the large scale and the majestic row of stags' heads. The marbleized wall, the white-painted steps, the metal balusters are all typical of the hard surfaces which Prince Albert liked.

63. *The Royal Dairy, Frogmore*

The marble tables bear great pans of Wedgwood queensware for the rising of cream. Only the electric drop-light is an intrusion. The portrait heads in white on a blue-green ground which punctuate the frieze are based on Wyon's silver medallions; blue-green also are the ventilating tile of the ceiling; the large relief groups of dancing children on the end walls are white on yellow; the borders have a good deal of deep red, which is echoed in the windows; and the cornices are black and gold.

64. *The Queen's Audience Chamber, Windsor Castle*

On the panels where we see small circular portraits of heads, the larger oval portraits of George III's family by Gainsborough were arranged when the room was new. For a time, both these and the Winterhalter portraits of Queen Victoria's children hung there. The chair and table seen in the modern photograph are George IV's, the music box is perhaps Queen Alexandra's, the vitrines George V's. The chandelier, a later insertion, rather suits the glitter of the room but is a little overwhelming. In the ceiling by John Thomas we see the Queen's head, over the door, flanked by the earliest and latest of her predecessors, William I and William IV.

65. *The Duchess of Kent's Mausoleum*

The old Duchess, the Queen, and Prince Albert were all parties to the programme for this temple-gazebo-tomb built on and in a mound which had been created about 1795 with excavated earth. The Prince's late works show his eclectic taste turning more and more to fine-scaled ornament. [This almost Louis XVI building is not far from the Prince's more informal and 'English' aviary of 1845.] He had always been fond of complicated stairs and rather taut surfaces; here, soon after the hard tiles of the Dairy and the satin-wood, enamel, and ormolu of the Queen's Audience Chamber, he called for a severe geometry of stair, precisely elegant ornament, and plain polished columns of a hard material. The photograph does not show the long zigzag steps leading down to the vault door.

66. Leonard Charles Wyon: *Silver Medallions*

Examples in bronze also exist; these profiles served later as models for the larger heads in glazed terracotta used as part of the decoration of the Royal Dairy at Frogmore. Several of the Wyons, including William and his son Leonard Charles, who worked for the Mint and other government departments, also served the Queen as engravers and medallists.

67. Franz Xaver Winterhalter: *The Prince Consort*

The Prince sat or stood several times during the second half of May 1859 for this state portrait, a replica of which is in the National Portrait Gallery. He wears the green Rifle Brigade uniform, and is surrounded by all the apparatus of majesty, including a Riesener desk. Winterhalter was allowed to flatter the Queen, but was given little leeway with the Prince, who was already exhausted by work though he stood straight and was still a proper figure of a man. Winterhalter let himself go with the ornaments, and in his obvious cribs from Rigaud, Largillière, and Boucher perhaps went too far.

68 and 69. Daniel Maclise: *The Meeting of Wellington and Blücher; The Death of Nelson* (details)

These great decorations, the designs of which were approved by Prince Albert not long before his death, are almost the only parts of the painted enrichment of the Houses of Parliament that remain in excellent condition and that also stand up to modern criticism. Both compositions, immensely long and not tall, are meant to be seen as one walks along them. Therefore Maclise gave them both the big scale of the figures and the action (like the big scale of a concrete dam) and the small scale of the rich detail (like the grain of the wood shuttering [forms] left in the concrete when one sees it at close range). In Maclise's day it was not expected that these pictures would be seen by many women, and they are not pretty as some of his earlier easel pictures were pretty. They have neither the false-Spartan nonsense of the Napoleonic *mystique* nor the military dandyism which is the other side of the same coin, but a masculine grace which is rare.
House of Lords, New Palace of Westminster

70. F. W. Sperling: *Imaum*

Herring was too much in demand everywhere to work very often for the records of the royal stables. In his stead, Sperling and Woodward produced many small horse-portraits in crayon or water-colour, sometimes (as here) approaching the *chic* sobriety of the previous generation.

71. John F. Herring, senior: *Said*

Foreign princes sending gifts to England occasionally added human attendants of whose later fate one hears nothing; the Tsar once sent a droshky complete with driver. *Said* had been presented to Queen Victoria by the Imam of Muscat in 1852; whether the groom shown was still attending the Arabian in 1856 is not clear; but Herring, who here provided one of his fine dependable horse-portraits, must have borrowed the rest of the setting, perhaps from Edward Lear; and he had trouble with the perspective of the tent.

72. Andrea della Robbia: *Cherub with a Bagpipe*

The bagpipe-sack is blue, the pipes yellow, the figure cream-white. The Prince, who had commissioned sculptured portraits of his children from the Thornycrofts, must have had a pang at parting from this enchanting piece if it remained in his hands for any length of time. But presumably it was bought for presentation, possibly on Cole's or Robinson's request.

Victoria and Albert Museum

73. *Venus Anadyomene*

This version of a favourite Hellenistic piece is close to the one in the Rhodes Museum, but it suffers from a rather odd restoration of the foot; otherwise it is charming. Gruner gave 150 guineas for it on the Queen's account when the contents of Stowe were sold to satisfy Buckingham's creditors. Prince Albert had greatly admired the sculpture during a visit to Stowe where the Duke had kept almost royal state.

74. Alfred Stevens: *Model for Prize Medal*

This and an oval sketch, also rather damaged by time, were for medals intended for local use in the Schools of Design superintended by Cole's Department. Stevens wanted to *cast* these medals as a move away from the over-precise *struck* medals of the time, which had a hard coin-like finish. This design seems to have been influenced by a Greek bronze mirror-cover in the British Museum.

The Tate Gallery, London

75. John Thomas: *St Eustace* or *St Hubert*

Along with similar reliefs of St George and St Andrew, this work is built into the granite walls of Balmoral. Though it suggests in a way the central panel of many an eighteenth-century carved chimneypiece, the presentation and iconology speak more strongly of the German 'little master' printmakers of the sixteenth century. Thomas, who had worked in a rather Grec style at Buckingham Palace, and who provided many Gothic statues for the Houses of Parliament, had indeed worked in every style on half the important buildings of his generation. These reliefs are among his happiest domestic works.

Balmoral Castle, Aberdeenshire

76. A. W. N. Pugin: *Chalice*

At the Crystal Palace in 1851, the 'Mediaeval Court', which was what we should now call an exhibition of liturgical art, was complained of by evangelicals as a lot of popery. When a committee was entrusted late in the year with the purchase of five thousand pounds' worth of objects for the purposes of Prince Albert's team, this chalice was one of several Mediaeval Court objects bought. The photograph, made by F. Bedford at Marlborough House in 1854, is part of an album made for the Prince as a record of one of the Department of Science and Art's exhibitions of works of art old and new. Though Pugin was an antiquarian, he was as willing as any designer-for-machine to pile on more ornament than his Gothic prototype would have been likely to possess; yet he had enough feeling for material to leave areas of plain metal in the cup.
Victoria and Albert Museum, London

77. *Billiards Table*

The smooth surfaces, plain blocks, and Renaissance ornament suggest both the architectonic bias of the Prince and the helping hand of Ludwig Gruner; the more usual treatment of the time would have called for stout turned legs. The original lamps, hanging from a shaft entwined in gilt-bronze ivy, had two clusters of three cone-shaped shades.

78. *The Refreshment Rooms* (part of the Arcades) *from the East Dome of the Exhibition of 1862*

Two days after the Prince Consort's death, the camera looked across the south-west corner of the Royal Horticultural Society's Gardens to the houses in Queen's Gate Terrace and contiguous streets. In the foreground is part of the roofing of the Nave which stretched east and west between the glass domes; in the centre we see the inside or back of the gateway which was the centre of the South Arcade. The whole garden project had been carried out between spring of 1859 and early June 1861.
Victoria and Albert Museum Library

79. *View across the Royal Horticultural Society's Gardens to the East Dome of the Exhibition of 1862*

The curved ribs of the dome had not yet taken shape, as they would

about New Year's Day 1862. We see about half of the east-west length of the Nave; at the right is the outside of Fowke's central garden entrance to the building, the back or inside of which we see (in pl. 78.) In the foreground are some of the patterned flower beds, young trees, and complex devices for changing levels which Nesfield designed at the Prince Consort's suggestion. It is difficult to realize from the photograph the great depth of the building under construction. Between Arcades and Nave were many parallel north-south exhibition rooms; and more on the other (south) side of the Nave, extending to the 'permanent' brick building in Cromwell Road.
Victoria and Albert Museum Library

80. *South-east Corner of the Building for the Exhibition of 1862*
Francis Fowke's building came to the very corner of Cromwell Road and what is now Exhibition Road, and we are looking, therefore, at a site which is now part of the garden around the Natural History Museum. Fowke's design suggests Dutch work enlarged to great dimensions; but he may have looked at such Dutch-influenced buildings as Kew Palace, Broome Park (Kent), or Swakeleys (near Uxbridge). As we can tell by counting the courses of brick, the height will have been a good fifty feet to the cornice. The clerestory is prettily related to the parapets of the towers. These Cromwell Road galleries were intended to be permanent, but they lasted not much longer than the temporary parts of the Exhibition.
Victoria and Albert Museum Library

Index

Note: Prince Albert himself is not indexed, as he appears on more than half the pages of the book, but subject headings will be found under his name